A PLACE IN THE SKY

A History of the
Arnold Palmer Regional Airport
1919 - 2001

Richard David Wissolik
General Editor

Contributing Editors:
David J. Wilmes
Mary Ann Mogus
Don Riggs
Julie R. Platt
Barbara Wissolik

Editors:
Gene Lakin
Erica Wissolik
John Ward
Mark Phillips
Michael Larson
Tim Shay
J. S. Downs and Associates

Financial Support for this publication was provided by the Pennsylvania
Historical and Museum Commission, the R.K. Mellon Family Foundation,
the Westmoreland County Airport Authority.

Publications of the Saint Vincent College Center
for Northern Appalachian Studies
Latrobe, Pennsylvania
2001

©PUBLICATIONS OF THE SAINT VINCENT COLLEGE CENTER FOR NORTHERN APPALACHIAN STUDIES

Saint Vincent College
300 Fraser Purchase Road
Latrobe, PA 15650
www.stvincent.edu

A Place in the Sky: A History of the Arnold Palmer Regional Airport
1919-2001

Cover Design: Michael Cerce
J.S. Downs and Associates

Printed by Sheridan Books
Ann Arbor, Michigan

Library of Congress Cataloging-in-Publication Data

Wissolik, Richard David, 1938-
   A place in the sky : a history of the Arnold Palmer Regional Airport and aviation in Southwestern Pennsylvania, 1919-2001 / Richard David Wissolik, David Wilmes ; editors, Mary Ann Mogus ... [et al.].
      p. cm.
   Includes bibliographical references.
   ISBN 1-885851-17-0 (alk. paper)
   1. Arnold Palmer Regional Airport--History. 2. Aeronautics--Pennsylvania--History. I. Wilmes, David. II. Mogus, Mary Ann. III. Title.

TL726.3.P4 W57 2001
387.7'36'0974881--dc21

                                        2001041641

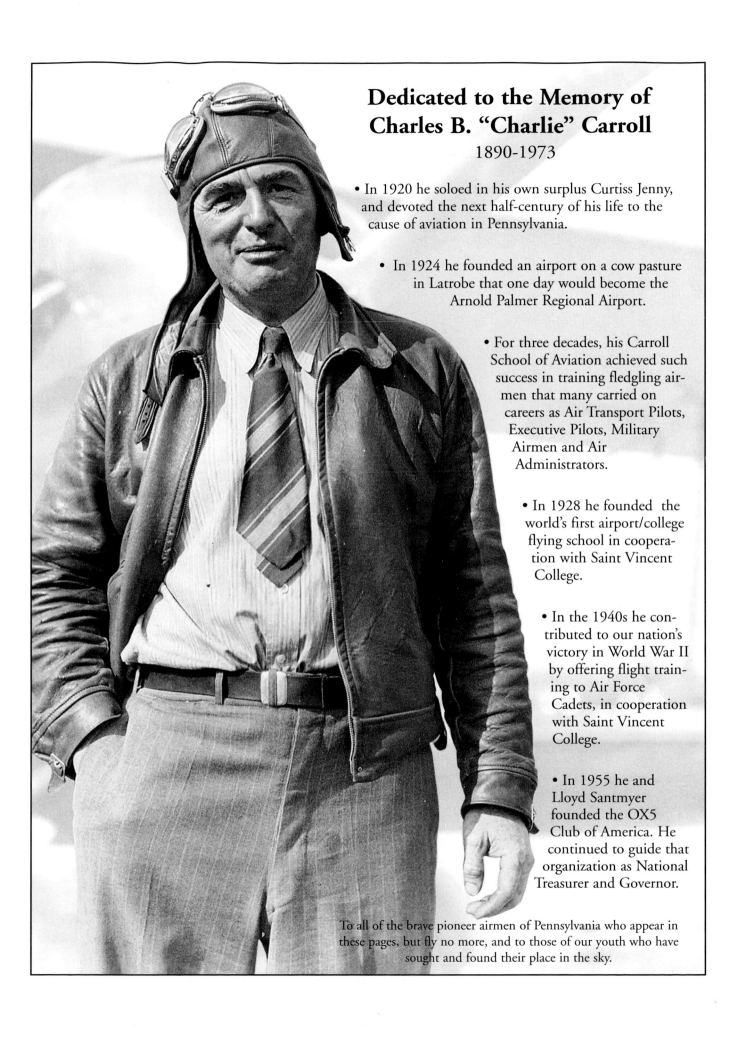

Dedicated to the Memory of Charles B. "Charlie" Carroll

1890-1973

• In 1920 he soloed in his own surplus Curtiss Jenny, and devoted the next half-century of his life to the cause of aviation in Pennsylvania.

• In 1924 he founded an airport on a cow pasture in Latrobe that one day would become the Arnold Palmer Regional Airport.

• For three decades, his Carroll School of Aviation achieved such success in training fledgling airmen that many carried on careers as Air Transport Pilots, Executive Pilots, Military Airmen and Air Administrators.

• In 1928 he founded the world's first airport/college flying school in cooperation with Saint Vincent College.

• In the 1940s he contributed to our nation's victory in World War II by offering flight training to Air Force Cadets, in cooperation with Saint Vincent College.

• In 1955 he and Lloyd Santmyer founded the OX5 Club of America. He continued to guide that organization as National Treasurer and Governor.

To all of the brave pioneer airmen of Pennsylvania who appear in these pages, but fly no more, and to those of our youth who have sought and found their place in the sky.

Table of Contents

THE KITTY HAWK MONSTER

I was walking my dog through the shifting sand one brisk December day,

When some men I'd never seen before ran out to block my way.

I'd climbed that hill a hundred times. I couldn't understand

Why anyone had any cause to bar me from the land.

And then I saw, up by the shed, a weird impressive sight;

I knew from pictures I had seen it was a huge box kite.

One man was stretched out in the thing while another stood and talked.

Then after a while, he looked around and to the back he walked.

He spun a funny looking fan that made an awful clatter.

In fact I think I saw two fans, but it really doesn't matter.

Above the din, I heard some shouts; I thought my ears would burst.

The man aboard blared, "Wilbur! I'm going to try it first!"

I couldn't think why grown up men would play with such a toy.

Then a man with a camera aimed at the kite called "Good luck, Orv, old boy!"

The monster started moving across the sand; it was headed straight for me.

I turned and ran down Kill Devil Hill as frightened as I could be.

I ran for miles. I never looked back. My feet scarcely touched the ground.

I made it home safely and locked the door just ten feet ahead of the hound.

There was nothing in the papers; I searched them through; and we had no radio.

I was NOT just imagination. Not at all!

I was there and I should know...

Years have come an gone since nineteen three,

and as I sit here reviewing,

I've often wondered to this day

what those two fools were doing.

- Russ Brinkley

Editor's Note and Acknowledgements

A Place in the Sky is about the aviation pioneers of Westmoreland County in the Commonwealth of Pennsylvania. They were a breed of courageous, adventurous, sometimes reckless men and women who flew "by the seat of their pants in aircraft that were little more than stiffened cloth stretched over wood and held together with baling wire. Their daring, their mistakes and successes, made aviation in the county what it is today. Moreover, this book is about the Arnold Palmer Regional Airport in Latrobe, and the role it played in developing and advancing aviation in Western Pennsylvania.

More than two years of research went into the publication of this history. Though our original purpose was to focus on the development of Latrobe's Arnold Palmer Regional Airport from the founding of Longview Flying Field in 1924, it was because the broader geographic area's early pilots and aviation pioneers were such a tight, mutually-supportive group that we found it necessary to include some of them, especially C.P. Mayer (Mayer Field, Bridgeville, Pennsylvania), and D. Barr Peat and Clifford Ball (Bettis Field, McKeesport, Pennsylvania).

By no means does this history purport to be exhaustive. It is, however, the most comprehensive one done to date on the development of the airport that today serves Westmoreland County and the region. Had we begun our work two or five years hence, what we have achieved in this volume would not have been possible.

Very little, if any, material on the days prior to 1980 was preserved in airport archives, and most of the principals involved in early developments had passed on around the same time Charles Carroll died in 1973. "Charlie" had preserved thirty-five years of airport history in an immense scrapbook, but it was lost after his widow, Grace, died in a nursing home in Florida some years after her husband's death. If we could have had that scrapbook, our task would have been much easier. Fortunately, six people (three of them in their nineties) who experienced the golden days of local aviation in the 1920s and 1930s were available for interviews; they were Lloyd Santmyer, Anna Mary Topper (widow of Carl Strickler), Ken Scholter, Frank Fox, Ed Blend, and Clyde Hauger, whose father, also Clyde, barnstormed out of the Longview Flying Field and J.D. Hill Airport in the waning years of the 1920s. Each presented us with extensive collections of photographs and other memorabilia. We are saddened that Frank Fox passed away before he could see himself and his old comrades honored in these pages.

We apologize for oversights and the kinds of errors that are sometimes unavoidable in historical reconstructions of this nature. We exerted every effort to contact people who could shed light on the airport's history. Among other approaches, our efforts included press releases, feature articles and advertisements in newspapers, public posters in the Palmer Airport terminal building, telephone contacts, and national and international outreach through the project's web site. Many came forward who were willing to share their memories and memorabilia. Many others supplied us with contacts. We examined more than 2,000 photographs and hundreds of letters, brochures, tabloids, newsletters, and holdings in county libraries, private libraries, and the archives of historical societies. We traveled Westmoreland, adjacent counties, and into other states to conduct research and interviews, and to spend endless hours in front of microfilm machines in libraries. Regretfully, we excluded material that we could neither identify nor corroborate. This material will be made available for public and scholarly examination in the Saint Vincent College Library.

With deep appreciation, we acknowledge the following:

The Pennsylvania Historical and Museum Commission, The R. K. Mellon Family Foundation, The Westmoreland County Airport Authority, and Saint Vincent College for the funds to undertake and complete the project; Gene Lakin, Gabe Monzo, Linda Brasile, Dorothy Zello for allowing free access to airport files and archives, and for their patience through countless phone calls and unscheduled visits from Center staff; Don Orlando, Theresa Schwab, and the staff of the Saint Vincent College Public Relations Office for their timely and efficient placement of publicity; Rita Catalano, Christine Foschia, Marsha Jasper, of the Saint Vincent College Office of Grants and Research for their expertise and assistance while the Center sought funds for this project; Patricia Dellinger, Gina Nalevanko, and the Saint Vincent College Business Office for their work in managing the funds of the Center; Rev. Chrysostom Schlimm, O.S.B., Rev. David Kelly, O.S.B., Margaret Friloux, John Benyo, Jack Macey, and all the others at the Saint Vincent College Library for their usual graciousness in assisting Center staff with research problems and obtaining often obscure inter-library loan materials; Saint Vincent College faculty secretary Shirley Skander, Lee Ann Ross and Kim Bobnar, of the college's Mailing and Duplicating department for their invaluable assistance in providing copies of the manuscript for the editors.

We are especially indebted to Mary Ann Mogus for her contribution concerning the life of J.D. Hill. Though Charles Carroll in 1928 renamed his Longview Flying Field after that Scottdale, Pennsylvania, airmail pilot, memories of Hill and his contributions to aviation had entirely disappeared from local memory. Dr. Mogus also brought to light many historically critical articles from the Scottdale Independent Observer published in the 1920s. Without these our reconstruction of events in the lives of Charles Carroll, Carl Strickler and Raymond Elder would not have been as thorough as they are.

Above all, we thank the following, without whose generous and gracious assistance, especially in providing many rare photographs, documents, and oral histories, this project would have been impossible; Rev. Omer Kline, O.S.B. (Saint Vincent Archabbey Archives), Rev. Roland Heid, O.S.B., Ken Scholter, Frank Fox, Ed Blend, Lloyd Santmyer, Clyde Hauger, Earl Metzler, James Carroll, Don Carroll, Dorothy Carroll Sadler, Janet Matchett, Carolyn Peat, Marcia Nair, Josephine Smart, Bob Downs, Robert Fisher, Lou Beamer, John "Reds" MacFarlane, William Strickler, Barry Elder, Anna Mary (Strickler) Topper, Don Riggs, Kip Barraclough, Victor Gasbarro, Eli "Babe" Krinock, Mansel Negley, Gene McDonald, Don Kane, Eleanor Ashbaugh, Jean Loughry, Harry Garman, Bruno Ferrari, Ronald Jasper, Dr. Walter Hazlett, Cliff Naugle, the New York Public Library, the West Overton Museums, the Latrobe Historical Society, the Greensburg Public Library, the Greater Latrobe Senior High School, the Westmoreland County Historical Society, the Scottdale Independent Observer, the Latrobe Bulletin, the Greensburg Tribune-Review, and many others, too numerous to mention, whose comments, criticisms, and leads were of invaluable assistance.

A Note From Gene Lakin

Executive Director, Arnold Palmer Regional Airport

My history of the Arnold Palmer Airport began in 1980. Bob Cheffins, the airport manager, offered me a job in the maintenance department, and we both agreed that it would be temporary employment. My wife, Ginger, and I, along with our two-year-old son, Jeff, were making plans to move to a warmer climate. My daughter, Amy, was born on July 31, 1980, my first day on the job.

My history of the airport centers around the people with whom I have been associated these twenty-one years. Many individuals come to mind. Terry Stuck, longtime maintenance worker taught me how to plow snow during my first winter at the airport. Terry, along with Tom Stynchula, Mike Umbaugh, and Moe Haas, today make up a unique group of maintenance workers truly dedicated to our airport; Charlie Green and his team of air-traffic controllers bring with them each day the loyalty, efficiency, and professionalism that are so important to any airport operation. My history also includes Gabe Monzo and Linda Brasile, who, along with me, make up the airport administration staff. The importance of Gabe (named 1999's "Airport Manager of the Year" by the Pennsylvania Department of Transportation's Bureau of Aviation) and Linda to the airport cannot be adequately described except by those who experience their dedication first hand. The success of our airport is attributable to this group of employees and to other special people who have been connected with the Airport Authority. In 1980, I was in the right place at the right time.

The Airport Authority was established in 1951. This year, 2001, marks our fiftieth anniversary. One day, I was discussing our anniversary plans with Saint Vincent College professor Dick Wissolik, whose wife, Barbara, had just finished a series of interviews with Gene McDonald, the airport solicitor since 1951. Dick suggested that we record a history, not only of the airport authority, but also of the airport since its earliest days. I knew that a great deal of Pennsylvania aviation history involved the old Latrobe airport, but a good historical record simply did not exist. The authority agreed that this was a perfect opportunity to research, compile, and publish a book about the characters and events that make up the history of the Arnold Palmer Regional Airport.

As part of my own research, I started reading the minutes of authority meetings that began to be officially recorded in 1953. As I read about the people, the projects, the problems and triumphs associated with those days, I developed a deeper appreciation of my own position at the airport. I only hope those who will someday succeed me derive from the following pages the same appreciation.

$\mathcal{L}$ooking Up for Eighty Years

When once you have tasted flight, you will forever walk the earth with your eyes turned skyward,
for there you have been, and there you will always long to return

- Leonardo da Vinci

More than eight decades ago, when the land had not yet been dug up, moved and shifted to suit the needs of commerce and progress, southwestern Pennsylvania was a quiet rural community settling down after the turmoil of World War I. Places like Greensburg, Latrobe, New Alexandria, Derry, Scottdale, Uniontown, Monessen, and Connellsville, had once been just towns on a map connected by miles of winding roads, and patched with cornfields and pastures. Automobiles were just beginning to change the lives of the American people. They were still a novelty of sorts, especially in rural communities where they still might turn a head or two, but they would not compare to what was about to burst upon the scene shortly after the end of the Great War. Suddenly, the new art of flying from town to town, practiced by discharged Army pilots flying surplus aircraft and giving the local populace a chance to touch the clouds, stirred the imagination of the inhabitants. No motor car, however strange or exotic, could ever manage to draw a thousand people of all ages to a roadside field or pasture, where a Curtiss Jenny in distress, or one whose pilot would sell rides for two or three dollars, made a landing. To pilots, especially, new realms became accessible by air, new lands were there to discover, new experiments and adventures possible to undertake.

In 1910, in Mt. Pleasant, Pennsylvania, Frisbee, "The Man Bird," made two flights a day at the Home Week Celebration.

On October 3, 1910, Wilbur Wright himself brought a new Wright Flyer to the Washington County Centennial Fair where his pilot, Walter Brookins, flew from Wallace Field to a height of 1,200 feet, a new record for Pennsylvania. Brookins' flight lasted twenty-two minutes.

Sometime in 1911, R.C. Jennings of Uniontown, Pennsylvania, got a second hand engine and fitted into a Bleriot-type monoplane. His engine was underpowered, so he switched to a forty-horsepower Gray Eagle, and made a few modifications to strengthen the plane's structure. Jennings claimed to have made flights lasting as long as forty-five minutes, using a golf course as a flying field.

In April 1913, Victor D. Herbster of West Newton, Pennsylvania, one of the first Navy aviators trained by Curtiss, set a seaplane altitude record of 4,450 feet.

On Columbus Day, 1913, in Connellsville, Pennsylvania, W.S. Minerly performed in a Kirkham tractor biplane, and Frank H. Burnside performed in a Thomas Pusher.

On April 16, 1916, at the height of World War I, DeLloyd "Dutch" Thompson of Washington County, dropped a paper bag filled with firecrackers over Washington, D.C., to demonstrate that American cities were vulnerable to air attack. Thompson also claimed to be the fourteenth man in history ever to pilot an aircraft.

At the end of World War I, a field in downtown Latrobe was used for passenger flights. The field eventually became the 800 block of Weldon, Spring, Chestnut, Walnut, Fairmont, and St. Clair Streets.

The Curtiss Jenny, the "Barnstormers," and the Air Mail Pilots

For three decades after the historic flight of the Wright brothers at Kitty Hawk, the air belonged to the "Barnstormers," aerial vagabonds who purchased war surplus Curtiss "Jennies" for little more than a song, then bounced from cow pasture to cow pasture putting on exhibitions and selling rides for whatever price they could extract from the locals. Of all the early barnstormers, a young man named Charles Augustus Lindbergh was the most famous. There were no regulations in place concerning aviation, nor were flying licenses required.

Anyone with the courage to take up an airplane could do so.

The Barnstormers flew in open cockpit aircraft, behind engines that could malfunction at any time, usually when it was most inconvenient. Their aircraft had limited range, and ground facilities and navigational aids were sparse. Pilots looked for the names of towns carved out in pastures or painted on the roofs of barns and other large buildings, or they followed highways, rivers and railways. Then, once confident that they had reached their desired destination, the pilots would circle a likely landing place, then swoop low and slow in order to locate wet spots, ditches, rocks, tree stumps, and to chase off any livestock grazing in the area. They called it "drag-

As aviation developed, it caught the attention of sundry people in the region, a number of whom had a clear understanding of the potential of aviation in the world of business and commerce. By the end of 1920, there were 271 airfields in the entire United States. Twenty-five were Army Air Corps fields, twenty-two were operated as mail service points and emergency fields (one of these was on the Saint Vincent College campus), and 224 were operated by individuals, companies, or municipalities.

In 1919, Bob Hancock helped form the Pittsburgh-based Kenny Aircraft Company with Roy Kenney and

The Curtiss "Jenny"

ging." If they did get lost, they would land anyway and ask a farmer for directions. They always drew a crowd. Later, the Barnstormers refined their performances with parachute jumps, wing-walks, and other dangerous stunts.

Any sort of flying in the early days was dangerous. The most noted of the professionals back then were the air-mail pilots. Thirty-one of the original forty were killed in crashes, many of them over the treacherous Allegheny mountains, an area most called the "Hell Stretch" and some called the "Death Stretch." Laurel Mountain and Chestnut Ridge, beginning just east of Latrobe, were especially feared.

Paul Milnor. Pilots Joe Slater and Bob Dake flew the company's Jenny to Altoona with Pittsburgh newspapers and sold them to the Pennsylvania Railroad's westbound passengers. To augment the company's income, Slater and Dake barnstormed county fairs in this region. Their efforts were not enough, however, to keep the company from bankruptcy. Railroads were still the transportation power in the United States, and any sort of airline was hard-pressed to survive more than a year or two.

One person who was able to make a living was Casper P. Mayer, the owner of a brickyard, who set up a "flying field" in Bridgeville, Pennsylvania. Mayer obtained a Laird biplane, then hired a pilot to begin a flying school and passenger business. True to the times, and in order to attract the public, Mayer held flying exhibitions on weekends. In addition to the usual aerobatics, G.H. "The Human Fly" Phillips, did headstands while his airplane did the loop the loop!

The 1920s brought more developments. An airfield opened in Ligonier in 1920. In 1921, the Irwin Aircraft Company, just to the east of Pittsburgh, started an air taxi, aerial advertising, and flying-school business on a small field. The dapper Neil McCray, who ran a flying school and passenger business in Erie, traveled the region selling used and new aircraft, and the Pennsylvania Aero Service stationed some Jennies at Latrobe, on the field that Charles Carroll established in partnership with Joe Maloy.

In June 1925, thirty-three-year-old McKeesport Hudson-Essex dealer, Clifford Ball, and D. Barr Peat, purchased a forty-acre tract just above Dravosburg, to use as an airport. Peat had been using the site since 1924 for an aerial sightseeing service, but had plans to develop a more permanent facility. With $35,000.00 in seed money, Ball and Peat built a hangar and machine shop on the field and named it the Pittsburgh-McKeesport Airport. According to form, they supplemented revenues with air shows, plane rides, and flying instruction. In November 1926, they renamed the field Bettis Field, after Lieutenant Cyrus Bettis who died in a plane crash near Bellefonte, Pennsylvania.

Also, in June 1925, the first municipal flying field was opened in the Fox Chapel area of Pittsburgh. The field was named Rodgers Field, after Calbraith P. Rodgers, a six-foot-four-inch aviator from southwestern Pennsylvania, and grandson of Oliver Perry, victor of the Battle of Lake Erie. In September 1911, Rodgers, piloting a Wright Model B, began what would become the first transcontinental flight, a promotional one for the Armour Company's soft drink "Vin Fiz." Rodgers christened the plane "Vin Fiz Flyer." Sixty-nine landings and fifteen crashes later (on November 5), Rodgers landed in Pasadena, California. He took the train home. Rodgers was killed two months later when he crashed into the Pacific Ocean after flying into a flock of seagulls.

Charles Bruce Carroll, Latrobe, and Longview Flying Field

In 1924 Charles Bruce Carroll established a flying field in Latrobe on a property that would evolve into the present day Arnold Palmer Regional Airport.

"Charlie" Carroll was a mechanic and automobile dealer from Scottdale, Pennsylvania. Like many of the aviation pioneers, Carroll's interest in flying led him to purchase an Army surplus Curtiss Jenny in 1919. Carroll half-flew, half-trucked the plane from New Jersey to Scottdale with Torrance Overholt, a veteran World War I pilot. The men organized the Scottdale Aerial Club soon after, and at five o'clock in the afternoon on September 2, 1920, Overholt dazzled the local citizens with a series of stunts.

Carroll's interest did not wane with a few hops into the air in his new plane. He had a vision. He knew aviation had a place in the rural areas of Westmoreland County. He began searching for a location among the rolling hills and pastures appropriate for a permanent aviation facility.

In 1920, the year of his solo flight, Charlie landed on a broad clover field situated on top of a hill on the Saint Vincent College Campus, now the site of the college's Rooney Hall. This clover field had been known as the Saint Vincent Aviation Field ever since two Army Pathfinders made an emergency landing there in 1919.

To the east of the Saint Vincent Aviation Field was the Kerr farm. According to maps of the day, the Kerr property bordered the Saint Vincent Archabbey farm. Before the historic Lincoln Highway was straightened in the 1930s and became US30, the road ran across the middle of the present-day airport, crossed the Manito Road (Route 981), and continued on through Youngstown, Pennsylvania. In 1924, with Joe Maloy as a partner, Carroll leased a cow pasture from the Kerrs exactly at the junction of these major highways. The word "airport" was not yet in use. Aircraft took off and landed on "aerodromes," "flying fields," "landing fields," or just plain "fields." Charlie called his leased field Longview Flying Field. It had easy access to Latrobe, Youngstown, Mt. Pleasant and numerous other towns. It was also close to the Pennsylvania Railroad.

Today, immediately after making a right onto 981 south, one can still see the overgrown area within the boundaries of the Arnold Palmer Regional Airport that marks the location of the old runway.

Carroll's "Hooligans"

With the help of his son Jim and joined by his friends, Scottdale pilots Carl Strickler and Raymond Elder, and Greensburger Lloyd Santmyer, Carroll built a hangar on the field. Within a couple years, Longview Flying Field would become home to Clyde Hauger of Donegal, Greensburgers Frank Fox, Dave Patterson, Lewis "Mickey" DeBurger, followed by Charles "Red" Gahagan, Russ Brinkley, Joe Crane, Dick Copeland, Clyde Goerring, Jack Frost and others. They would come to be known as the "Longview Boys" or "Carroll's Hooligans," as one old neighbor still calls them.

The Longview Boys stunted at the air shows they sponsored on weekends, walked on wings, and parachuted out of airplanes. The wingwalkers and jumpers formed the "Tombstone Club," a gutsy bunch who had accepted the fact that their next barrel-roll, their next jump, their next wingwalk, could be their last. They chased trains, flew under bridges, and never abandoned a troubled plane once in the air. Three of the best of them–Carl Strickler, Mickey DeBurger, and Clyde Hauger–would die in crashes.

By 1926, Longview Flying Field had four aircraft, the fourth highest total in Pennsylvania. The field was also fourth highest in number of flights (1,483), third in number of passengers (1,408), and fifth in number of miles (25,000). All of this was achieved without a serious accident. Like most of the other owners of an FBOs(Fixed Base of Operation), Carroll supplemented his income through air exhibitions, mechanic services, and fuel sales.

According to those who knew him, Charlie was an excellent pilot and promoter. According to Lloyd Santmyer, he bought a carload of surplus Jennies and made them ready to fly. He cannibalized wrecks for parts. He sold cars and became an agent for various aircraft manufacturers, including Waco. In 1926, he would give Westmoreland County its first air race, and a major air show in each year of the remaining 1920s.

Aviation pioneer Ken Scholter says, "everybody knew Charlie." Earl Metzler, a friend of Carroll's from the early days says, "Charlie knew everybody." "Everybody" included Russell Brinkley, D. Barr Peat, Clifford Ball, Ken "Curley" Lovejoy, Merle Moltrup, Dewey Noyes, C.P. Mayer, and most of the other aerial pioneers of the day.

J.D. Hill Airport, the New Alexandria Airport, and the World's First College/Airport Aeronautics School

In June 1928, Longview Flying Field was renamed J.D. Hill Airport, after James DeWitt Hill, the "Bird Boy of Scottdale," a friend of Carroll's. Hill was an air mail pilot who was killed in an attempt to fly across the Atlantic to Rome.

The year 1928 also saw Saint Vincent College become involved in aviation. Carroll, Russ Brinkley, and Thomas E. Whiteman, the *Latrobe Bulletin* publisher, met with Archabbott Aurelius B. Stehle, OSB, president of Saint Vincent College, to establish the world's first college/airport curriculum in aviation. Stehle agreed, fore-

seeing what an asset such an enterprise would be for the college. He had the notion that aviation would give missionaries access to remote areas. He wanted Saint Vincent College to be the first to utilize this new machine to benefit Benedictine missions around the world, especially those in China.

After the meeting, Carroll applied to Rand-McNally to place the Saint Vincent Aviation Field on their aero-map as "Hill Airport at Saint Vincent College." Unfortunately, Carroll's association with Saint Vincent College ended after a few months because of personal financial exigency. Carroll traveled to Florida during the winters to work as a mechanic with Pan American Airways, and fly copilot with for his friend, Ed Musick.

In 1929, Saint Vincent College carried on without Carroll and soon acquired its own plane, a New Standard biplane designed by Charles Day that they christened *The Spirit of Saint Vincent*. The student body was introduced to their new mascot in dramatic fashion one fall afternoon when the plane cruised overhead before a football game, the pilot dropping the game ball onto the field. The flight school was moved to the newly opened Pittsburgh-Greensburg Airport, where Lieutenant Jack Bessey and Jacob Lythe were the flight instructors. Unfortunately, the Great Depression intervened and the program closed in 1930.

Financial exigency became the least of Carroll's problems in 1930. In that year, Charlie nearly lost the lease on the Kerr property. The Kerrs made plans to either sell the property that housed the J.D. Hill Airport or allow it to revert to pasture land. The situation forced Carroll to look for a site in a good location. He and Lloyd Santmyer found one not far away on Route 22 (William Penn Highway) in New Alexandria, on property owned by Howard Cox and John Giffen.

Lloyd Santmyer describes what took place:

It looked like the airport would revert back to being a farm. Right about that time, the William Penn Highway was getting more and more popular, and it looked like it was maybe going to be the main highway, instead of the Lincoln Highway. So Charlie and I decided that maybe we ought to go over there and find a field, which we did. We located the field there on the Griffin farm, east of New Alex, a couple miles on the right-hand side. The building is still there. It adjoined another farm, owned by the Cox family. So Charlie made a deal with the two families to take down a fence and make a strip. Actually, we made an X-shaped field there. Charlie had access to one of the Meadow Mill buildings down in Scottdale, where a steel factory closed down and left a couple steel buildings. Charlie bought one of these buildings and got Joe Reedy and his brother, good metal workers, to go tear the building down and bring it to New Alex for a hangar. They built a refreshment stand there. Frank Fox managed the airport for a couple years.

Security at Last

For a couple of years Carroll and Lloyd worked both the New Alex and Hill Airports, but two events prompted him to lobby Latrobe Boro to transform Hill Airport into a municipal entity.

The first event occurred in the last week of April 1931, when the *Latrobe Bulletin* prematurely reported that the Howard Gasoline and Oil Company of Jeannette, Pennsylvania, had purchased the seventy-five acre J.D. Hill Airport site. The company's plans were to improve the property in anticipation of the straightening of the Lincoln Highway and its re-routing to the north of the airport. Carroll approached the Borough of Latrobe, doubly convinced of the importance of the Hill Airport's location to its success and benefit to the community.

Carroll met with Cyrus McHenry, secretary of the Chamber of Commerce and officials of the Howard Gasoline and Oil Company, to work out a suitable plan. Carroll pointed out that the Howard company's plan to remove a hump from the field would make it possible to expand the runway from 1,500 feet to 2,500 feet. For some unknown reason, the sale never took place. No record of it exists in borough or county records, and the company, still in existence, has purged all of its older records. At any rate, Carroll's visit to the Chamber of Commerce certainly must have planted a seed in the right places.

The second event occurred when Franklin Delano Roosevelt established the Works Progress Administration. The WPA would issue no funds for the development of any airport not under the auspices of a municipality. The borough, given the impetus of Works Progress Administration funds, purchased the airport site and much of the remaining Kerr property for the nominal sum of one dollar, with the proviso that it could buy the property fifteen years hence for an agreed upon sum of $22,500. J.D. Hill Airport was renamed Latrobe Airport on November 30, 1935. Two runways were put in and blacktopped. The main strip was 2,200 feet long and the secondary 1,400 feet. Today, these would not even qualify for taxi strips, but in the 1930s they were more than adequate for the type of aircraft using the airport.

The relationship between Carroll and Saint Vincent College resumed in 1939 with the Civilian Pilot Training Program. Furthermore, the United States entry into World War II a few years later transformed pilot training at the college into a military program. Air Cadets took ground school at Saint Vincent College and flight training at the Latrobe Airport.

All American Aviation and the World's First Air Mail Pick-up

In the mid-1930s, a few miles west of Latrobe on Route 30 in Irwin, Pennsylvania, another visionary of aviation had his own dreams. Dr. Lytle Adams, a dentist and aviation enthusiast, had been experimenting with a nonstop, airmail pick-up system in the 1920s, though some say earlier. Adams hoped that his system would provide airmail and express service to rural communities isolated from main roads and railroad lines. Dr. Adams' method was well-known.

On May 12, 1939, the world's first scheduled airmail pick-up by All American Aviation, using Adams' system, occurred at Carroll's Latrobe Airport. Lloyd Santmyer, Clyde Hauger, Raymond Elder and Dave Patterson, four of the Longview Boys, established solid reputations as pilots for AAA. The nonstop airmail deliveries would continue until 1949 when All-American Aviation converted to passenger service. Eventually, All-American Aviation would develop into All American Airways, then into Allegheny Airlines, and finally into US Air, an airline that is today a household word: US Airways.

Airports at Greensburg, Pennsylvania

The Pittsburgh-Greensburg Airport was dedicated on September 20-21, 1929. At the time, it was Pennsylvania's largest airport, but it would have a short, sometimes exciting, but, at length, an undistinguished history. Though the airport was located in Greensburg, it was altogether a Pittsburgh project, inspired and developed by the Aeronautics Committee of the Pittsburgh Chamber of Commerce and the Main Aeronautics Company.

In June 1928, in response to overtures from the Pittsburgh Chamber of Commerce, H. Raymond Mason, secretary of the Greensburg Chamber, sent to Pittsburgh a list of five sites in the Greensburg area that would be suitable for an airport. These sites were:

1. The McNary/John Robertshaw farm bounded by the Hannastown and New Alexandria roads (Rts. 819 and 119), 2.7 miles from Greensburg and consisting of 233 acres.

2. The Little Farm, consisting of 170 acres, located at the Radebaugh station on the Pennsylvania Railroad, three miles from Greensburg and close to the Jeannette Road.

3. The John C. Andrew property, consisting of fifty-two acres, located five miles from Greensburg on the Mt. Pleasant Road, near United, Pennsylvania.

4. The Keaggy property, consisting of seventy acres, located two miles from Greensburg on the West Newton Road.

5. The Youngwood Land Company property, four miles from Greensburg, and paralleling the Southwest Branch of the Pennsylvania Railroad

The principals involved visited the sites. For a time the McNary property was favored, and a large air meet took place there on June 26, 1928. Eventually, Frank Wilbur Main of Main Aeronautics purchased a site at Dry Ridge, just southeast of Greensburg, and announced on May 29, 1929, that he would construct a $2 million airport there. The Pittsburgh-Greensburg Airport had an auspicious beginning; not only did it host commercial, express, airmail, and private flights, but also the Main School of Aviation.

For many years, the Pittsburgh-Greensburg Airport was managed by Norman ("Happy") O'Bryan. In the last few years of its existence, it was managed by Earl Metzler.

Increasing costs, the development of airports closer to Pittsburgh, the termination of airmail and airmail pick-up services, more efficient and aggressive planning at the Latrobe Airport through the decades of the 1930s and 1940s, reduced the Pittsburgh-Greensburg airport to use by weekend pleasure-flyers.

In early 1954, a Pittsburgh real estate agency, C.A. West, purchased the 700-acre Pittsburgh-Greensburg airport after the area was rejected as a home for a Nike missile battery. West then built a residential complex there that he called West Point. It would be surprising if more than a few of today's West Point residents know that their homes had been built atop the airport's runways.

Lloyd Santmyer and Clyde Hauger opened a second Greensburg airport in 1947 in the community of Carbon. Today, Greensburg Central Catholic High School occupies the site. Though opened with much hope for the future, the airport closed within a few years.

This was all happening at a time when local government officials believed that airports located close to small towns could be financially supportive to the community. This was certainly true for many communities, but many felt more could be done by converting one of those airports into a facility that would service an entire county or region. Such thinking was especially evident at Latrobe.

The Tri-City Municipal Authority

In the late 1940s, interest in pioneering a county airport brought together several important figures in Westmoreland County.

On November 30, 1950, Latrobe Borough purchased the Kerr property for $22,500.00, the amount agreed upon by the borough and the Kerr family in 1935.

Allan Scaife, Richard Mellon, and Jim Underwood, an industrialist from the Latrobe area, wanted the airport at Latrobe to become a facility serving all of Westmoreland County. There had been some interest in expanding the airport at New Kensington into a county facility, but the commissioners gave their approval to Jim Underwood's proposal in January of 1951.

Once this was done, Underwood, Scaife and Bruno Ferrari formed a seven-member airport authority called the Tri-City Municipal Authority encompassing Latrobe, Greensburg and Jeannette. In order to ensure a quorum, the group made a gentleman's agreement that members of the authority would come from the Greensburg, Latrobe and Ligonier areas. Eventually, Carroll, who had spent so many years building his airport, would get left out of this new era of expansion.

The authority knew that it needed to survey and purchase more land. Most state and federal money for aviation in Pennsylvania went to either Pittsburgh or Philadelphia. Jim Underwood and his companions in the airport authority had to become "scroungers." Much to the credit of authority soliciter Gene MacDonald's philosophy to purchase land at what it would be worth ten or fifteen years hence rather than at present value, the authority was able to avoid a considerable amount of litigation. Under the Tri-City Municipall Authority, the construction of the runway began to a specification of 3,600 feet. The length turned out to be too short. The authority added an additional 800 feet for an overrun to be used in case of emergency or overshooting by pilots.

Bruno Ferrari, Latrobe Construction, and Expansion

The construction and later expansion of the runways became a reality mainly through the auspices of one man, Bruno Ferrari. The Latrobe Airport was fortunate to have him. As many say, Ferrari was the godfather of today's airport. Ferrari started a construction business in 1928 in West Virginia called B. Ferrari, but he later moved it to the Latrobe area. In 1940 his company became Latrobe Construction. Latrobe Construction owned and operated a 2,700 acre bluestone quarry near Latrobe. The output of this quarry was immense. The quarry produced one-and-a-half-million tons of stone a year. Other enterprises of Ferrari's were Latrobe Road Construction and Latrobe Aviation, Inc.

On October 30, 1958, the Westmoreland-Latrobe airport officially opened to the public with Ferrari and Latrobe Aviation as manager. Ferrari was selected because of proved financial responsibility, outstanding reputation in road construction and willingness to take on most of the operating expenses of the airport. Ferrari accepted a salary of zero dollars a year and the perk of having a place to park his airplane.

Ferrari made numerous improvements during his tenure. He renovated buildings, constructed new hangers, established a service and repair facility, installed an approach landing system, and built the framework for a state-of-the-art portable control tower, really a mobile home equipped with a communications center.

Ferrari's Latrobe Construction also made all the improvements and expansions to the runways over the years. Ferrari always managed to make the lowest bid, happy just to break even. When the airport went to 5,500 feet in 1968, Ferrari's company did the work. In 1985, when the runway was expanded to 7,000 feet and reinforced to accommodate jets the size of a 727, Ferrari again did the work. Not only was it fiscally convenient for the future development of the airport to have Bruno Ferrari manage it, he was a man who could get things done, and who had an interest in improving the operation of the Latrobe Airport.

The year 1978 was a milestone year in aviation. It was the 75th Anniversary of the Wright brothers first powered-airplane flight. Celebrations of the historic event were on the agendas of many aviation clubs and airports around the country. In that year, Latrobe Airport officially became the Westmoreland County Airport. Also in 1978 Saint Vincent College renewed its relationship with the airport by offering ground-school courses in cooperation with Vee Neal Aviation.

Recent Developments

From 1958, the date of the opening of the Latrobe-Westmoreland Airport, to the year 2000, the airport authority received $17,782,333 million in federal funds. In the late 1990s, the authority approved $1.75 million bond issue, thus completing funding for a $4.7 million project that doubled the size of the existing terminal.

In 2001, U.S. Representative John Murtha announced that the Arnold Palmer Regional Airport was awarded $1 million a year for five years to smooth plans to extend its primary runway by 1,500 feet.

Rostraver Airport

In November 1963, the Rostraver Township Board of Commissioners became keenly aware of the declining economic conditions in Pennsylvania's Monongahela Valley. Because of the dispersal or closing of mills, factories, mines and businesses, many once bustling communities fell into decline. Seeking a means to stimulate growth in the area, the commissioners requested that the Federal Aviation Administration investigate possible sites for the development of an airport, one that would provide suitable facilities for present and projected needs. The FAA had long recognized the need for an aviation facility in the valley, and had included a proposed airport in its National Airport Plan beginning in 1955.

The FAA completed its study in February 1964, recommending the Rostraver site over two others because of its proximity to the area to be served, its potential for expansion, its economy of construction, and its operational safety. Initially, the site was a privately owned field known as the J.S. Thompson Field with the FAA designation, Monongahela. The field had two grass landing strips, one running NE/SW for 1,750 feet, and the other running E/W for 1,600 feet.

Based on FAA recommendations, the Rostraver Township Commissioners solicited support from area municipalities and Westmoreland County officials. The county extended a grant of $75,000.00 over a three-year period. The local municipalities, however, though expressing support for the project, were unable to provide financial support.

Rostraver Township Airport Authority

In May 1965, the commissioners created the Rostraver Township Airport Authority for purposes of proceeding with the development of an airport at the Thompson field. The Authority included the following five members: Peter Buck, Chairman; J. Bachman Brown, Vice Chairman; Ignatius Mattes, Secretary; Michael Sweeney, Treasurer; John Porter, Assistant Secretary/Treasurer. Andrew Solan served as Deputy Secretary of the Authority.

The Authority accomplished three major phases of construction between 1965-1974. These included Project 01 (1965-1967) land acquisition, construction of a 3,200-x seventy-five- foot Runway 7-25, an apron and taxiway, an access road, and field lighting and rotating beacon; Project 02 (1967-1969) an 800-foot extension of Runway 7-25 to the west, turnaround taxiways, and land acquisition for the approach to Runway 7; Project 03

(1971-1974) a parallel taxiway to runway 7-25, and associated lighting and marking.

In addition, the Authority carried on interim work that included the construction of a hangar and administration building, fuel facilities, and utility lines. Private individuals also constructed hangars for their use on land leased by the Authority.

The Westmoreland County Airport Authority and management officially assumed operation of Rostraver Airport on February 13, 1986, aided by a $1.3 million grant from the Commonwealth of Pennsylvania.

In 1987, a $650,000.00 Federal Airport Improvement grant made it possible to rehabilitate the runway, taxiways, and aircraft parking apron. Since that time, more than $6 million in Federal and State grants have transformed Rostraver Airport into the first-class general aviation airport that exists today. A recent study by the Commonwealth of Pennsylvania calculated the economic impact of the Rostraver Airport to the communities surrounding the airport at nearly $8 million annually.

A Dream That Became Reality

The Arnold Palmer Regional Airport could not have come into being as the modern facility it is without the time and effort of many. Bruno Ferrari, Jim Underwood, Alan Scaife, Gene McDonald, Arnold Palmer, Jim Cavalier, Bob Cheffins, today's airport administrators, members of the Westmoreland County Airport Authority, and many others too numerous to mention were and are vital to the airport's continued success.

At some point along the way, Westmoreland County would have developed a regional airport in one of its townships. That it did so in Latrobe was because a thirty-four-year-old Scottdale aviation visionary leased a farm property at the junction of two major roads in Unity Township.

Charlie Carroll started his Longview Flying Field on a dream that turned into a landmark to the thousands who live in Western Pennsylvania. He was one of those pioneers who always looked up in expectation of the next flight and what new discoveries could be made in the sky.

Westmoreland County Airport Authority Members and Terms of Office

1951-2001

James Underwood (1951-1976)
Bruno Ferrari (1951-1957)
Francis J. Harvey (1951-1975)
Paul J. Abraham (1951-1975)
John W. Stader (1951-1970)
Charles Dobernik (1951-1970)
Alan M. Scaife (1951-1959)
Victor B. Stader, Jr. (1957-1974)
Leonard Bughman (1959-1977)
B. Patrick Costello (1965-1982)
Arnold D. Palmer (1970-1984;
1996-Present)
Charles A. Higgins (1970-1979)
Thomas A. Whiteman (1970-1979;
1982-1988)
George M. Blair (1970-1974)
Dean P. Nieman (1974-1975)
Richard B. Guskiewicz (1976-1984)
Michael Watson (1976-1987)

Donald C. Madl (1977-1991)
Earl F. Rectanus (1978-1986)
John H. Dent (1979-1984)
P. Benjamin Johnston (1980-1989)
Gerald A. Ficco (1985-1986)
Donald J. Rossi (1985-Present)
Dennis Manown (1985-1999)
Dorothy Zello (1987-Present)
Francis Barch (1986-1989)
Michael Salvatore (1988-1993)
C. Philip Weigel (1988-1995)
John R. Finfrock (1989-Present)
Mike Smith (1990-1995)
Philip Morrow (1992-Present)
Mark Gera (1992-2000)
Janice Smarto (1994-Present)
Oland Canterna (1996-Present)
J. Clifford Naugle (2000-Present)
Anthony Ferrante (2001-Present)

Airport Management

1924-2001

Charles B. "Charlie" Carroll (1924-1959)
Bruno Ferrari/Latrobe Aviation, Inc. (1959-1972)
James Cavalier (1968-1976)
Robert H. Cheffins (1976-1985)
Gene Lakin (1985-Present)
Gabe Monzo (1997-Present)

A SPECIAL PICTORIAL

ABOVE: The 1919 landing field in downtown Latrobe, now the 800 block of Weldon, Spring, Chestnut, Walnut, Fairmont, and St. Clair Streets, taken from the front yard of M.W. Saxman's residence on East Main Street. The field is where Lieutenant Grow sold rides in his Curtiss Jenny for three dollars per person. BELOW: The same general vicinity in 1900, taken from Fairmont Street.
(Courtesy of the Latrobe Historical Society).

Lloyd Santmyer and Clyde Hauger's Greensburg City Airport at Carbon, 1947 *(Courtesy of Clyde Hauger).*

Rodgers Field, Aspinwall, PA. Pittsburgh's first municipal airport. *(Courtesy of Ken Scholter).*

C.P. Mayer at Mayer Field
Bridgeville, Pennsylvania
ca. 1922. *(Courtesy of Ken Scholter).*

Clifford Ball. *(Courtesy of Ken Scholter).*

D. Barr Peat, Philadelphia Air Show, 1926.
(Courtesy of Carolyn Peat).

J. D. Hill Airport in the early 1930s just after the re-routing and straightening of US Route 30 (Lincoln Highway). The original Mission Inn, with its horseshoe-shaped dance and concert area, is in the foreground. At the east side of the junction of Rts. 30 and 981 Peretto's gas station. The old Lincoln Highway cuts across the airport property at the top of the photo. *(Courtesy of Don Carroll)*.

A DeHavilland DH-4 at Rodgers Field. *(Courtesy of Frank Fox)*.

RIGHT: Alan Scaife in the 1940s at Latrobe Airport with his Stinson Voyager. While at Yale, Scaife was a classmate of Juan Trippe. In 1951, Scaife served on the Pennsylvania Aeronautical Commission under Governor Fine together with John Henry Leh, John "Reds" MacFarlane, Herbert Spencer, Ralph C. Hutchinson, Andrew J. Sordoni. Also a member of the Tri-City Municipal Authority in the early 1950s, he was instrumental in the establishment of the Westmoreland-Latrobe Airport. *Courtesy of Kenneth Scholter).*

LEFT: Lieutenant Cyrus Bettis, U.S. Army Air Corps, after whom Bettis Field (Pittsburgh-Mckeesport Airport) was named. Bettis won the Pulitzer Trophy in 1925 with a world record flying speed of 249.342 miles per hour. He participated in the opening ceremonies for Pittsburgh-Mckeesport Airport in June 1925. On August 12, 1926, Bettis was leading a formation of three Army planes from Philadelphia to Michigan when they encountered poor weather near Bellefonte, PA. Lost in the fog, Bettis hit a treetop and crashed in the Allegheny Mountains. After regaining consciousness, he waited for search planes flying overhead to find him, but they failed to do so because of the dense woods. The injured Bettis crawled toward the sound of automobiles, but did not reach the road until the next morning. He finally made it to the road where he was rescued. He died from complications on September 1, 1926. *(Courtesy of Kenneth Scholter).*

Staff and Instructors, Main School of Aviation, Pittsburgh-Greensburg Airport, 1930 *(Courtesy of Frank Fox).*

Clyde Hauger measures a portion of the quonset hut for the Greensburg-City Airport at Carbon, ca. 1946/1947. *(Courtesy of Clyde Hauger).*

Lloyd Santmyer hands flowers to Westmoreland County Commissioner Mrs. Jean Whited on the day Greensburg City Airport opened in 1947. *(Courtesy of Clyde Hauger).*

Captain Frank Fox makes the first landing at Greenburg City Airport at Carbon in a Capital Airlines DC3, September 28, 1947. Today's Greensburg Central Catholic High School is built on the site. *(Photo by Howard Smeltzer. Courtesy of Frank Fox).*

A group of Greensburgers at the opening of the Greensburg City Airport at Carbon. Frank Fox stands seventh from right. He and First Officer William Richey (center), also of Greensburg, took the group for a ride in the Capital Airlines DC-3. The plane still bears the Pennsylvania-Central Airlines monogram. *(Courtesy of Clyde Hauger).*

Commonwealth of Pennsylvania

DEPARTMENT OF COMMERCE
PENNSYLVANIA AERONAUTICS COMMISSION
HARRISBURG

AIRPORT LICENSE

NO. 82

THIS IS TO CERTIFY THAT ON APPLICATION OF WESTMORELAND AIRCRAFT SALES

GREENSBURG CITY AIRPORT

LOCATED AT GREENSBURG, WESTMORELAND COUNTY, PENNSYLVANIA

HAS BEEN FOUND ADEQUATE AND PROPERLY QUALIFIED AND SAFE FOR PRIVATE OPERATIONS

AND IS HEREBY LICENSED TO OPERATE AS

A PRIVATE AIRPORT

THIS LICENSE IS ISSUED SUBJECT TO COMPLIANCE WITH THE RULES AND REGULA-TIONS OF THE COMMISSION, THE PROVISIONS OF WHICH ARE MADE A PART HEREOF AS THOUGH WRITTEN HEREIN, AND WILL REMAIN IN FULL FORCE AND EFFECT FROM THIS DATE AND WILL BE RENEWED ANNUALLY UNLESS REVOKED FOR CAUSE.

PENNSYLVANIA AERONAUTICS COMMISSION

INSPECTOR'S RENEWAL	DATE
Robert E. Zook	1-1-47

BY *Wm L Anderson*
EXECUTIVE DIRECTOR

NON-TRANSFERABLE

THIS LICENSE MUST BE CONSPICUOUSLY DISPLAYED AT THE ABOVE LOCATION

Clyde Hauger and Lloyd Santmyer's 1947 PCA license for the Greensburg City Airport, the year the airport opened. *(Courtesy of Clyde Hauger).*

ABOVE: On the left is Greensburg's Dick Coulter, with his brother Jack, founder of Central Airlines, which merged with Cliff Ball's Pennsylvania Airlines in 1936 to become Pennsylvania-Central Airlines. In 1948 PCA changed its name to Capital Airlines. In 1960 the airline was taken over by United Airlines. Coulter died with a student pilot in a crash at Bettis Field when the controls on his Piper aircraft failed. Student pilots accidentally bent the framework on the rudder while moving the plane. They straightened the bent frame instead of reporting the damage, according to Lloyd Santmeyer, who was an instructor at Bettis Field at the time. On the right is Helen Richey of McKeesport, Pennsylvania. She was hired by Coulter in 1934. Richey became the first woman to fly for a regularly scheduled airline, and the first woman sworn in as a pilot flying the U.S. mail. As a woman, she faced discrimination from many male pilots and was denied membership in the Airline Pilots Union. She resigned in October 1935. BELOW: A PCA Douglas aircraft at the Latrobe Airport. *(Courtesy of the Latrobe Historical Society).*

Bruno Ferrari in his office at Latrobe Airport, 1947. *(Courtesy of Clyde Hauger).*

BELOW: Clyde Hauger, left, with Bruno Ferrari and his all-wood Cessna UC-78, the "Bamboo Bomb." The Latrobe Construction Company plane was housed at the Latrobe Airport in 1947. *(Courtesy of Clyde Hauger).*

INSERT: The same plane in profile. *(Courtesy of Bob Downs).*

Official opening of the Westmoreland-Latrobe Airport, October 30, 1958. LEFT TO RIGHT: E.B. Elias, Mayor of Jeannette; Victor B. Stader, Burgess of Latrobe; Mrs. Cordelia Scaife May; James M. Underwood, Tri-City Authority Chairman; Homer Ruffner, Mayor of Greensburg. *(Courtesy of Latrobe Historical Society).*

1970s. Members of the Westmoreland County Airport Authority pose after approving the airport's terminal bond issue. SEATED: United States Congressman John Dent. STANDING LEFT TO RIGHT: Ed McMillan, Richard Guskiewicz, Gene McDonald, Benjamin Johnston, Earl F. Rectanus, Mike Watson. *(Courtesy of the Westmoreland County Airport Authority).*

Westmoreland County Commissioners and members of the Airport Authority participate in the groundbreaking ceremony for the new terminal building which was dedicated on November 14, 1972. FRONT ROW (left to right); James Kelley, Bernard Scherer, Leonard Bughman, John Le Carte, Francis Harvey. BACK ROW (left to right); James Underwood, Tom Whiteman, Arnold Palmer, Robert Lightcap, Gene McDonald, Victor Stader, B. Patrick Costello, John Ridilla. *(Courtesy of the Westmoreland County Airport Authority).*

County commissioners, airport officials, and government officials at the ceremony opening the runway extension, May 1986. LEFT Bruno Ferrari with his dog, "Pepe," stands next to U.S. Representative John Murtha, who is ready to cut the ribbon. *(Courtesy of the Westmoreland County Airport Authority).*

TOP: Westmoreland County Airport, ca. 1972, showing the North Hangar which dates from the WPA days in the mid-1930s. *(Courtesy of the* Latrobe Bulletin*)*.

ABOVE: Construction crews at work, ca. 1970s. *(Courtesy of the* Latrobe Bulletin*)*.

RIGHT: Early 1980s. construction of what will become the John Dent Tower.

Bruno Ferrari (insert) poses with his ever-present Chihuahua in front of his early mark Lear Jet. *(Courtesy of Bruno Ferrari).*

Westmoreland County Airport Authority members, administrators, and maintenance staff, 1987. SEATED: Francis Barch, Dennis Manown, Ben Johnston, Don Rossi, Dorothy Zello. STANDING: Gene McDonald, Bill Hallowell, Charlie Stockdale, Charlie Green, John Finfrock, Don Madl, Philip Weigel, Mike Salvatore, Gene Lakin, Linda Brasile, Gabe Monzo. *(Courtesy of the Westmoreland County Airport Authority).*

Today's Arnold Palmer Regional Airport front office trio at the 1989 air show. LEFT TO RIGHT: Executive Director Gene Lakin; Administrative Assistant Linda Brasile; Airport Manager Gabe Monzo. *(Courtesy of the Westmoreland County Airport Authority).*

Township, county, state and airport officials pose for a photo at the Ground breaking ceremony for the Rostraver Airport sewage project, December 9, 1995. LEFT TO RIGHT: Andy Temoshenka, Phil Morrow, Dennis Manown, Frank Irey, Gene McDonald, Dorothy Zello, Richard Vidmer, Gene Porterfield, Mike Smith, Herman Mihalich, Ted Simon, Nick Lorenzo, Jack Hazelbaker, Carl Russell, Regis Serinko, Austin Cratty. *(Courtesy of the Westmoreland County Airport Authorityy).*

Westmoreland County Airport Authority, 2001. SEATED LEFT TO RIGHT: Anthony Ferrante, Arnold Palmer, John Finfrock. STANDING LEFT TO RIGHT: J. Clifford Naugle, Oland Canterna, Janice Smarto, Phil Morrow, Dorothy Zello, Donald Rossi. *(Courtesy of Dorthy Zello).*

Arnold Palmer Regional Airport maintenance staff, 2001. LEFT TO RIGHT: Mike Umbaugh, Terry Stuck, Moe Haas, Sean Phillips, Tom Stynchula. *(Courtesy of Dorothy Zello).*

Arnold Palmer Regional Airport control tower staff, 2001. SEATED (left to right); Bob Novitsky, Paul Salonick, Charlie Green. STANDING (left to right); Paul Johns, Greg Retallick, Rich Fleischer. *(Courtesy of Dorothy Zello).*

Don Rechichar (far left) and Jim Gavatorta (far right) maintenance staff at Westmoreland County's Rostraver Airport pose with Gene Lakin and Gabe Monzo. *(Courtesy of Dorothy Zello).*

A Beginning in Chance and Hospitality

It was five o'clock in the afternoon. The military Curtiss Jenny raced against the storm. A threatening, gray sky followed not far behind. Below, in the late afternoon light, among the rolling fields and hillsides, lush with summer crops and foliage, was the campus of the Saint Vincent College and Archabbey. Lieutenant Pearson was piloting the struggling Jenny. He could hear, even above the sound of the Hispano-Suiza engine, the thunder rumbling at his tail. Pearson tapped his observer, Sergeant Weidencamp on the shoulder. Weidencamp turned to the rear cockpit, and understood that the lieutenant wanted to land. Pearson was gesturing toward a broad clover-field on the college campus. It looked like a good place to hold up for the night. The Jenny would not last long in the storm rolling in from the west, toward Chestnut Ridge. Besides, the Benedictines were well known for their hospitality to travelers. Pearson banked toward the clover field, hoping there wouldn't be a crosswind. It could be murderous.

The Jenny caused quite a stir among the locals. Even though airplanes loomed in the public imagination, they were a rare sight in rural Western Pennsylvania. Only sixteen years earlier, the Wright brothers took their Flyer to the air at Kitty Hawk, and the Great War had just ended nine months prior. In that conflict, the actions of America's air hero, Eddie Rickenbacker had thrilled the American populace. Flying machines appealed to the adventurous spirit in all people, not least of all the monks who came out to watch the Jenny struggling to land.

Alphonse Farley, O.S.B. looked up. He saw the dark wings of the Jenny silhouetted against the graying sky. Alphonse, together with his confreres, Cuthbert Gallick and Ruppert Stadtmiller, made their way up a steep hillside on the northside of the college campus. As they neared the top, they saw the now silent Jenny in the clover field. Two men were standing in conference near the aircraft. The three clerics approached the two men in greeting. Some local farmers were approaching across the adjoining fields, a few from the Kerr farm less than a mile away. Little did they know it at the time, but the Kerr family would play an important role in the future of aviation in the area.

Pearson and Weidencamp explained their hasty landing to the monks. They were one of a squadron of All American Army Aerial Pathfinders that left Long Island, New York, a week earlier. Their mission was to map air mail routes and chart emergency landing fields. Without hesitation, and true to the reputation of their community, Farley invited the weary airmen to have dinner and spend the night at the college.

It was August 21, 1919. It was the first day Saint Vincent College became associated with aviation. Somewhere in Scottdale, PA, a young man named Charlie Carroll was taking flying lessons from Torrance Overholt, a veteran World War I pilot. The day also marked the humble beginning of the Arnold Palmer Regional Airport.

> *"The Jenny would not last long in the storm rolling in from the west, toward Chestnut Ridge. Besides, the Benedictines were well known for their hospitality to travelers. Pearson banked toward the clover field, hoping there wouldn't be a crosswind. It could be murderous."*

The *Latrobe Bulletin* next day reported, "As soon as the weather gave promise of turning fair, Lieutenant Pearson and Sergeant Weidencamp resumed their flight to Columbus, Ohio, yesterday. Accompanied by all of the residents of the Archabbey, the two fliers proceeded from the college to the field, tuned up the engine a little, and then started on their way, making a nice ascent. A big crowd witnessed their departure. The aviators headed immediately for the railroad, and followed it toward Pittsburgh."

Later, Pearson related his experience to his superiors, and the clover field at Saint Vincent became an official emergency landing area for the American Army Airplane Service and the Postal Air Service. Both Army and civilian pilots thereafter regularly used the field. It came to be called the Saint Vincent Aviation Field.

Charlie Carroll soloed in 1920. He had friends in Latrobe. When he came to visit them in his surplus Jenny, he landed on the clover field at Saint Vincent. It wouldn't be long before he saw some potential in a cow pasture on the Kerr farm, at the junction of Old U.S. Route 30 and State Highway 981, in the Borough of Latrobe.

This is the Curtiss "Jenny" JN4-H that landed on the clover field at Saint Vincent College, 21 August 1919. The plane contains a Wright-Hispano engine ("Hisso"). Planes of this type were retained by the military after World War I because they were considered to be too "hot" for civilians. Surplus Jennies with the OX5 engine were released for sale to the public. This model became the plane used by the "Barnstormers." Typical of the military type, this Jenny carries an auxiliary fuel tank under the center of the top wing. Together, the main and auxiliary tanks carried twenty-two gallons of fuel, sufficient for two-and-one-half hours of flying time. The Benedictine monks accompanying local farmers are (left to right) Alphonse Farley, Rupert Stadtmiller and Cuthbert Gallick *(Courtesy of the Saint Vincent Archabbey Archives)*

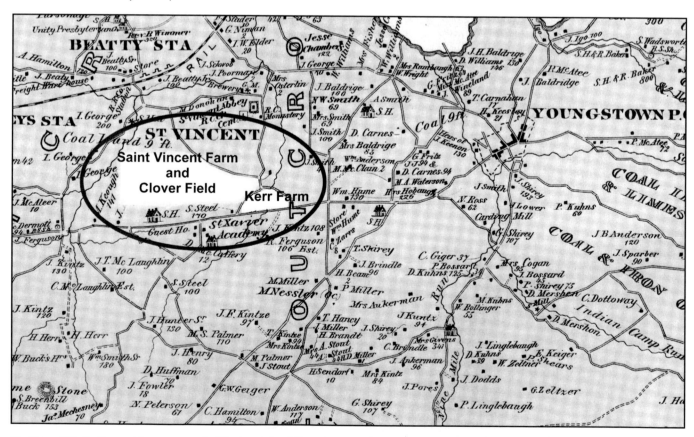

Portion of Unity Township on an early Westmoreland County map showing the location of the Saint Vincent clover field in relationship to the Kerr property.

Charles B. Carroll

Charlie Carroll was a thirty-year-old mechanic in Scottdale, in partnership with a man named Torrence Overholt. Anything with an engine in it appealed to Charlie, but he was developing a fascination with the Flying Machine. The Army had used the rugged Curtiss JN-4s during the Great War as trainers for its fledgling Army Air Service. With the ending of the war, the government offered their OX5 powered "Jennies" at a cheap price to anyone who wanted to buy one. Charlie jumped at the chance. Pilots' licenses were not required in those days; that would not happen until 1927.

Charlie, Torrance Overholt, and the First Jenny

Sometime in 1919, Charlie and his partner, Torrance Overholt, a pilot and World War I veteran, went to New York to pick up Charlie's new Jenny. On the way back to Pennsylvania, the Jenny developed magneto trouble, and the pair made a forced landing on a farm in New Jersey, running into a fence in the process. The damage to the plane was extensive enough that take off was impossible. Charlie and Torrence had a truck come out from Scottdale, loaded the plane on the flat bed, brought it home, and kept it on Felger's farm.

Charlie had gotten a little formal instruction from Torrance but presumably not enough to go it alone. He would learn much of what he knew through trial and error. One day, Charlie had the plane out, starting and stopping the engine and taxiing around trying to get the feel of the controls. Charlie pushed the throttle. The OX5 engine sputtered and the airframe shook. The Jenny bounded over the uneven pasture, gaining speed. A sudden, strong wind lifted the Jenny off the ground like a leaf. Charlie found himself on his first solo flight, all because of a whim of the weather, a whim that would secure his place in aviation.

To Find A Landing Field

Charlie made a safe landing. He practiced more and more, getting to know the Jenny inside and out. A plan developed in his mind. Charlie was quick to realize the commercial importance of aviation to Western Pennsylvania, and he believed an airfield in a rural community with easy access to a major road and railhead would benefit the area. He flew his Jenny over the rolling countryside in search of a field that would suit his purpose. He crisscrossed the skies many times, buzzing low over the small communities that dotted the landscape. The sight of his Jenny, moving like a slow, watchful bird across the sky had become familiar to those below.

Charlie often flew to Latrobe where he had friends. When he did, he made good use of the Saint Vincent Aviation Field. He knew well the story of the two airmen who had made a forced landing there.

The Kerr Farm

It didn't take Charlie long to realize the potential of the area, conveniently located near the Pennsylvania Railroad and two major roads US Route 30 (The Lincoln Highway) and State Road 981 (Manito Road). The roads provided easy access to a number of communities throughout Westmoreland County and beyond. Could there be, he wondered, a place nearer their junction?

Less than a mile away from the college field and located exactly at the junction was the Kerr farm. One day, Charlie landed in their cow pasture.

Perhaps in some dusty folder in borough or county archives are the legal details of Charlie's lease with the Kerrs, but except for Lloyd Santmyer's recollections, the human details would have been lost to us. Here is the way Lloyd remembers the day Charlie landed:

So Charlie came up here and was flying around Route 30. It was the Lincoln Highway back then. It went right through Saint Xavier's, across the Kerr farm, and on into Youngstown. Charlie saw this pasture out there at the crossroads of the Lincoln Highway and 981, which was then the Manito Road. There were a couple of cows in the field. So he landed in there. Andy Berzda, who lived on a farm across the way (where they built Mission Inn later), came over to Charlie.

Charlie said, 'I'm Charlie Carroll from Scottdale. I'm looking for a field to fly out of around here. Is this your field?'

And Andy said, 'No. It belongs to the Kerr family right below here. That's their house and barn down below.'

Charlie said, 'Do you suppose they'd be down there?'

Andy said, 'I don't know. Why don't you just park here and go down and see.'

So Charlie walked down to see them. He introduced himself and told them what he was looking for.

They said, 'We farm the field. We plant corn there and everything. Right now, it's our pasture and we're feeding up our cows. We'll talk it over with our family and see if it's all right for you to fly in and out of here with passengers and stuff.'

So, that was the beginning of it, and that was 1924. So they made a deal with Charlie to come over and fly out of the field. Which he did. And I have been a part of the old airport ever since it was there, clear up to now. I learned to fly there. Raymond Elder taught me. And I worked with and for Charlie into the 1930s. We were buddies. He called the place Longview Flying Field.

Longview Flying Field

The roots of the first airport grew deep into the ground where they would remain and continue to grow. Longview Flying Field was exactly that. The word "airport" had not yet been coined, and the common terms of the day were "flying field" or "aerodrome." Charlie's field was the typical FBO (Fixed Base of Operation) of the time. Charlie's dream slowly took shape. He had established his flying field, now he needed to maintain it. To keep his flying field operating, he bought and repaired Jennies and other kinds of early airplanes; he sold airplanes, rented airplanes, did charter work and sold airplane rides to the curious and fascinated public. Almost from the day he opened the Longview Flying Field, Charlie put on air shows, complete with barnstorming, fly-ins, parachute jumps, wing-walks, and other kinds of exhibitions. All of Pennsylvania's aviation pioneers and promoters came to those shows. They included Dewey Noyes, Merle Moltrup, Al Litzenberger, Clifford Ball, D. Barr Peat, Russ Brinkley, Kenny Scholter, and others. Many of them became Charlie's friends and would remain so for the next four or five decades, until their deaths.

Welcoming Charles Lindbergh

The year 1927 was the year that Charles Augustus Lindbergh flew nonstop across the Atlantic in his Ryan monoplane *Spirit of St. Louis*. Aviation was never the same after that. Charlie and Russ Brinkley (together with thousands of others) wasted no time in getting to Washington, D.C. to welcome Lindbergh back to the United States. They piled into seventy-eight-year-old Scottdale First National Bank director Burt Keister's straight-eight Paige automobile and set off, with Charlie behind the wheel, Keister next to him, with Detroit parachutist Steve Boudreaux and Russell Brinkley in the back. Brinkley wrote of the trip in the June 14, 1927 edition of the *Scottdale Independent Observer*:

Charlie Carroll at the wheel makes a Pullman car ride like an old time 'iron tire' wagon by comparison. We made the trip to Washington, over mountains and all, via the Lincoln route, in little less than seven hours, and came back via the National Pike in less than six hours, to Scottdale. And our seventy-eight-year-old aviation booster was as chipper as a 'sixteen year old' when we finished the trip. We wonder if the people of Westmoreland County believe that aviation is confined to the respective trips of Lindy, Chamberlain, Byrd, and Charlie Carroll's Long View Flying Field.

Florida, Ed Musick, and Pan-American

While business was good at times, it was difficult to keep the dream in flight. The winter months from 1926 to 1931 were the most difficult. Most people found it a chore getting around on the ground, let alone subject themselves to an open-cockpit Jenny in freezing weather. To make ends meet, Charlie traveled to Florida and flew copilot with Ed Musick for Pan-Am on Fokker Trimotors and Sikorsky S-38 Flying Boats. Early February 1929 must have remained a special time for Charlie. That was when he met Charles Lindbergh, who was blazing a route for mail and passenger service into Central America. Concerning that occasion, Mr. and Mrs. A.C. Farmer of Scottdale, in Florida at the time, wrote home to two friends, Teddy and Ellwood:

I was sure glad to hear from you and am going to send you some pictures of "Lindy" and the aeroplane that he flew to Porto Rico. Charlie Carroll put all the gas and oil in the ship for him just before he took off. How would you like to be Charlie?

New Alexandria Airport

In the early 1930s, there arose the possibility that Charlie would lose the lease on the Kerr property, so he and Lloyd Santmyer started the New Alexandria Airport. Joe Reedy helped put up the metal hangar.

The "Longview Boys" shuttled back and forth between the two airports, performing their usual antics. A young Frank Fox became airport manager. A big attraction was Dr. Smith's big Ford trimotor flown by Al Litzenberger and Ken Scholter. On September 10, 1930, residents between the New Alexandria and J.D. Hill Airports felt what they thought to be raindrops. They were mistaken. The refreshment stand at New Alex had run out of ice, so Charlie hopped in *Miss Tydol*, his OX5 Jenny, flew to Hill Airport, then sent someone to the Latrobe Ice and Provision Plant for ice. Charlie loaded the ice on his plane and returned to New Alex. What the locals thought was rain, were really drops falling from the melting ice.

J.D. Hill Airport

A friend of Charlie's from the early days was J.D. Hill, an airmail pilot from Scottdale. Hill was a great pilot who pushed his machines to the limit. He earned the nickname the "Bird Boy of Scottdale" for his daring achievements in early aviation. The same year Charles Lindbergh made his historic flight, Hill was killed in his own attempt to cross the Atlantic to Rome, Italy. One imagines that Carroll realized early in his career as a pilot that flying was a dangerous profession, that there was always going to be something beyond the control of even the most skilled pilot. It was the price one had to pay to fly.

In early June 1928, amid great celebration, Charlie renamed Longview Flying Field in Hill's honor. It would be called Hill Airport at Latrobe until 1935, the year Charlie and Latrobe Borough expanded the runways with Works Progress Administration money and renamed it Latrobe Airport.

The End of the Glory Days

By 1935 the glory days were just about over. The rest was business. Apart from his other achievements, Charlie Carroll managed the same airport for nearly thirty-five years. He retired in 1959 at the age of sixty-nine. He would have gone on longer, but the Tri-City Municipal Authority that would create the Latrobe-Westmoreland Airport required that all interested in the position of manager should submit applications. Charlie's application was rejected. "Babe" Krinock remembers that day: "Charlie had tears in his eyes. 'They didn't take me, Babe,' he said."

B. Patrick Costello, a prominent Greensburg attorney, former World War II pilot, and Airport Authority member for eighteen years, remembers Charlie, wearing a straw hat and sitting in a favorite chair just inside the North Hanger, managing, organizing and, surrounded by admirers seated in folding chairs, reminiscing.

Don Riggs describes the reception Carroll received in 1965, when he returned to Latrobe from his retirement in Florida to attend the tenth anniversary of his founding of the OX5 Club: "All those old timers said, 'Charlie, you're still around, and we're glad.' I mean. They revered the guy!"

Earl Metzler tells this story:

Charlie knew all the important people in aviation. All of them came out to his airport in Latrobe. He was a good mechanic. He must have rebuilt twenty planes out there. He would go down to Florida in the winters in the early days to earn extra money flying and maintaining engines. He was a chief maintenance superintendent at Pan-American in Florida. He always came back to run his airport, though. Around 1955 I asked him: 'Why didn't you stay with Pan-American, Charlie? You'd be a big-wheel by now?' He took his pipe out of his mouth, looked at me for a couple seconds and said: 'All my old buddies are dead.' I think I know what he meant.

Charlie Carroll died in 1973 in Florida. He was eighty-three years old. Charlie's youngest son, Captain Don Carroll, a retired airline pilot, tells of an eight-inch-thick scrapbook filled with photographs and news clippings that Charlie kept of his aviation days. Grace Carroll, Don's mother, aviatrix and OX5 Club charter member, cherished the scrapbook for many years, until her death at ninety-five in a retirement home in Florida. Today, no one knows what happened to that scrapbook, though it is thought that it was taken from her during her last days by someone unknown. Who knows what treasures of aviation history were contained within it.

Charlie Carroll posing beside his war surplus Jenny at the time of his solo flight in 1920. He landed on the Saint Vincent Aviation Field, now site of present Rooney Hall. *(Courtesy of the Saint Vincent Archabbey Archives).*

Charlie Carroll in 1924, when he leased the Kerr farm cow pasture. He called the field Longview Flying Field. He has landed on the Saint Vincent Aviation Field. The farmhouse in the background, now the site of Green Meadows retirement complex, was then occupied by the Zuercher family, according to Rev. Roland Heid, O.S.B. *(Courtesy of Dorothy Carroll Sadler).*

Charlie Carroll sits in the front cockpit, and Carl Strickler is in the rear. The photo was taken in 1925 on Felger's farm in Scottdale when Charlie was a partner with Joe Maloy in a Flint automobile dealership. *(Courtesy of Frank Fox).*

Fédération Aéronautique Internationale

United States of America

ANNUAL SPORTING LICENSE ISSUED TO

Mr. C. B. Carroll.......

Place of Birth Uniontown, Pa.

Date of Birth Jan. 6, 1890.

Contest Committee Chairman

Orville Wright

Year of 1927

F. A. I. Certificate No. 6577

Issued by N.A.A.

Type of Aircraft Airplane

Signature of Licensee

License No. 130.

Valid until December 31 of the year of issuance, 1927

Charlie Carroll's pilot's license number 130, signed by Orville Wright. *(Courtes of Marcia Nair).*

To Frank Fox From Chas. B. Carroll. Soloed 1920

Charlie Carroll greets Frank Fox just after Frank landed at the Latrobe Airport. The photo was taken in the mid-1950s. Frank wrote on the back: "Charlie always greeted me at the airport." Charlie inscribed photo and recorded the year of his solo flight. *(Courtesy of Frank Fox).*

PAN AMERICAN AIRWAYS. INC.

PILOT: **MUSICK**   CO-PILOT: **CARROLL**

PLANE: NC- 396-E DATE: 3-19-31 TIME: 9:00

WEATHER REPORT

	STATION		
ALTITUDE	MIAMI	KEY WEST	HAVANA
SURFACE	N 2	N 10	NW 7
350	ENE 8	N 14	
600			NNW 9
700	SE 14	N 17	
1200			NNW 9
1350	1050 SSE 17	N 14	
1800	1700 SE 21		NNW 11
2000		N 8	
2400	2350 SSE 18		NNW 9
2600		NE 5	
3000	SSE 14		SW 18
3200		NE 4	
3700		NW 8	
4500	4200 S 10	WNW 12	WNW 8
6000	5000 S 11	NW 15	NW 15
8000		WNW 17	
CEILING		Unlimited	SC.-2500
VISIBILITY		12 mi.	5 mi.

STEWARD: **LAWRENCE**   OPERATOR: **MURPHY**

NO. OF PASS.: 10   NO. OF ALIENS:

LOAD: 4757   145

Charlie Carroll and Ed Musick's flight log for March 19, 1931 for Miami, Key West, and Havana. *(Courtesy of Don Carroll).*

ABOVE: Charlie Carroll and his son Jim, Sarasota Florida, 1969.

LEFT: Captain Don Carroll, Charlie's son, and Charlie's grand-daughter, Tricia. *(Courtesy of Don Carroll).*

BELOW: 1965. Charlie Carroll holds the OX5 commemorative plaque presented to him at the ten year celebration of the founding of the OX5 Club of America at Latrobe on August 27, 1955. *(Courtesy of Don Carroll).*

J. D. Hill Airport: Dedication Day June 2, 1928

It was June 1, 1928. Charlie Carroll walked across the field toward the hanger. Dew soaked his boots. The cool June morning filled the air with a promise of a beautiful day. Across the rolling fields of the Kerr property, Carroll saw the spires of the Saint Vincent Archabbey glow with the first rays of the sun. To his left he heard an automobile on the Old Lincoln Highway. He hoped that in the next couple of days that road would be packed with cars coming to his airfield.

In the hanger, Carroll's Canuck biplane waited. He stood there for a moment staring at the silent aircraft. He thought about how just five years before he founded the Longview Flying Field, the first real airport at Latrobe. Tomorrow he would rededicate the airfield in honor of his friend, J.D. Hill, who had been killed the previous summer in an attempt to fly nonstop across the Atlantic to Rome.

It was going to be a big day for aviation in Pennsylvania. He wished J.D. could be there to see it.

June 2, 1928 "Angels Or Gods..."

Music from the American Legion band swelled as crowds of spectators milled around aircraft at the west end of the landing strip. Pilots from Pennsylvania, West Virginia, Ohio and beyond stood around their machines, talking with fascinated people. A troop of boy scouts from Scottdale, there as part of the day's festivities, eagerly pressed the pilots for tales of adventure. The pilots in their flying suits, leather caps and goggles resembled to the scouts the romantic aces of the Great War as they were portrayed in films and books. For the younger people it must have been like meeting angels or gods.

June 2, 1928, the time of the dedication of the J. D. Hill Airport , Latrobe, formerly Longview Flying Field. This group is gathered by *The Pride of Pittsburgh*, a Ryan Brougham monoplane and replica of Charles Lindbergh's *Spirit of St. Louis*. The plane was owned at the time by C.P. Mayer, who brought it to Latrobe on many occasions from his field in Bridgeville. TOP ROW, LEFT TO RIGHT, as identified by Ken Scholter and Lloyd Santmyer: Unidentified, unidentified, J. W. Smith, Bill Day, C.P. Mayer, Charles Carroll, D. Barr Peat, Carl Strickler, Clyde Hauger. BOTTOM ROW, LEFT TO RIGHT: Hub Morgan, Merle Moltrop, Curley Lovejoy, unidentified, Christenson. In 1928, Clifford Ball bought the craft for use on his CAM 11 mail route from Pittsburgh to Cleveland.

(Courtesy of Ken Scholter).

Charlie Carroll and Russ Brinkley, field manager of Longview Flying Field, were pleased with the turnout. The airport had grown in the consciousness of the local population for the past five years. The sounds of airplanes overhead had become almost commonplace. But the winters were still financially tough for the airport. Brinkley and Carroll knew those months would be difficult for the next couple of years, but they were sure that the airport would survive.

Charlie was admired by many aviators from the tri-state area, but after the weekend events of June 2 and 3, 1928 his reputation was sure to be enhanced. The pilots in attendance were the ones responsible for the array of aircraft present for the dedication. The public would see the likes of such aviation pioneers as C.P. Mayer, Clifford Ball, Carl Strickler, Dewey Noyes and Raymond Elder. The celebration was also because no one had yet been injured or killed in the airport's five years of operation. Considering the dangers of early flight, this was indeed an impressive figure.

It was a quarter till twelve. The aerial parade over Greensburg and Latrobe was to begin at noon. The time had come to get the pilots together and prepare their machines for flight. A tremendous excitement charged the cool June air. It was a dream come true for local aviation enthusiasts.

Engines pulsed to life. The odor of exhaust wafted into the crowd. Planes moved forward toward the runway. Carroll sat in the Canuck. He would be racing in the craft the next day in the twenty-five-mile race. He felt a moment of expectation mixed with a little fear. This was the biggest event ever to take place at his airfield. He hoped everything would be all right. He saw the boy scouts from his hometown of Scottdale enthusiastically waving to the pilots. Carroll smiled and hit the throttle of the biplane's OX5 engine.

The aerial parade marched into the sky. "Crates" of all types took flight. Jennies, OX5 Challengers, Wacos, Canucks and the Brougham Monoplane, *The Pride of Pittsburgh.* Some planes circled overhead waiting for others aircraft to gain altitude. Thousands of eyes turned upwards and followed the progress of the machines as they made their way toward Greensburg. In backyards, fields and roads, people stopped to look up, gesture in amazement or cheer. More than one spectator was with the planes in spirit as they defied gravity.

The spectacle drew people to the airport like pilgrims to a holy site. The *Greensburg Morning Review, Latrobe Bulletin,* and the *Scottdale Independent Observer* did their part, too. For days, the newspapers stirred up excitement over the events.

As the aircraft returned to the airport from the parade, workers made ready the speakers' platform. Speakers included Wesley L. Smith, manager of the National Air Transport; Frank Hill, brother of J.D. Hill; Clifford Ball, Charlie Carroll, C.P. Mayer and Russ Brinkley. After all the words were spoken, the aerial exhibition continued. One of Hill's airmail buddies flew Hill's airmail plane over the field and dropped roses.

The crowd heard a lone airplane overhead. Shielding their eyes, they peered into the bright sky for the aircraft. It came out of the sun like a pursuit plane of the Great War looking for its next victim. An Eagle Rock biplane descended low over the gathering, Carl Strickler in behind the controls. Strickler waggled the wings, then put the plane into a loop the loop. Carl filled the sky with Immelman turns, a maneuver made famous in the Great War by one of Germany's early air aces, Max Immelman. His expertise as a pilot was already well-known, but his flying display at the Hill Airport dedication amazed all present, even his pilot comrades. Not to be outdone, several performed stunts just as incredible, terrifying and breathtaking.

Russ Brinkley, relieved of his organizational duties, took to the air that day as well. He ascended with Raymond Elder, got to altitude, then stepped out onto the wing of the plane and gave a deft demonstration of wing walking. Other wing-walkers performed their stunts along with Brinkley. They were entered in "the daredevil program." There were prizes for the most daring, but history does not record the winners, only that all made it safely back to the ground.

Other daredevils included parachutist Clarence Brown of Kansas City. His exhibition was initially planned for the June 2 ceremonies but had to be canceled because of high winds. The following day, Clarence would live up to his reputation by amazing the crowds with his incredible free-falls.

After all of the speeches, aerobatics and aerial stunts concluded, Charlie hosted a dinner and reception at the nearby Mountain View Inn. Clifford Ball was master of ceremonies, and Russ Brinkley was toastmaster. Wesley Smith spoke about the importance of commercial aviation. Charlie Carroll, C.P. Mayer and Carl Strickler gave responses to Smith's speech. The evening wound down with performances by musicians and vaudeville acts.

The following day brought more excitement. The June 2 ceremonies caused quite a stir in the communities surrounding the airport. People were talking with awe and fascination about the aerial parade. Many wanted to get a closer look at the machines and the daring pilots who flew them. The next day the Old Lincoln Highway would be choked with cars just as Charlie Carroll had hoped.

June 3, 1928. Race in the Sky

The State Police patrolled the Old Lincoln Highway attempting to keep the traffic moving. Cars were bumper to bumper for four miles. Heat rose in eerie waves from the roofs of the vehicles.

The events lined up for Sunday, June 3, were very similar to the previous day's. Another noontime aerial parade passed over Greensburg and Latrobe. This time, however, many of the people who witnessed the parade the day before would now be seeing it from the fields surrounding the Hill Airport or from automobiles backed up for miles on the Old Lincoln Highway . After the conclusion of the parade, a demonstration of formation flying led up to the events everyone was talking about—the aerial races.

Commercial planes raced first. A ten-mile course took the planes out over the rolling hills of Westmoreland County. The next race of twenty-five-miles had the likes of Charlie Carroll and Raymond Elder in it. Carroll flew the Canuck and came in second. Elder also flew a Canuck and won the race. The highlight of the day was the fifty-mile race over a triangular course. The entries all exceeded speeds of 100 miles per hour, which for 1928 was faster than most people could imagine. The fifty-mile race had generated a lot of publicity in the newspapers. The rivalry between the Dewey Noyes, an airmail pilot on Clifford Ball's Cleveland-Pittsburgh route and

Carl Strickler got special attention. Both of these men expected to beat the other in a "spite race," but they would have competition. Clifford March of Cleveland had won every high-speed race in which he flew. In his Whirlwind Laird machine he was the favorite.

As starting time drew near, the crowd became more agitated. The pilots revved their engines. The race was being called a "free-for-all," meaning that throttles would be wide open all the way. Carl Strickler sat in his Eagle Rock preparing for the flight. Dewey Noyes listened to the smooth action of the engine in his Whirlwind Laird. Clifford March calmly checked the instruments of his craft and waited for the signal to start.

The race was close. It concluded with Dewey Noyes as the winner taking home $500.00 cash. Strickler took $250.00 in prize money.

It is not known where the course took the pilots. It is plausible that at some point the planes roared over Greensburg and Latrobe like the aerial parades of June 2 and 3. The length of the race would certainly take the pilots over many other communities in Westmoreland County.

The opportunity for people to be a part of the dream Charlie, had created with the Hill Airport was undoubtedly a reason for the fifty-mile race.

The airport had now become a part of the community. It supported the notion that almost anything was possible.

Charlie Carroll watches as an aircraft warms up on the J.D. Hill Airport dedication day. *(Courtesy of Lloyd Santmyer).*

A Douglas O2-B at J.D. Hill Airport, June 2, 1928. *(Courtesy of Lloyd Santmyer).*

Fueling a Pitcairn Mailwing flown by Dewey Noyes in the J.D. Hill Airport dedication day air race. *(Courtesy of Lloyd Santmyer).*

Raymond Elder sits in the rear cockpit of Dave Patterson's American Eagle. The plane was used in the air race on dedication day. Charlie also parked the aircraft near the junction of the Lincoln Highway and U.S. Route 981 as an attraction for tourists and those eager to fly in an airplane. *(Courtesy of Lloyd Santmyer).*

C.P. Mayer's Pride of Pittsburgh circles the J.D. Hill Airport, June 2, 1928. *(Courtesy of Lloyd Santmyer).*

Skywriters at work over the J. D. Hill Airport, June 2, 1928. *(Courtesy of Lloyd Santmyer).*

A Boeing B-1 bomber brought in for the dedication of the J.D. Hill Airport. Military aircraft, then as now, were prime attractions at air shows. *(Courtesy of Lloyd Santmyer).*

A Curtiss Jenny (left) and Charlie Carroll's OX5 Challenge, Miss Tydol, lined up at J.D. Hill Airport, *(Courtesy of Anna Mary Topper).*

A speaker, possibly J.D. Hill's brother, at the dedication ceremony, J.D. Hill Airport. *(Courtesy of Lloyd Santmyer).*

Charlie Carroll and a group of young admirers on dedication day, J.D. Hill Airport. *(Courtesy of Lloyd Santmyer).*

James DeWitt Hill. *(Courtesy of Jesse Davidson Archives).*

James DeWitt ("J.D.") Hill

Old Glory stood ready on the hard-packed sand. She was a Jupiter powered Fokker monoplane, gold and silver, with an eagle-wreath insignia and her name painted beneath her wings. Forty-five year old James DeWitt Hill, from Scottdale, Pennsylvania, had won the toss from Lloyd Bertaud to pilot her from Old Orchard Beach, Maine, on a transatlantic flight to Rome sponsored by the publisher, William Randolph Hearst. The day was September 6, 1927. This would be the last flight J.D. would ever make.

J.D. had been flying since March 1909, when, at Hot Springs, Arkansas, he took up his airship, afterwards writing to his father about the flight. J.D.'s colorful career included training under Glenn Curtiss at San Diego, where J.D. earned his Aero Club Land Plane certificate number 234 in 1913. Later, J.D. worked for Curtiss at his Hammondsport, New York factory before and after World War I. During the war, J.D. was a civilian instructor, and a number of famous World War I aces received their training from him.

After the war, J.D. served a stint as test pilot with Air Service Engineering at Dayton Field in Ohio, then rejoined the Curtiss Company. J.D. flew in various air races, and for the Oregon, Washington, Idaho Airplane Company, a Curtiss branch. He joined the United States Air Mail Service July 1, 1924. At 42, he was the service's oldest pilot.

J.D. became famous for his cigar-chomping antics, using the cigars to time flights between refueling stops on the Air Mail Services "Hell's Stretch" over the Allegheny Mountains. There were many times when J.D. and his friend, Bertaud, passed each other in the air over the Alleghenies, J.D. flying west to Cleveland, and Bertaud flying east to Hadly Field.

When he was very young, J.D. borrowed his mother's favorite tablecloth and used it to parachute from the roof the family stable. The attempt failed. Then J.D. persuaded his brother to the same. Frank also failed. Paternal intervention finally put an end to the experiment. Perhaps that experience created in J.D. an aversion to jumping from a plane. He never parachuted from any plane he flew, even if it was damaged, preferring instead to ride the plane to a landing, something he was often forced to do. Once, during a 1919 air race to Canada, his Curtiss Oriole went into a spin. Too low to recover, J.D. braced for the inevitable crash. The plane was a total loss, but J.D. and his passenger walked away without a scratch. A week later, undaunted by his experience, J.D. chose the same Curtiss type to fly from Buffalo to Syracuse, with silent screen film star, Hope Eden, as his passenger.

J.D. was a colorful, well-known aviator and aeronautical engineer when he and Bertaud made plans to cross the Atlantic Ocean. This came after Charles Levine, owner of the Bellanca built Columbia (the same plane first considered by Lindbergh before his historic flight in the Spirit of St. Louis), bumped Bertaud from a flight designed to best Lindbergh's transatlantic record. Instead, Clarence D. Chamberlain, with Levine as passenger, successfully piloted the Columbia across the ocean to Berlin. Thus it was that J.D. and Bertaud made their own arrangements to fly the Atlantic to Rome. In June 1927, Hill contacted Columbia designer, Giuseppe Bellanca, and asked him to build a plane capable of flying nonstop to Rome. Bellanca, however, needed more time than J.D. could spare. So Bertaud made arrangements with Philip Payne, the managing editor of the Daily Mirror, a Hearst paper. In exchange for a plane, the Mirror could use the flight for publicity. Payne insisted on going on the flight, against the objections of Hearst, who was also beginning to object to the flight itself. Payne won out.

On that day in September, with festivities accompanying the takeoff, with J.D. at the controls, with Bertaud on the radio, and Payne stretched out beneath the fuel tank (there was no passenger seat), the overweight Fokker monoplane rumbled down the hard-packed, natural runway at Old Orchard Beach, Maine. *Old Glory* flew low, maintaining a speed of about 100 miles per hour. To the uninitiated, this seemed excellent time. But J.D. must have sensed that the plane was far too heavy, and that altitude and speed were not enough to get them to Rome. If he had those thoughts, they probably would not have much concerned him. After all, J.D. had had experience landing on the sea. He trained in seaplanes as early as 1913, and though *Old Glory* was not a seaplane, it did have the latest in survival equipment, an actual radio station with the call letters WRHP (William Randolph Hearst), and a waterproof, automatic transmitter powered by a wind generator. On board, the transmitter was to send out the station's call letters in Morse code, allowing stations along the way to track the plane's progress.

Unfortunately, neither expertise nor equipment was enough to save *Old Glory* and her crew. Early on September 7, 1927, a cold, misty day, *Old Glory* and her crew went down in the rough waters of the North Atlantic. Though parts of the aircraft were recovered, J.D., Bertaud and Payne were lost forever.

In June 1928, Charlie Carroll renamed his Latrobe Longview Flying Field after his friend and sometime instructor. In a couple months, people seemed to forget about J.D. J.D. Hill Airport in Latrobe came to be called just plain "Hill Airport," and visitors thought that was because it sat at the top of a grade of the Lincoln Highway as it came in from the west. That, too, would pass. Less than a decade later, J.D. Hill Airport would become the Latrobe Airport.

On October 18, 1970, a day perfect for flying, citizens, politicians, officials, old friends, aviation representatives and representatives for the Hill family gathered around the gazebo in Scottdale to dedicate a monument to James DeWitt Hill, the "Bird Boy of Scottdale." Within the stone monument, faced with a bronze plaque of J.D., they placed a speech written by J.D.'s old friend, A.G. Trimble, the names of the donors of the memorial, and a flag that had flown over the North and South Poles.

J.D. Hill preparing for a night airmail flight. Postmaster Harry New hands J.D. some commemorative covers. *(Jesse Davidson Archives).*

Navigation by Cigars

During his air mail days, J.D. Hill used a cigar as an instrument of navigation. A Pittsburgh newspaper dated Thursday May 19, 1938, in a series honoring National Air Mail Week, tells the story: "Hill...took off from Cleveland one day for Hadley Field, New Brunswick, with a load of mail and a pocket full of cigars. He was told that he would have clear weather until he reached the mountains and that he would have to fly over clouds while crossing the Alleghenies to the coast. Before he started down the runway at Cleveland he lighted a cigar. It lasted until he reached Mercer, PA....He glanced at his clock. It had stopped....He had to know the time so that he would know when to come down through the clouds....He recalled that his cigar lasted from Cleveland to Mercer. 'Cleveland to Mercer,' said Hill to himself, 'that's 75 miles. I have about 255 miles to go. Let's see—75 into 255—is 3 and 30 left over. That's—let me see—30-75s..two fifths. If I smoke 3 and two fifths cigars, I should be over Hadley Field, if I'm on my course.' Hill took four cigars from his pocket. Three he placed beside him and the fourth he lighted. When it was finished he lighted another and on he went, chain-smoking over the clouds. When two-fifths of the fourth cigar was gone, he came down through the clouds and there, welcome sight, not far away, was Hadley Field." *(Courtesy of Lloyd Santmyer).*

TOP: J.D. Hill's commemorative plaque in Scottdale, Pennsylvania. *(West Overton Museums).*

BOTTOM: Suspended from a clothesline outside the Hill residence in Scottdale is a model of an aircraft designed by J.D. *(West Overton Museums).*

Carl Strickler

It was not the kind of day to be driving. The wind kept trying to toss my car to the side of the road. The sky was gray. Rain spattered against the windshield. The heater refused to function, and the cold was like a needle through my forehead. It was a typical late fall day in Western Pennsylvania.

I was driving east on Route 30. To my immediate left, the spires of the Saint Vincent Basilica came into view. Ahead, to my right, was the flat plain of the Arnold Palmer Regional Airport. Directly in front was Chestnut Ridge of the Allegheny Mountains, the "Death Stretch" of the early airmail pilots. The "Ridge" was surrounded with thick, ominous fog. It was as if someone had stretched a monstrous sheet of dirty cotton over the top. Bare treetops ripped huge gaps in the sheet. The fog was creeping down and filling the bowl of the lower lands. The airport was socked in, and the Basilica seemed to be balancing a cloud on one of its spires.

Above me, just below the solid cloud cover, a tiny, single-engine plane moved soundlessly on its approach. This was not a good day to be driving. It certainly wasn't a good day to be piloting a small aircraft. It was on such

a day that one of Western Pennsylvania's aviation pioneers was killed flying a Challenger aircraft from Maryland to Bettis Field. His name was Carl Strickler. I could not help but think of him when I saw that aircraft, alone against the leaden sky.

Back in my office I look at a collection of old photographs, portraits and vignettes from the life of Carl. In one of the pictures, he has on a leather flying cap and goggles, and is not looking directly at the camera. He is looking to his left, his eyes slightly raised as if in expectation of his next flight. It is a romantic photo of a man who led a romantic life.

Carl Strickler was from Scottdale. When he was a boy, his obsession was flight. He waited eagerly for the barnstormers to land their planes when they flew overhead. He learned to fly by watching these men and other pilots. He often persuaded them to take him up in their "crates" so that he could study how they mastered their machines. Later, when he began to fly on his own, he and Charlie Carroll built "homemade" planes out of the wreckage of crashed planes.

In the early 1920s, Strickler got a job at the Longview Flying Field as chief pilot. He developed a splendid flying record. He thrilled the local populace with his daring stunts and aerial exhibitions that Charlie and Russ Brinkley, the field manager, held on holidays and air shows. Undoubtedly, his death-defying displays inspired many young people to consider flying as a pastime, if not a career. Clyde Hauger was one of his student pilots, as was Carl's wife, Anna Mary, now ninety-seven years old. Carl continued instructing after the Longview Flying Field became the J.D. Hill Airport.

In the late 1920s, Carl became the chief test pilot for the Kreider-Reisner Aircraft Corporation of Hagerstown, Maryland. On November 28, 1928, Carl, twenty-five years old, was flying one of two OX5 Challenger aircraft from Hagerstown to Bettis Field when he encountered a heavy fog in the Laurel Mountains. Ahead of Strickler in the other Challenger was A.H. Kreider. They lost each other in the fog. Kreider landed safely at Bettis, and waited for Carl. He did not come.

In the plane with Strickler was Michael MacIntyre, an electrician from Kreider-Reisner. He was also Carl's mechanic. In her oral history, Anna Mary (Strickler) Topper describes Carl's last flight:

> They were flying low through the fog when Michael shouted to Carl to turn back. Carl put his finger to his lips, and must have been distracted. There was a burned-out area on the mountain, and the plane's wing hit the top of a tree. The plane tipped over and went down. Carl was killed when his head hit a sharp rock.

MacIntyre told all this to Anna Mary the day after the accident, while he lay in the hospital. He, too, would die of his injuries sometime later. The crash occurred somewhere between Ligonier and Laughlintown.

Carl Strickler's daring nature and love of flying influenced many other renowned local aviation pioneers. The list of men who were pallbearers at this funeral speaks for itself. They were: Charlie Carroll, Raymond Elder, Richard Copeland, Clyde Goerring, Clyde Hauger, and Jack Frost. Who can tell what the future held for Carl Strickler had he not died before his prime.

On the day Charles Lindbergh arrived in America after his historic transatlantic flight, Charlie Carroll and Russ Brinkley traveled to Washington, D.C., to witness the event.

Charlie Carroll sent a postcard to Carl, dated July 11, 1927 and addressed simply "Carl G. Strickler, Longview Flying Field, Latrobe, Pa." It said, "Your're [sic] next, Strick!"

–David Wilmes

TOP: An OX5 Challenger of the type Carl Strickler flew for Kreider-Reisner.

CENTER: The identification plate from the plane in which Carl Strickler flew, retrieved and given to Anna Mary Strickler by Lloyd Santmyer.

BOTTOM: Carl Strickler's crashed OX5 Challenger in the Laurel Mountains near Laughlintown.

(Courtesy of Anna Mary Strickler Topper).

Raymond "Pappy" Elder

According to some biographical notes he sent to the All American Aviation newsletter *The Pick-Up*, August 1944, Ray Elder drove a truck for the Blue Ridge Gas Station in Blairsville, Pennsylvania, while he learned to fly on a Canadian built Curtiss Jenny, otherwise known as a "Canuck." He kept the plane on the family farm in Scottdale and, after his day job was over, he cranked up the Canuck and flew out to Longview Flying Field to meet the other original "Longview Boys," including Charlie Carroll and Carl Strickler, who was Ray's instructor. Ray, Carl and Charlie were also "Scottdale Boys," like J.D. Hill.

This is how Lloyd Santmyer describes Raymond's "flight training:"

Raymond and Carl Strickler were school buddies. Strick was already flying. He learned from "Pop" Cleveland down at C.P. Mayer's field in Bridgeville. Strick could fly that Canuck Raymond bought, and he finally soloed Raymond. Raymond also had some time in with Cleveland. This was back before 1927, before the new license rules came into effect. Anybody who was already flying and had enough hours could automatically get a license if he could answer a little bit of rules and regulations. That's how Raymond and Charlie both got their FAA, CAA licenses. So Raymond had a lot of good experience flying locally. After Carl went down to Hagerstown, Charlie had a couple different guys flying for a little while to try out for Strick's job, and then Raymond started, and Raymond got the job. Raymond made a name for himself. He was a good instructor, a good flier, a good pilot. He was as good as the next guy, and fearless. Of course we did a lot of stump jumping, and he always was pilot when Russ Brinkley did his wing walks for the air shows.

Jim Carroll, one of Raymond's students who got his license in September 1929, relates this story:

Raymond would yell at me, 'You're not getting your tail down when you go down to land.'

I'd yell, 'Well, I have it back as far as it goes, right back so far that my elbow hits the cowling around the seat.'

He'd yell, 'You're not supposed to do that!'

It was a bucket seat, and it had a metal hinge on it. I hit that with my elbow and quit, thinking I couldn't go any further. After I got straightened out, Raymond said, 'Jim, now that you learned to get your tail down, I'm gonna let you go. You go on and take the plane up.'

I said, 'Raymond, are you sure?'

He said, 'I'm absolutely sure.'

So I went up solo. While I was flying, my dad flew back from the New Alexandria Airport and landed. He saw his Challenger up there and he said (he told me later), 'Raymond, I see the Challenger is up there. Who's in it?'

'Jim,' answered Raymond.

'Jim who?'

'Your son, Jim!'

'Hell, he doesn't have enough time in.'

Raymond said, 'Watch him land; then tell me that!'

One time Raymond took me up and the magneto quit on the engine. Raymond said, 'Jim, we have to find a field to land in.'

We were somewhere over Pleasant Unity, I remember. I saw this nice field and I yelled, 'Raymond! Right down there. See! There's a big, long field.'

Raymond shook his head. Finally, he worked the plane down into another field.

I asked him, 'How come you didn't land in the other field?'

He said, 'It was a good field, but did you notice the grass was mostly brownish except for a big green patch. That meant there was water there. If we had landed there, we might have sunk into some mud and nosed the plane over. That's something you need to remember.'

Another time Raymond and I were coming back from New Alexandria, and I smelled gasoline. I was in the front cockpit, and I could see gas dripping out onto the floor.

Raymond said, 'Jesus! I don't know if we can make it back to Latrobe!'

Raymond headed for Saint Vincent Lake. He skimmed the treetops and the water, got up in the air again and headed for the airport. We landed safely. When we got out of the plane, Raymond told me, 'I figured that we could catch a spark and the whole plane would have gone up in flames. I figured to ditch in the lake, but changed my mind.'

Old Raymond. He was a helluva guy!

In the early 1930s, Ray gave up passenger flying and instructing at Latrobe and moved to West Palm Beach to pilot flying boats between Miami and Bimini for Roosevelt Flying Service.

In 1934, Ray returned to Western Pennsylvania to become Pilot-Instructor at the Pittsburgh-Greensburg Airport and Bettis Field. At Bettis he joined his former student, Lloyd Santmyer, an instructor there. When the airmail pick-up began in 1939, Ray signed on as a reserve pilot, becoming one of the company's respected pilots.

Clyde Hauger, pilot Clyde's son, was a flight engineer on AAA's pick-up planes. He describes one of Raymond's feats:

Raymond perfected what he called 'The Dipsy Doodle.' He'd come in and make a pick-up the regular way. Then he'd go into a steep climb, stall the plane, turn, then zoom down and make another pick-up! Everytime the AAA people had a banquet, that 'Dipsy Doodle' would be a topic of conversation. One time he lost the engine, and had to make a forced landing. He took the plane between two trees and took off both wings!

On January 29, 1942, Pittsburgh was, as usual, socked in with smog and smoke. Somewhere in the air was an Army plane, long overdue at the airport. All AAA planes had reached their holding points at the last pick-up stations nearest Pittsburgh, and were being held up by Airway Traffic Control until the lost pilot was located. Raymond had just made his last pick-up at the Pitcairn station, when he saw the Army plane apparently trying to make an emergency landing at a golf course. Elder immediately radioed the Pittsburgh Control Tower, suggesting that the Tower call the Army pilot and advise him to follow him to Pittsburgh. The Tower made the call. Immediately, the Army pilot pulled into close formation with Raymond, who led him to Pittsburgh Airport. The Army plane had less than five minutes fuel supply when Raymond found him.

Seven days later, Raymond "Pappy" Elder became Raymond "The Flying Fire Chief" Elder. Flying Route B near Gallipolis, Ohio, Raymond noticed a burning house, the residence, as it was later discovered, of one J. L. Coleman, of Bidwell, Ohio. Since he saw no activity on the ground, Raymond assumed that the owner was away, and no one had as yet discovered the fire. Raymond dove and circled, trying to attract attention, but without success. Finally, he radioed AAA's Pittsburgh radio operator, Jimmy Ray, and gave him the information. Ray called the Pennsylvania State Police, who immediately contacted the Ohio Highway Patrol, who sent fire trucks to the scene. Fire fighters managed to save much of the owner's personal property.

Many years earlier, in the mid-1920s, after a day at Longview Flying Field, Raymond took off in his Canuck, bound for the family farm at Scottdale. Lloyd Santmyer picks up the story from there:

Raymond used to come over to Longview in the evenings. That must have been around 1926 or 1927, when I used to come out here every evening. Raymond would fly up from his farm. He was driving a truck for a fuel company, and in the evening he'd get the Jenny out, and he'd fly it up to Latrobe here, and then pilots from different places around would congregate and come over.

Sometimes there'd be three or four strange pilots in the evening, and I rode with all those guys, and Raymond would come over, and about dark he would leave and go back to the farm and put the airplane in an old wooden barn. Raymond was on his way home this one evening, and the wind had shifted, and he was landing on the side of a hill down beside the barn, and it wasn't the best place in the world to fly, but it was good enough. By Gosh! He cracked it up going in. The cockpit fell in on him and knocked him out. I think his dad was always, more or less, against aviation. While they took Raymond to the doctor, the old man went down and chopped the thing up with an axe.

'That's the end,' his dad told Raymond. 'That's the last time you are going to fly in one of these damn crates!'

Raymond and his brother got out and collected the OX5 engine and the fittings and put it out in a shed. Later the shed became a sheep shed, and the engine and parts got covered over with straw and manure.

When we started the OX5 Club, Charlie and I got Raymond's permission, and I went down there to see if I could find the engine. I was at Allegheny Elizabeth at the time. I went down with my mechanic from Allegheny, George Markley, and Johnny Trunk from Clarion. Johnny was a contractor and had a pickup truck. Here, the farm had been sold. The sheep shed was still there, though, and so was the engine.

'Well, that's valuable to you is it?' the farmer asked.

I said, 'Yes, we want that for a keepsake for our club.'

And the guy said, 'If it's worth money to you, it ought to be worth something.'

So, he wanted a hundred dollars for it or something like that.

I said, 'Oh, my goodness, that's junk, I couldn't do that.'

He said, 'Well, I'll take fifty, otherwise I'll sell it for junk.'

So, we gave him fifty dollars for it, and that's how the OX5 club got their engine. Johnny cleaned it up with steal wool, and built a display case for it.

Looking back, all who knew Raymond Elder will agree it was good fortune that he followed his own dream, rather than his father's stern wishes.

TOP LEFT: Captain Raymond "The Flying Fire Chief" Elder, All American Aviation. *(Courtesy of All American Aviation* The Pick-Up).

BOTTOM LEFT: Raymond Elder and a cousin at J. D. Hill Airport. *(Courtesy of Barry Elder).*

IMMEDIATELY ABOVE: A young Raymond Elder and his "Canuck" Jenny at Scottdale. *(Courtesy of Russell Brinkley,* Quadrant Aerographic, *July, 1962).*

Lloyd "The Saint" Santmyer

I never thought I would live to retirement.
None of us, me, Raymond, Clyde, Dave, Carl,
thought we would live very long.

Today, Lloyd Santmyer is ninety-one, a spry, humble, kind man who gets a twinkle in his eye whenever someone brings up the subject of airplanes; he has done as much for aviation as anyone in history.

Jim Carroll, Charlie Carroll's oldest son who is now in his nineties, tells of a conversation he once had with his father:

> Santmyer learned to fly right after I did. He had the same teacher, Ray Elder. He was a biscuit salesman for biscuit company in Greensburg, and he was a good boy, a good pilot, single. He left Latrobe and he went to work flying blind flying equipment for a company that made it. When the war broke out my dad met a friend named Larry Morrow in Export and asked, 'Where did Lloyd get to?' He left here and went south, but I don't know where he is.'
>
> Morrow said, 'He's down in Miami in the Air Force. He's pushin' a pencil.'
>
> My dad said, 'He's doing what? Pushing a pencil? He loves his airplanes. Hell! Lloyd had more blind flying experience than anyone in the country!'

Charlie was probably right. While in the Air Corps, Lloyd was given an "honorary" Doctor of Blind Flying degree by the Gore Field Institute for the Blind. In tendering the honor, James D. Rogers, Director of Instrument Flying of the 7th Ferrying Group at Great Falls, Montana, cited Lloyd's "unerring instinct to achieve the station in nocturnal and sub-weather conditions." A great deal of Lloyd's non-military blind-flying experience came without the benefit of instruments. He devised a way of getting past the dangerous ridges of the Allegheny Mountains by practicing on clear days a system of timing, then repeating the process when it was foggy. He also devised a method using signals from electric lines. Both methods are detailed later in the chapter on the air mail pick-up.

Carl Santmyer, Lloyd's son, describes a moment when, as a boy, he watched the air mail pick-ups at Latrobe:

> Once in a while my dad would be piloting the pick-up plane. If the fog was in, you could hear the plane, but you couldn't see it. Then, suddenly there it was, right between the posts. He'd drop a bag, and make the grab. Then he would disappear into the fog, and all you heard was the sound of the plane growing fainter and fainter. I was amazed that he even knew where he was, let alone be able to hook that rope.

Mail wasn't the only thing Lloyd and the other pilots picked up. Carl Santmyer continues:

> My dad flew through the apple growing areas during apple season, and often the people there would send up a second pick-up bag along with the regular bag. The second bag would have warm, apple pie and a tub of ice cream for him and the flight engineer. This was in appreciation of the good mail service these brave and dedicated pilots provided in all types of weather.

Boyhood in Mt. Pleasant, Pennsylvania

Lloyd grew up in Mt. Pleasant, Pennsylvania. His family home was next to the National Guard Armory. As World War I approached, Lloyd would watch the boys of Company E Militia drill prior to their departure for the fields of France. Too young to go himself, Lloyd followed the war from home, and was especially fascinated by the accounts and illustrations of early airplanes involved in dogfights. After the war, the Barnstormers began to make their rounds of America's rural communities.

By 1927, Lloyd's family had moved to Greensburg. Lloyd enrolled at Greensburg High School. His studies were important, but 1927 was the year of Charles

Lindbergh's transatlantic flight, and Lloyd, like many of his generation eager for similar adventure and glory, longed to fly. Only eight miles east on the Lincoln Highway was Charlie Carroll's Longview Flying Field. Nothing could keep Lloyd away from the place.

Lloyd started out at Latrobe as a "lineboy," selling tickets for rides, washing and fueling planes, and cranking engines. Occasionally, Raymond Elder would take him up for some "stick time."

Lloyd recalls those days:

I graduated from high school in 1927, and Lindbergh flew in May of 1927, and I was still going to school and, cripes, I couldn't study those last days. I had been going to Charlie Carroll's airfield since 1926. I used to come out there all the time. That's when Charlie had just the Jennises and the old LS-5. That's when Hodge Smith used to come out in the Jennies from Pittsburgh. I got to selling tickets and carrying gas and cranking the props, and helping Charlie work on them and all that stuff, and worked my way in. So I got to flying with all those guys, getting some stick time and everything, and while I was with the National Biscuit Company, I settled down in earnest and got enough time in to get my commercial license, and start teaching the students. But, up until then, I was hopping around pastures and stuff. But I'd be with Elder all the time. Elder and I flew a lot, barnstorming around the country, and going over to New Alex and everything. So, once in awhile he'd let me fly. So in order to do it, to get it done and over with, I said, 'Raymond, we gotta take enough time to get it going right.'

Elder honored Lloyd's request and began giving him full-time instruction. After Lloyd got both a mechanic and pilot's license, he stayed on at Latrobe as an instructor and mechanic, during which time he helped Charlie Carroll start the New Alexandria airport a few miles away on Route 22 (William Penn Highway).

Down to Bettis Field

Lloyd stayed on at Latrobe until 1935, when he went down to Bettis Field to help organize and instruct at a flight school owned by Becker Aviation. Among his many students were a couple of Lithuanians and some members of the Hitler Youth over here to get some flight training (the United States was still on good terms with Nazi Germany).

Lloyd always insisted that his students deliberately cause their aircraft to go into a spin, once to the right and once to the left, recovering each time. Today, Lloyd still believes that there are far too many licensed pilots who have never experienced a stall and spin, and wouldn't

know how to recover if they did experience one. At Bettis, Lloyd met fellow Greensburger, Dick Coulter, founder of Central Airlines. The association would be a fruitful one for Lloyd.

The Instrument Landing System ((ILS)

In 1938, the U.S. Department of Commerce realized the need for radio instrument landings that would allow pilots to land in poor weather conditions. The Bureau of Standards issued a contract for such a system to the Washington Institute of Technology who developed the system in their College Park, Maryland lab. The system consisted of a directional beam that aligned an aircraft with the runway, and an inclined beam that guided it to a proper landing point. Air Track Manufacturing at the Allegheny County Airport built the first system. Lloyd, realizing that the system would have a significant impact on aviation, applied for and got the job of testing it. He spent the next year testing the system with a Stinson Reliant as his mount, flying with a shield placed over the windows of the cockpit. He was totally reliant on the ILS, or Instrument Landing System. Toward the end of the test period, Lloyd taught the famous racing pilot, Jacqueline Cochran, head of the U.S. Women Air force Service Pilots (WASP), to fly blind. The ILS remains in use today.

Pennsylvania-Central Airlines and All American Aviation

In 1940, after testing the ILS and completing reserve military duty at Wright Field in Dayton, Lloyd piloted Boeing 247s and DC3s for Dick Coulter's new Pennsylvania-Central Airlines. For anyone else, the job with PCA (later Capital, then United Airlines) would have offered security, but Lloyd couldn't resist a new aviation adventure. In the same year, he signed on with All American Aviation to do airmail pick-ups. Lloyd jumped at the opportunity to join his instructor, Ray Elder, on the pilot roster. "Besides," Lloyd says with pride, "It was a service second to none!"

Service in World War II

When World War II began, the Air Corps, impressed with his success in testing the ILS and his reputation as an instructor, activated Lloyd's reserve status, gave him the rank of Captain, and assigned him to train the first night fighter squadron at Fighter Command School in Orlando, Florida. Lloyd developed a curriculum that combined instruction in the use of instruments, radio operation, and radar. Lloyd's squadron went to Italy in 1942, but Lloyd was asked to stay behind and work on a troop glider pick-up system that the Air Corps was developing at Wright Field.

The Glider Pick-up

Richard du Pont, owner of All American Aviation, had been appointed Civilian Advisor for Gliders on the staff of Air Corps Chief of Staff, "Hap" Arnold. Du Pont, a skilled glider pilot, had been asked to assist the U.S. government with glider assault and paratroop operations. Du Pont convinced Army brass that All American's air mail pick-up system would work just as well in picking up gliders. It was only natural that Du Pont remembered his former employee and recommended him to the Air Corps as test pilot. Norm Rintoul also worked on the project.

Lloyd describes the day of the first test:

The All American engineers took the kind of equipment we used in the air mail planes and made it much bigger in size. Then they put it in the bomb bay of a B23 bomber. We set us a glider on the ground. Du Pont was part of the ground crew, all the brass was there, and a bunch of photographers and movie people. Fred Dent, the colonel who headed up Glider Test Branch, decided to fly the glider. It would be on his shoulders if the whole thing failed. I flew that B23 just like it was the old mail plane and grabbed up that glider on the first try!

The B23 was just an interim airplane until the military could ready a Douglas C47 in time for the invasion of Sicily. When it was, Lloyd and a crew flew the Douglas to North Africa, where he trained men of the Troop Carrier Command in the new system.

Lloyd describes the trip over:

I took the first big C47 that we had equipped for picking up the big gliders on the fly. On the way over to Africa, we were way overloaded. Between Greenland and Iceland, the weather came in, a bad front. We thought we left it behind in Greenland, but it was closing in everywhere. We were past our point of no return. No way was I going to try and make it back to Greenland. We were on an empty tank, and we were going down in the drink if we didn't do something. I told the crew, 'We're going down into Iceland.'

Finally, we were at zero-zero, and still about half-an-hour from Iceland. I radioed in for clearance. What I did was use a little of the ILS beam system. The rain station was only about a mile from the airport, so the beam as narrow at that distance, and it lined up with the airport, and the altitude was right and everything. I figured out what my altitude was and how much descent it would take and how many minutes and seconds.

'We can't give you clearance,' they said. 'The field is closed.'

I said, 'You call the C.O. and tell him we're coming in. Otherwise, I'm gonna have to declare and emergency, and they don't like that because there's a lot of paper work and everything!'

They said, 'OK, OK. C.O. says you can have clearance to make one approach.'

I reported my position, came in over the rain station, went back out, made my turn, got down low and up and everything, then came in, like we did in the B23. So many minutes, so many seconds, then BOOM! On the ground! We had to stop fast, because at our speed, we'd go off the runway pretty quickly. But I got us stopped. There we were, sitting in the fog. I call in, 'We're here. Send some Jeeps.'

They answered, 'We can't find the Jeeps. We can't see them.'

So we waited for about ten minutes. They finally came with some Jeeps. I said to the Army fellas with me, 'Don't say anything. Let me do the talking.'

The Operations Manager asked me, 'What airline did you fly for?'

I said, 'All American.'

He said, 'Boy, You know your business!'

Then we went on down to England, and landed for fuel. They told us about German fighters that were after our transports and ferry planes. Of course, we had no guns on the planes. We took off at night, in overcast, thinking they wouldn't find us. Just off the coast of Spain, one came out at us. We dropped down to about 6,000 feet, into the overcast, no lights, not even one to light a cigarette. After about an hour, we figured his fuel was low and he had to go back. I took one more look out of the astral hatch. It was all clear. We made it into Africa.

After North Africa, Lloyd returned to the States at the request of Admiral "Bull" Halsey, who was anxious to use the pick-up system in the Pacific island-hopping campaign. Lloyd met Halsey at Mustin Field in Philadelphia and gave him a demonstration.

Lloyd finished his military career flying supplies in the China-Burma-India Theatre for Air Transport Command. When the Allied Powers met at Potsdam, Lloyd flew the China delegation back from the meetings. His plane ran into heavy turbulence, and he became worried about his VIP passengers. Lloyd turned the aircraft over to his copilot, and went back to check on them. To his surprise, they were picnicking on wine and other provisions that they had packed in straw baskets. They gave Lloyd their broadest smiles and thanked him for the wonderful flight.

Return to AAA

After the war, Lloyd, now a major, went back to All American Aviation. By now they were using twin-engine Beechcraft, and were making pick-ups at 200 mph. Also, All American was slowly switching to passenger service. Lloyd was made chief check pilot. His duties included laying out service routes connecting small towns. He also advised airport owners on the sorts of electronic equipment that would complement receivers on the planes. When All American became Allegheny Airlines, Lloyd was made their Training and Civil Aeronautics Board Check Pilot for Douglas DC-3s.

Allegheny-Ludlum Steel

In 1951, Lloyd joined Allegheny Ludlum Steel Corporation as a pilot. Like many pilots of his generation, he learned in a Curtiss Jenny and finished his career in the jet age.

Lloyd's career was virtually accident free, but it was not for lack of trying. After all, he was one of the "Longview Boys," one of "Carroll's Hooligans." Once he tried to get permission from authorities in Washington to do a special stunt at an air show. What he wanted to do was secure a woman to the wing of a plane, then swoop in upside-down and have her pick up an American flag from the ground. They refused, adding, "And you're an airline pilot! What would people think?!"

Another time he cranked the prop on a plane. When the engine didn't kick over, Lloyd was set to make another attempt when suddenly the engine kicked in, prop spinning. "I was so close I couldn't even bend my knees. All I could do was sidle back a bit, then run like Hell! I was lucky the plane didn't lurch forward! All I could think of was the guy I saw once whose hat blew off after he started a plane. Without thinking he bent over to get it. You figure the rest!"

Once, while in Florida training night fighter pilots, his open-cockpit P-12 had a just-repaired brake system. On the check-out flight, the brakes locked when Lloyd was making a full-speed landing. The plane flipped over. When it finally came to a stop, Lloyd's flying helmet was worn through to his scalp.

Also, Lloyd delighted in flying fighter planes low and upside down. He tells this story:

> We did a lot of upside down flying, close to the ground. I had one real good army plane that was real good at doing that, the Boeing P-12. Boy, was that ever a sweet plane. I'd go down along the highway there in

Virginia, down below Washington, upside down, close to the ground, practicing, getting used to that thing, and the people would be sitting on their front porches, and they'd be waving. It would be in the cool of a summer evening. You just had to remember to push the stick forward!

"My God! I've Killed the Saint!"

One other time, during a glider pick-up, the glider pilot flew above Lloyd's plane instead of behind. The tail of his pick-up plane nearly destroyed, Lloyd released the glider. The glider pilot continued on his way, but Lloyd's plane went into a full-speed nose dive. Lloyd recovered barely 200 feet from the ground, a fact which was not known by the glider pilot, who radioed back to the field, "My God! I've killed the Saint!"

Captain Lloyd Santmyer, All American Aviation.
(Courtesy of Carl Santmyer).

TOP: Lloyd Santmyer poses with his OX5 Waco 10 at J.D. Hill Airport.
BOTTOM: Lloyd in the cockpit of the same plane. *(Courtesy of Clyde Hauger).*

Lloyd Santmyer *(Courtesy of Clyde Hauger).*

Clyde Hauger

Seventeen-year-old Clyde Hauger dashed down the stairs of his home in Donegal. He stopped in front of the hall mirror to adjust his collar. He had to look important. Clyde had been taking flying lessons from Carl Strickler, borrowing flight hours from the young pilot in an OX5 Challenger at Longview Flying Field. However, Clyde wanted to be able to take to the air anytime, anywhere.

Clyde's father called from outside. Clyde slung his bag onto his shoulder and hurried out the door to his father's waiting truck. Today, he was going to get a plane of his own.

Two years later, Clyde was flying in his Eagle Rock biplane, out of his own hangar on the Ulery Farm in Donegal Township. Clyde and his father had originally built the hangar in the middle of Donegal borough, much to the dismay of the residents of Donegal, who forced them to move it to the farm.

In 1934, while a huge crowd watched, Clyde flew over downtown Greensburg and dropped a wristwatch from one thousand feet. The Greensburg *Morning Tribune* had run an ad claiming that the watch would still run, even when dropped from such a distance.

In the late 1930s, Clyde developed a landing strip on property owned by the Niederheizer family in Donegal Township. The landing strip became somewhat of a local attraction, with stands selling beer and sandwiches to onlookers. On Sundays and holidays, Clyde would haul passengers out of the park in his Taylor Cub. However, these seemingly leisurely trips were not without peril. Once, Clyde flew in too low. While the crowds looked on, Clyde hooked the undercarriage of his airplane on a fence. The Cub was damaged, and Clyde's wife, who had been flying with him, broke her collarbone.

Clyde began flying the airmail pick-up for All American Aviation in 1941. Clyde quickly became a top pilot for All American. Along with flight mechanic Raymond Garcia, Clyde was chosen to staff the operations department of All American's Brazilian subsidiary. For months, Clyde and Raymond trained Brazilian pilots in Rio de Janiero to perform the air pick-up, while developing pick-up routes in Brazil.

After Clyde's return from Brazil, he moved immediately to another project. Along with his friend Lloyd Santmyer, Clyde founded the Greensburg City Airport on Carbon Hill, just a five-minute drive from the County Courthouse. The Carbon airport, developed in 1947, was built on property leased from the Repaski family, and included a converted barn for storage of airplanes. Eventually, Clyde and Lloyd built a Quonset hut hangar that held eight or nine airplanes. The Carbon airport offered flying lessons and classes, which were supported by funds from the GI bill.

Clyde and Lloyd acquired a Link Trainer and stored it in a rented building in Greensburg. The device, a small cabin-type affair containing an instrument panel, was used to simulate blind-flying. Clyde often instructed novice pilots in the state-of-the-art machine before taking them out into the sky.

In 1950, the Carbon airport came under consideration for development into a city-county airport. It looked hopeful. However, the closeness of the airport to the town caused some to complain about the noise, and the project was abandoned. Unfazed, Clyde and Lloyd transformed the airport into Westmoreland Aircraft Sales. The two men sold Cessna aircraft out of the airport until its dissolution in 1952. Today, the site is the home of Greensburg Central Catholic High School.

Clyde Hauger was notorious for crash landings. While flying for All American, Clyde's planes were forced down thirteen different times, whether from leaking oil, inclement weather, or stuck landing gears. After leaving All American Aviation following the end of the airmail pick-up, Clyde flew as the chief pilot for Bruno Ferrari's Latrobe-Dill Construction.

On January 16, 1957, Clyde was flying Bruno Ferrari's twin-engine Beechcraft over Charleston, West Virginia, on his way home from Florida. He and his passengers, John Stacio and Harry Ridilla, found themselves stuck underneath two heavy cloud layers. Ice was beginning to form on the wings of the Beechcraft, and the plane was losing altitude. Clyde spotted a nearby hillside, covered with snow. He tried a belly landing on the hillside. The plane crashed, gas tanks bursting immediately into flame. Clyde, just forty-seven years old, was killed.

ABOVE: Clyde Hauger's ID badge from All American Aviation. *(Clyde Hauger, Jr. Collection).*

RIGHT: Teenager Clyde Hauger. *(Clyde Hauger, Jr. Collection).*

BOTTOM: Clyde Hauger and his Eagle Rock biplane. *(Clyde Hauger, Jr. Collection).*

Russell Brinkley

Newspaper reporter, barnstormer, aviator, instructor, airport manager, public relations expert, promoter, air show announcer, author and editor, TV weatherman, first president of the OX5 Club, founder of Silver Wings Fraternity--Russ Brinkley was all of these. And he wasn't shy about it!

Russ started out writing for newspapers in Jamestown and Olean, New York, then drifted down to Clarion, Pennsylvania, where he did similar work. Or, it might have been the other way around. Apparently, Russ never talked much about his personal life. Even among his surviving friends, Lloyd Santmyer, "Reds" MacFarlane, and Lou Beemer of HarrisburgJet, such knowledge is hazy. Most of what appears in this biographical note has been gleaned from Russ's 1960s aviation magazine, *Quadrant Aerographic*, conversations with Lou Beemer, "Reds" MacFarlane, Lloyd Santmyer, and references in the *Latrobe Bulletin*.

Russ and Bettis Field

In 1925, Russ, just hired by the *McKeesport Journal*, talked his boss into letting him cover the opening of Bettis Field. On his first visit, Russ met pilot Merle "Mope" Moltrup, a friend of Eddie Stinson who was just then building his first biplane at Detroit. It was a cold day and Russ watched Moltrup try to take off in a old Standard biplane that had been sitting tied down during the first snow of the season. There was a steep embankment on the field. Moltrup headed down the field toward the embankment, but he was having great difficulty getting the right wing up. He stopped the plane, got out of the cockpit, pulled a knife from his flying suit, and slit the trailing edge of the lower right wing. Out poured a couple gallons of water. The rotted wing fabric, once covered by snow that had since melted, had allowed water to seep in. Only Moltrup's quick thinking avoided a potentially fatal crash. At Bettis, Russ also met a teenager who spent more time at the field than at school. The truant officers always knew where to find him. After a small building was erected on the field, the boy managed to create a hiding place in it, a small cubby-hole unknown to his searchers. The boy would grow up to be one of the most respected pilots in the area, an aviation historian of merit, and a successful airport operator. His name was Ken Scholter.

Shortly after covering the dedication of Bettis Field, Russ lost his job at the *McKeesport Journal*. He offended the higher-ups by selling an advertisement rather than referring the matter to the advertising department. Worse than that, he wrote nice things about the Postmaster, a mortal enemy of the City Editor, McDonald.

Russ got another job with a newspaper in Swissvale, a suburb of Pittsburgh, this time as an editor. The community was strange to Russ, and he was hard-pressed to fill up an eight-page weekly with local news. To compensate, he lifted stories from other neighborhood publications. One on unfortunate occasion, he reprinted a story about a couple who, as he says: ". . . had not undergone the benefit of clergy." After that, Russ was on the road again.

On to the Waco Factory

Turning his interest once again to aviation, Russ hitchhiked to C.P. Mayer's field in Bridgeville to seek advice from "Pop" Cleveland and Jim Wagner, two noted airmen of the day. They directed him to the new Waco factory in Troy, Ohio. Russ made his way there and was hired at the handsome wage of twenty-cents per hour, for as many hours a day he wished to work, and he worked many. He started by covering and sewing fabric on the wings of the final 100 Waco Nines and the first 100 Waco Tens. By mid-summer Russ had developed such a deep tan that he was accused of being a Negro by some of his more racially motivated colleagues. In spite of that, or because of it, he was given a foreman's position, one that required harder work. He was given the task of supervising the cleaning of a barn-full of war-surplus Curtiss engines that were to be used to power the Wacos. With that task finished, Russ looked forward to once again joining the production line. He was disappointed. The chief supervisor had other plans. Russ was to remove rusted farm machinery, old automobiles, and assorted junk from the main floor of the barn to make room for wings and spare parts. As Russ tells it: "I took one long last look at the foreman, walked back to the factory office and drew my pay!"

Chance Visit to Longview Flying Field

The same night, Russ rode the electric tram to Dayton, Ohio. To pass some time, he went to the theatre to watch the famous Two Black Crows. As chance would have it, a old vaudeville act that had once played in Russ's home town was on the bill. Russ had become acquainted with them back then, and decided to relive old times. Backstage, the troupe invited him to ride along with them to New York. Russ took them up on it. That was 1927. He might have gotten there, too, had it not been for an empty gas tank, impatient traveling companions, and a hung-over driver.

This is how Russ tells the story:

I held firmly to the door handle as we wended our way along the narrow Lincoln Highway, narrowly missing adventure at every turn in the snaking road. By 11 a.m., we had traversed approximately forty miles and the driver decided that we needed some gas. Fortunately, the first service station ahead [*owned by Michael Peretto*] was situated at the edge of a field [*Longview Flying Field*] where two World War I biplanes and a shiny, new American Eagle [*Dave Patterson's*] were parked in a line to attract passing motorists. While my companions had the car serviced, I wandered up to the airplanes and found a couple of men engaged in repairing a tire on the new airplane. On several occasions, I heard my party calling to me, but I ignored their summons. The next thing I noted was my bag being dropped out of the car as it sped off in the direction of New York. I was filled with mixed emotions. I was glad to be rid of the drunks and at the same time, I realized I was a long way from New York and with limited resources.

Once I became acquainted with the men at the airport, I learned that they worked at other trades during the week, and spent their Saturdays and Sundays building up flight time [Raymond Elder drove a truck; Lloyd Santmyer worked for a Greensburg biscuit company]. They made no particular effort to attract passengers. If

someone showed up and asked to be taken for a ride, they were accommodated. They had never been subjected to the kind of pressure I had learned to apply. In my opinion, the boys might have done well to go after more business. Since the Lindbergh flight, the public was becoming air-minded and many people were eager to get off the ground. Business was picking up at other small airports across the nation. I offered my services to see what could be done on the local level. My offer was accepted and my first act was to stand along the highway to attract passing cars onto the field. Visitors who weren't interested in taking a ride might at least want a drink or a sandwich, both of which were available at the field refreshment stand.

Within a few minutes, I had a goodly crowd on the parking line and our guests were in a receptive mood. We set ride prices at three and five dollars, and by the time the sun went down, the two pilots [Ray Elder and Carl Strickler] were drooping in their tracks. I had my nicker pockets filled with crumpled banknotes, and all concerned were eager to get to the nearest beanery.

By the time we had eaten and counted the day's receipts, all of us were ready to turn in. I found a hotel room nearby and, before by new associates had taken their leave, each of them had shaken my hand and left in my palm the equivalent of a week's salary at Waco. What was more, they invited me to stay around in hopes that I might effect permanent association with the field. That was my introduction to the airport at Latrobe, Pennsylvania.

There was little or no weekday activity at the airport for some time after my arrival. It left me with plenty of time for other things, so I found time to renew my old practice of writing for the aviation magazines.

During the year that followed, the airport became one of the most-extensively known aviation bases in the nation. Each weekend assured an air show for the visiting crowds that we gleaned from the Lincoln Highway. Our regular bill-of-fare included such attractions as parachute jumps by Joe Crane and Smiles O'Timmons, supplemented by wingwalking by visiting daredevils and aerial acrobatics by Carl Strickler and Ray Elder.

All the aviators and promoters from the area were regular visitors to the airport during the heyday of the barnstormers; Cliff Ball, D. Barr Peat, Dewey Noyes and Blanch Noyes, C. P. Mayer, Merle Moltrup, and many others. There was a huge crowd when Longview Flying Field was renamed J.D. Hill Airport.

Russ took some flying instruction from the pilots at Longview Flying Field, but did not pass his pilot's test until 1934, after formal instruction at the American School of Aviation in Chicago. While at Longview Field, he took a job as a columnist with the *Latrobe Bulletin*. Through his columns, Brinkley played a major role in developing publicity for the dedication of the J.D. Hill

Airport. While in the area, Russ traveled to many air-shows, including those at Elmira, Cleveland, and Teterboro. On some of these trips he was accompanied by Latrobe's young pilot, Lew Strickler, and Livingstone "Pops" Clewell, of the neighboring town of Kingston.

Pittsburgh-Greensburg Airport and Beyond

In 1929, Russ became Commercial Manager for the Pittsburgh-Greensburg Airport. He was back on the payroll at Hill Airport in 1930. From there, Russ moved on to New York where he edited several aviation magazines, including *Air Transportation Weekly*. In the years that followed he flew to nearly every airport in the United States, Canada and Mexico as a charter pilot, writer, and flying instructor. Eventually, he settled in Harrisburg, Pennsylvania, where he published his own aviation magazine *Quadrant Aerographic*. In 1960, at Harrisburg, Russ set a world record by flying forty different models of aircraft, including antiques and helicopters, all within a twelve-hour period. He eventually produced a manuscript for a book titled *Wings Over Main Street*, an account of his experiences in aviation.

Russ Brinkley with Lou Strickler (left), Pennsylvania's youngest licensed pilot, at the Teterboro, New Jersey air show, 1930.
(Courtesy of Lou Beemer).

The book was never published, but it was serialized in issues of *Quadrant Aerographic*. Unfortunately, the manuscript has been lost and there are many gaps in the one remaining microfilm version of *Quadrant* in the New York Public Library.

Russ's relationship with Carroll and the airport at Latrobe would continue for many years, and his association with Latrobe and Saint Vincent College would continue into the 1980s. Russ was on hand on August 27, 1955, the day Carroll's brainchild, the OX5 Club was founded. Russ was elected president. A few years later, disappointed and angry at not being re-elected, Russ resigned and formed the Silver Wings Fraternity. By that time, Charlie Carroll, not included in the new plans for what had become the Latrobe-Westmoreland Airport, had retired with his family to Florida. Russ was back in Latrobe in 1962 publicizing his book. He came again in 1978 to award the Rev. Alcuin Tasch, O.S.B. a Silver Wings Fraternity certificate for Tasch's work in aviation instruction. Russ, Father Alcuin, and Charlie Carroll had started the world's first college/aeronautics school fifty years earlier at the J.D. Hill Airport.

Russ Brinkley at the Pittsburgh-Greensburg Airport, 1929.
(Courtesy of Lou Beemer).

Frank Fox

*"Choose a job you love, and you will
never have to work in your life."*

A father and his two sons climb aboard a Curtiss OX5 Seagull. The year is 1921. The place is Atlantic City, New Jersey. The six-year-old dons a World War 1 pilot's cap. The pilot revs the OX5 engine, the Seagull takes the waves smoothly, then bounces, picks up speed, and is airborne. It circles over the boardwalk, banks, and heads out to sea. The six-year-old and his brother look over the sides of the flying machine, fascinated by the whitecaps and the tiny sailboats below. After about thirty minutes, the machine gradually loses altitude as the pilot prepares for a landing. The plane drifts down and seems to hover for a few seconds. Then, as if an invisible hand had taken charge of events, the machine gently sets down in the inlet and taxis to a stop. The six-year-old climbs out of the plane onto the quay and runs up to his father.

"Dad! You know what! I'm going to be a pilot!" he says.

And so he did. He became one of the best. The six-year-old was Frank Fox from Greensburg, Pennsylvania. A couple of years later, Frank and his brother George took to hanging out at Longview Flying Field in Latrobe where they watched the planes coming and going, never missing an air show, and getting to know Charlie Carroll. Charlie welcomed kids at Longview. They were ready to do a few chores in exchange for being allowed to hob nob with the pilots, or sit in cockpits, or even go up for a spin. Who knew? Maybe one of them would grow up to become another Eddie Rickenbacker. When he got old enough to fly himself, Frank and Charlie became friends, and they stayed friends until Charlie died in 1973. When Charlie retired in 1959, it was Frank Fox who bought Charlie's OX5 Challenger.

As a youngster, Frank and two buddies built a glider in the Fox basement. They took the contraption to the hill at the State Police Barracks in Greensburg. Frank, of course, was the pilot. There was some advance publicity and a large crowd was on hand to watch the demonstration. The wind was right, and Frank's friends pushed him off. Frank never got to enjoy himself because his first public appearance as a pilot lasted less than a second. The glider's wings folded, and the craft came to an ignominious end. It would be different next time. Next time his aircraft would have an engine in it.

Frank soloed in 1931, after four hours of instruction from Dick Coulter of Greensburg. Frank was sixteen. His plane was an E-2 Club. Frank's Atlantic City dream had come true, but he would go on dreaming.

Frank graduated from Greensburg High School in 1933, where he lettered in basketball and track. Then he attended Saint Vincent College from 1935-1936. At Saint Vincent they called him "Streaky," because he had great speed as a football and basketball player. But college wasn't for him. He couldn't stand "working on the ground," not when there was work to do "in the skies."

In 1936, Frank joined Central Airlines in Detroit as an agent. In 1941, Frank's good friend, Lloyd Santmyer, helped him get hired as First Officer for Pennsylvania-Central Airlines Detroit operation. It was the airline founded by his flight instructor, Dick Coulter. In Detroit, Frank flew DC-3s, then received his Airline Transport Rating for the Boeing 247-D. He became a Captain July 1942. Frank stayed with the airline during its changes through Capitol Airlines to United, and retired at the mandatory age of 60. He had come a long way from that rumbling OX5 in Atlantic City fifty-five years before.

Frank and Evelyn Fox finally settled in Rockville, Maryland, but the memories of those early years at

Longview Flying Field would never leave Frank.

He landed there a couple or times in the early eighties in his restored Waco. "I often thought what Charlie would say now!" Frank said.

There would be no retirement for Frank. He continued to participate in aircraft restoration, flying meets, and the activities of numerous aviation associations. In his lifetime, he logged 42,000 hours in one kind of airplane cockpit or another. He made nonstop flights from Baltimore to Hawaii in United Airlines DC-8s. He flew Lowell Thomas around for a week's tour of the United States. In 1942, he demonstrated a Harlow aircraft for his hero, Charles Lindbergh. He made five forced landings. He made a parachute jump at Kenny Scholter's Butler Airport in 1948. He was a charter member of the OX5 club and the OX5 Aviation Pioneers Hall of Fame, the Aero Club of Pittsburgh, the Antique Aircraft Association, the Experimental Aircraft Association, the Quiet Birdmen, the AOPA, the Aviation Historical Society, the Bonanza Society, the Soaring Society of America, the Wings Club, the Pennsylvania Pilot's Council, and the ALPA. In 1999, Frank was given the Wright Brothers Master Aviation Award.

BOTTOM: Frank Fox (center of the cockpit), age 6, ready for is first flight in a Curtiss OX5 "Seagull, Atlantic City, New Jersey, 1921. *(Frank Fox Collection).*

TOP RIGHT: Frank Fox on the day of his retirement. *(Frank Fox Collection).*

Joe Reedy

Joe Reedy loved to fly upside down. He thrilled crowds during aerial exhibitions at the Latrobe Airport in the 1930s with his inverted stunts. Flying upside down, however, had its problems; the carburetor only operated for a short time in such a position, then the engine shut off. Undaunted, Joe built a carburetor that could function in any configuration. The engine still quit, but it engaged again almost immediately. The brief pause was enough to make air show crowds anxious. With his invention, Joe flew upside down for as long as he desired, which was often, according to the recollections of his daughter, Janet Matchett.

Joe Reedy offered more to aviation than just a few tricks and thrills. A brilliant inventor, instructor, engineer and pioneer aviator, Joe Reedy is important to the story of the Latrobe Airport and aviation in Pennsylvania.

Joe came from a hard-working family. His father was a steel worker. Joe himself was a paradigm of the American self-made man, never having gone beyond the seventh grade, yet achieving an international reputation as an engineer. After suffering a debilitating injury on the job, Reedy's father had to stay home to recuperate. Joe and his brother picked up where their father left off. Joe

became an renowned structural-steel worker and field superintendent.

Joe began flying in the late 1920s at the Hill Airport. He developed friendships and associations with Charlie Carroll, Raymond Elder, Russ Brinkley and Lloyd Santmyer. He taught George Allen, the first African-American commercial pilot in Pennsylvania, meteorology and navigation so George could pass his flight test. He taught Greensburg's Dick Coulter, the founder of Pennsylvania-Central Airlines, how to fly. In 1930, he helped Charlie Carroll set up a steel hangar at the New Alexandria Airport.

When the United States became involved in World War II, Joe offered his services to the U.S. Army Air Corps as an instructor, but his knowledge as an engineer proved too valuable. In 1939 he built the largest crane in the world. His designs for coal tipples got him involved in the coal industry during the war years. As a result of these great engineering feats, he stayed on the home front. It must have been difficult for a man like Joe Reedy, whose mind was always affixed on the next flight, to be told he was more valuable in an area other than aviation. Nevertheless, flying remained his number one passion, and on the weekends, when he was not busy with war work, he still did stunt flying.

His daughter remembers his ability to build airplanes from scratch. Cannibalizing parts from other aircraft, Reedy constructed his own creations at home. The glue and "dope" used on the fabric of these planes filled the house with unpleasant odors, but the end result carried Joe off on new adventures in the sky. Once, at the Pittsburgh-Greensburg Airport, he crashed one of his "home-made" jobs. He came home unfazed by the accident to an anxious family that feared him dead. He suffered only a cut finger, and the incident had already slipped his mind. He was already thinking about his next flight, his next invention.

"You have to realize," says Janet Matchett, "this was a man who worked hundreds of feet in the air for a good bit of his life. Why would an airplane crash bother him?"

Most of the early pilots were like that, possessing the ability to shrug off danger and mortality like a shiver. Either that or they made a joke of it. Joe is reputed to have flown under more than one bridge in Pittsburgh. His upside-down feats are still well-known. When the era of the air mail pick-up was in full swing Reedy, jokingly unimpressed with the skill of the pilots, attached a hook to the tail of his plane and made a pick-up flying upside down! It was all in good fun!

Joe Reedy amassed more than 14,000 hours in the air. He remained a constant out at the Latrobe Airport until his death at the age of seventy-five. At his funeral, a procession of aircraft flown by pilots who knew him well in his lifetime circled his grave site to honor a man who gave most of his life to aviation.

RIGHT: Joe Reedy as "Uncle Sam" at an early airshow, J.D. Hill Airport. *(Courtesy of Janet Matchett).*

BELOW: Joe Reedy with a Waco aircraft at Latrobe Airport, 1940s. Joe was seldom without his cigar, except on occasions when he quit smoking in order to save money to purchase parts for his homebuilt aircraft. *(Courtesy of Janet Matchett).*

Earl Metzler

*I've been flying with the wing spring for years,
and they won't even look at it.*

Earl Metzler was born along Hill Creek in Somerset County a little more than ten years into the new century. In 1914, he moved with his family to Greensburg, went to school there, and helped his father and brother in the family ice and coal business. Nineteen-twenty-seven and Charles Lindbergh changed his life. Shortly before he died in February 2000, Earl admitted, "Lindbergh was my hero, the All-American Hero, and I wanted to emulate him, and become an airplane pilot. So, in the summer of 1928, I went out to the Hill Airport in Latrobe."

When Earl got there, he walked up to a young man, Dick Copeland, who was standing by a Curtiss Jenny. Copeland took Earl for ten-minute, three-dollar ride, one that stretched into half-an-hour because Copeland wasn't making the kinds of landings he wanted to. He would simply touch down for an instant, then take off again. When they finally landed, Copeland informed Earl that he had just soloed himself the day before.

Shortly after, Earl saw an ad in the newspaper stating that the Chicago Aeronautical Service was taking students and promising them jobs in Chicago. That was enough for Earl. He signed up, and in the winter of 1929, went to Chicago where he got a job and took flying lessons at the Cook County Airport, flying in open cockpits, often in ten degree weather. Then, as Earl describes:

In the spring, my brother wanted to go away, so he asked me to come home and work the family trucks. I went back to Hill Airport and took more flying lessons. Ray Elder was my teacher. We flew a Waco 10, a nice-flying machine. On that humpbacked field it made nice landings. I flew for fifteen minutes at a time. It cost me seven dollars and fifteen cents. On September 25, 1929, Ray decided that I should fly alone. I soloed with three other men, one of them Charlie Carroll's son, Jimmy.

Though he soloed that day, Earl didn't get a license until much later. The Great Depression had set in, and he simply didn't have the money. He went into the long-distance trucking business with his brother, but aviation remained his first love. An idea slowly formed in his mind:

I found out that the Ryan Lindbergh flew across the Atlantic was an unstable airplane. It didn't have the kind of dihedral angle that gives stability to an airplane. He actually wanted it that way so he didn't have to work to stay awake. Cliff Ball had one of these Ryans, and his mechanics were adjusting the dihedral by threading out the threads on the struts. I said to them, 'Why don't you just have a hydraulic jack there to give you any kind of dihedral you want?'

I decided to get a patent on what I called a wing-adjusting device that would increase the dihedral in flight to give you exactly the kind you wanted. So, in 1931, I applied for and got a patent on a wing-adjusting device for monoplanes.

Charlie Carroll and the people at Latrobe Airport helped me out. I got FAA approval and sold a number of kits to Taylorcraft. Then I started putting them on Cessnas. I got a 170-B, put the shock-absorbing struts on it, and it came out very stable. It practically flew by itself. The Army looked at it for a while, but became disinterested. I just couldn't do the two inches of paperwork to get grants for the project. All my patents ran out.

Earl Metzler stayed around aviation for a long time, eventually managing the Pittsburgh-Greensburg Airport during its final days in the 1950s. He opened a machine shop in Pleasant Unity, Pennsylvania, which he called "Wings With Springs." He continued trying to market his invention into his later years, always without success, always with frustration. "No one will listen," he said. "No one will give it a fair try. Some are even afraid to go up in an airplane installed with the spring. Someday, someone will listen and respond."

But few people did.

Among Earl's papers is a copy of the January 1985 issue of The Vintage Airplane. In it is an article by Ruby Garrett of Clinton, Arizona, a retired TWA captain. For thirteen years, Garrett flew his Cessna 180 from the

Midwest to California each January. On several of occasions, Garrett had to delay his flight because of dangerous mountain turbulence. His article reads in part:

In 1981, my regular January flight over mountain and desert became a new experience in comfort and security. The flight was made in the same air of previous years, but this 1981 flight never required a power reduction in either rough air or in let-down from cruise altitude. My head didn't hit the headliner, the seatbelt never tugged my back to the cushion, and the cabin never sharply jolted me once during some thirty hours of flying desert thermals, crossing mountain ridges, and cruising beneath the overcast layers where the choppy air lives.

The difference was a modification called 'Wings With Springs,' and oil-damped air spring built into the lift strut of the Cessna. The idea goes back at least to Waldo Waterson and possibly further, but the modern development and subsequent STC was accomplished by Earl Metzler of Pleasant Unity, Pennsylvania.

We found no negative aspect to this modification, and now that I've been exposed to the benefits, I would honestly prefer not to fly a light plane over that route without 'wings with springs.' This has been an easy way to add utilization, comfort, safety and value to the grand old Cessna.

Earl died just short of his ninetieth year, refusing treatment for a heart ailment. Until the end, he visited his shop in Pleasant Unity every day. His files were full of correspondence with FAA officials, military departments, aircraft manufacturers, colleagues. In the corners of the shop stood his invention in various stages of assemblage. He loved to talk about his Wings With Springs, but even more, he loved to talk about airplanes and flying, and all the old-timers he got to know back in the days just after Charles Lindbergh flew the Atlantic. After all, he was one of them.

TOP: Logo for Earl Metzler's "Wings With Springs."
CENTER: Earl Metzler's shock absorber apparatus mounted to the wing of a Cessna aircraft. The shock absorber uses oil to slow the movement of the wing strut and compressed air provides the spring action.
BOTTOM: Earl Metzler's invention mounted on his Aeronca, pictured at the Pittsburgh-Greensburg Airport in the early 1930s.
(Courtesy of Earl Metzler).

George Allen

George Allen was an African-American, and like many black citizens of his generation, he suffered for it. In the end, he triumphed. He was more than just an aviator. He paved the way for many other African-American pilots. He would become the first African-American commercial pilot in Pennsylvania, and one of the first in the country.

While a drummer with various dance bands from the Pittsburgh area, George managed to squeeze in some flight lessons. He made his first solo flight in a Waco 10 OX5 in 1933, at Bettis Field. His flight instructor was aviation Hall of Famer, Lloyd Santmyer.

Santmyer describes the day George got his pilot's license:

I took George down to Bettis for his test. As George waited by the plane, the licensing official asked me, "Lloyd, can that boy fly?"

'Just watch,' I answered.

Now, I always made sure my students could get out of a spin. Too many people are flying today who can't do that! Anyway, I had my students do two spins and recover, one from the right and one from the left. I had them get the hanger in their sights then climb, stall the plane, then recover. I had them do that twice. I told George to make sure to close the engine vents on the Waco because if it cooled down in the spin it would cut out. The first stall went OK. On the second one, the engine cut out.

Now there wasn't really a place at Bettis where you could do a nice glide down. George got the plane righted and did a beautiful spiral all the way down.

He got out of the plane and came over to me. I said, 'George, I told you to close the vents so the engine wouldn't cut out. Now go up and finish your test.'

He went back up. I went into the office. The official asked, "Where's your boy?"

I said, 'He's finishing his test.'

He said, 'Hell, after what I just saw, I signed his license. It's back there on the desk!'

The same year he got his wings, George bought an old Eaglerock OX5 laying neglected in the corner of a hanger out at the Latrobe Airport for $300 dollars. He overhauled and repaired the aircraft to make it flight-worthy and was soon regularly logging in hours in the skies above Latrobe. In 1937 George acquired a transport license Number 32630. Then, Charlie Carroll hired him as an instructor at the Carroll School of Aviation, where George taught Civil Air Patrol students from Saint Vincent College. Among George's other students was Fred Rogers of the PBS television series Mister Roger's Neighborhood.

At the outset of World War II, the need for experienced pilots was tantamount. George served as Chief Pilot for Civil Pilot Training and Flight Examiner at the Tuskegee Institute in Alabama, the famed, segregated flight school for blacks. The airmen who graduated from Tuskegee went on to achieve legendary fame in overseas service during World War II, being feared and respected by German pilots in the skies over Europe. They were the only fighter outfit in World War II to never lose an escorted bomber to enemy fighter planes. In 1943, George was appointed Squadron Commander at Tuskegee's Primary Flight School. While at Tuskegee, George flew PT-17s, AT-6s and C-45s.

After the war, George returned to the Latrobe Airport to continue his work with Charlie Carroll. In 1955, he joined the OX5 Club as one of its charter members.

George Allen was a well-respected pilot. He was admired by all who worked with him at the airport and beyond. Lou Strickler, one of the local legends of aviation in Western Pennsylvania knew him well. He saw in Allen a kindred spirit. There's one story about the two men that speaks well for the camraderie binding these early pioneers of aviation together. Lou and George entered a restaurant once. Allen was refused service because of the color of his skin. Lou Strickler took George by the arm and left. If his fellow pilot wouldn't be served, neither would he.

ABOVE: Lloyd Santmyer (left) and George Allen at the Westmoreland County Airport, May 12, 1989, the fiftieth anniversary of the first officially-scheduled All American Aviation airmail pick-up. In attendance were members of the 49'ers, an organization of pilots and staff who were employed by AAA during the ten pick-up years, and the OX5 Club, founded at the airport on August 27, 1955. Lloyd and George flank a plaque commemorating the first 100 charter members of the OX5 Club. *(Courtesy of Dorothy Zello).*

RIGHT: George Allen (right) and his former student, Mansel Negley at the Westmoreland County Airport. *(Courtesy of Mansel Negley).*

Dave Patterson

Dave Patterson had a chance connection to aviation from the moment of his birth. Born in 1903, the same year the Wright brothers took their first hesitant steps in powered flight, Dave seemed to have had wings waiting for him in his future. With an astounding 27,000 hours of flying time and more than four million miles traveled upon his retirement in 1962, Latrobe's Dave Patterson blazed some trails.

He earned his wings in 1927 at the age of twenty-four. Under the tutelage of instructor Raymond Elder at Longview Flying Field, Dave quickly learned the mechanics of flight. He barnstormed out of the same field in his own American Eagle biplane. He became a regular at the holiday and weekend air exhibitions at Hill Airport.

Flying was not all loops and daredevil stunts for Dave, though. He began giving flight lessons at the Latrobe airport and became one of Charlie Carroll's chief instructors at the Carroll School of Aviation in the 1930s.

His duties as instructor expanded with the times in the 1940s. After the Japanese bombed Pearl Harbor, the military suddenly and desperately needed pilots. Saint Vincent College became a training ground for these prospective aces, bomber pilots and instructors. The cadets got ground instruction at the college and flight instruction at the Carroll school. Dave Patterson taught hundreds of them before they were shipped off to overseas duty in all the theaters of operations.

The non-stop airmail pick-up began in 1939. By 1942, the year of Dave's first flight with Triple A, the routes were well-established, but still dangerous. That never changed. Flying through "Hell's Stretch," hopping over the ridges and skimming the valleys of Western Pennsylvania, West Virginia, Ohio and Maryland, Dave faced hazards on every flight. Improvisation was all a part of flying the non-stop pick-up routes, often making the difference in the mail getting delivered or even whether or not the next pick-up would result in a fatal crash.

One story tells of Dave flying a route through West Virginia when suddenly his Stinson's Lycoming engine just shut off. With only fifty feet of altitude to work with, Dave realized he had to bring the Reliant down immediately. Dave remained calm and quickly searched for a landing site. A little knoll presented itself between the trees and Dave made for it. With no room to spare, the Reliant came to a stop on the knoll without being seriously damaged. All-American Aviation, alerted that one of their planes had gone down, sent out the necessary parts for repairs. The next morning saw Dave ready to resume his flight. He wanted to fly the Reliant off the knoll, but realized some landscaping had to be done first. The locals cleared some brush and filled in ditches. When they were finished, Dave took off.

Dave's short lay-over on that hilltop in West Virginia stimulated the curiosity of the locals. When asked by the citizens of the near-by town if the knoll he landed on could be an airstrip, Dave replied in the affirmative. Following some advice from Dave, the townsfolk made some necessary improvements to the area. They called their airstrip Patterson Field, in Dave's honor.

Dave Patterson chalked up an impressive seven-year stint doing the pick-up. In 1949, All-American Aviation converted to passenger service and changed its name to All-American Airways. Dave's days of "trimming the hedges" in his Stinson Reliant were over. He made the transition to the larger passenger DC-3s and settled into calmer flights to Philadelphia and Boston.

Dave continued to fly for All-American Airways through its many transformations and developments. In 1953, All-American became Allegheny Airways. The company bought newer and bigger aircraft.. In 1959, the fast Convair 540 turbo-props were added to Allegheny Airways' inventory. Dave checked out on these as well and flew the first flight of a Convair out of Greater Pittsburgh Airport. For the next three years, Dave flew the Convairs between Pittsburgh, Philadelphia and Boston. To the passengers who frequented this service, Dave must have been a familiar sight.

In 1962, Dave decided to hang up his wings. For thirty-five years, Dave Patterson had an impact on aviation in Pennsylvania and beyond. He instructed both civilian and military pilots, was a pioneer airmail pilot and flew thousands of hours of commuter service. When he landed on his last flight for Allegheny Airways in 1962, dozens of fellow pilots were there to salute an impressive career in aviation.

RIGHT: Dave Patterson and Lou Strickler (right) at the J.D. Hill Airport, ca. 1930. *(Courtesy of Lloyd Santmyer).*

BELOW: March 30, 1962. Dave Patterson (right) with his copilot Captain John Semenko, on the day of his retirement flight with Allegheny Airlines. The flight was a Pittsburgh-Philadelphia round-trip. *(Courtesy of Clyde Hauger).*

Lou Strickler

L ou Strickler was a Latrobe boy, the son of David E. Strickler, a prominent local druggist, who was credited with inventing the banana split. Lou had his own claim to fame. He started flying when he was in high school, and at sixteen, he became Pennsylvania's youngest licensed pilot, soloing at Parks Air College in St. Louis, Missouri. Some said he was United States' youngest pilot. Others said he was the world's youngest pilot. Whatever, Lou Strickler was flying solo in an airplane at an age when most young men and women today are just getting their drivers' licenses. And he was setting records in the sky, and winning races. At New Jersey's 1930 Teterboro Air Show, Lou, chaperoned by Russ Brinkley, was featured as the "World's Youngest Exhibition Pilot" by the sponsoring organization, the Hackensack Lodge of Elks. On July 19 and 20, Lou succeeded in breaking his own junior altitude record of 14,000 feet. He donated his fee to the local "Crippled Kiddies Fund."

Lou's father liked pilots, and had no objection to his son being one, even though, as he said of a temporarily insolvent Tony LaVier, later a Thompson Trophy winner and Lockheed test pilot who stayed a couple of nights at the Strickler's, "Boy, these flyers don't make enough money to buy their own salt!"

On June 26, 1931, Lou's father purchased an Aeronca monoplane for him through the Morris Flying Service in Aspinwall, Pennsylvania. Lou and Ray Elder went out to Cincinnati, Ohio, to get the plane and fly it back to Latrobe, where it was hangared. Lou's ambition was to enter government service as a mail or transport pilot, and he needed the plane primarily to practice flying and increase his air time. Four months after he got the plane, Lou flew it from Bettis Field in McKeesport, Pennsylvania, to the J.D. Hill Airport, covering the thirty-mile air route in just six minutes. Eventually, he and Charlie Carroll managed the Aeronca agency in Westmoreland County.

Bill Strickler, Lou's brother, remembers that the Aeronca had only a forty-horsepower engine that went:

Putt, putt, putt. It was like a lawnmower with wings. The old pilots would say, 'Hey, Lou, wind up the rubber bands and let 'er go! One time we flew to New York. I was only about twelve or thirteen. Bill wasn't more than seventeen. We were flying along and there was a car down below. We flew some more, and I looked down, and there was that car again. That's how slow we were going. We landed in Newark. I said, 'Holy Heck, Lou, somebody is going to land on top of us!' It was like a mosquito landing on a table top. 'No, we're all right. Trust your brother,' Lou said.

When I went up with him, he'd do loop-the-loops, and whip-stalls. He'd whip, and the change would come out of his pockets. I'll tell you! Those pilots back then were a different breed!

They say that Lou used to fly under the Kingston Bridge. They said that about quite a few pilots from the Hill Airport. Those things were just rumors, but nobody ever denied it. I think where it got started was one day when I was in a small boat fishing just above the bridge. Lou came down low, I stood up and the boat capsized. When I got my bearings, I saw Lou's Aeronca past the bridge and climbing. I asked him, 'Lou, did you fly under that bridge?' He just gave me a smile. I don't think he did, to tell the truth.

On November 23, 1931, a terrible thing happened to eighteen-year-old Lou Strickler. Although he had more than fulfilled the twenty-five-hour transport pilot requisite for night flying, Lou felt that an additional twenty-five hours would enhance his chances in securing a government pilot's position. Taking advantage of a clear, moon-bright night, Lou went to the J. D. Hill airport with a couple of friends, Jerry Smith and Edward Thomas of Greensburg. Lou took off at about 11:00 p.m. with Thomas in the passenger seat. Smith sat in a car near the hangar, waiting to drive Lou back to Latrobe.

The little Aeronca got to altitude and circled Latrobe. The townspeople had heard the plane on many nights, and they knew who it was. Joe Roddy was still at work on a rush job at his garage when he heard the plane. "That's Lou Strickler," he said. With him were his twenty-four-year-old mechanic, Phil Duffy, Bob Pescatore and Allen Feathers, both employees of Vanadium-Alloys Steel. One of them suggested that they go to the field. Lou would surely give them a ride in the plane.

By the time they arrived, Thomas had gone home, and Lou was standing by the side of the Aeronca, talking with Smith. Lou agreed to take them up: first Pescatore, then Feathers, then Roddy. Duffy, Pescatore and Feathers watched the takeoff, but, despite warnings from Smith who had returned to his car, the trio remained on the runway, their backs to the approach lane.

No one witnessed the accident. Smith had shifted his attention to something else, and neither Lou nor Roddy saw the three men standing on the field as they descended. Lou felt a bump beneath the plane. "Joe," he yelled. "We've struck something, but we're not on the ground!"

Roddy yelled back, "Keep your head, Lou. Go up again and we'll see!"

The Aeronca nosed up. Roddy leaned out to check for damage.

"Lou, I don't see any problems, but I can't be sure. Bring it down and brace yourself, just in case!"

Lou brought the plane down to a gentle landing, and he and Roddy got out. To their horror they saw in the bright moonlight the bodies of their three friends sprawled on the runway turf. Pescatore had been decapitated, and Duffy's skull crushed. Feathers would die of a broken neck and fractured skull in the Latrobe Hospital. The next morning, Lou and Roddy made formal statements at the office of Justice George K. Braden.

Bill Strickler remembers being awakened by his father on the night of the accident:

> The old man woke everybody up. We all were in a sweat. He said, 'Lou just had an accident up at the airport and killed three fellows!' We were worried. Everyone was worried. The old man was just sick. Lou got sick and had nightmares after that. I used to sleep with him. I couldn't sleep with him after that night. Jesus! He had to wait with the bodies until the coroner came. Next day this guy was selling Pittsburgh Sun-Telegraphs out on Ligonier Street in front of our house. We wanted to get him out of there. He was yelling, 'Crash! Three people killed!' My neighbor came over there and ran this guy off.

Charlie Carroll was over at the New Alexandria Airport and didn't hear of the accident until the next morning. Charlie, the State Aeronautic Inspector Larry Faurot, and Eugene Scroggy, Department of Commerce, concluded that the deaths of the young men were a regrettable accident, and that they violated airport rules by standing on the runway. Charlie determined that the landing wheel on the left side of the Aeronca, and the two rear flying wires on the left-hand side of the plane had struck the men and, with a few more inches of altitude, the accident would never have happened. Why they had not heard the approach of the plane remained a mystery to Charlie and other investigators. Sam Bigony, a pilot for Pittsburgh Airways and a friend of Lou's, flew down from York, Pennsylvania to, as the Latrobe Bulletin reported, "lessen the strain under which Lou is now laboring." Expert flyers commended Lou for the way he managed to land the damaged aircraft. The jury at the coroner's inquest exonerated Lou.

Lou flew for a long time after the accident, but he never really got over what happened that November night in 1931. He managed the New Alexandria airport for a time, and signed on as a pilot for the airport in Greensburg. He got to know Chalmers "Slick" Goodlin, the Bell XS-1 test pilot from Greensburg/New Alexandria. He ferried aircraft for the United States government in the early 1940s, and piloted for a time with Capital Airlines. He taught flying for the government in Baltimore. When the Naugles built their experimental plane in Latrobe, Lou was their test pilot. Lou finally married, and started to raise a family. One day he said to his sister, "I think my number's up. I'm going to get killed in a plane."

Then he quit flying, and opened a garage near Irwin, Pennsylvania. One night in 1953, as he was driving home, his car collided with a trailer rig. Lou was killed. He was forty years old.

Lou Strickler with his new Aeronca. *(Courtesy of Bill Strickler).*

Elmer Ashbaugh

The story of Elmer Ashbaugh and his daughter Eleanor begins in an old log cabin without electricity and ends with a Space Shuttle flight that almost was.

Elmer was born in the log cabin in 1897. After an eighth-grade education in a one-room school house, he eventually got his start in the automobile industry. He studied auto maintenance in Detroit, then returned to the area and established his own garage in Harrison City. After marrying and having three daughters, Elmer developed his interest in aviation. He frequented the J.D. Hill Airport, the new Pittsburgh-Greensburg Airport, and associated with World War I pilots and the likes of Dave Patterson, Norman "Happy" O'Bryan, Clyde Hauger and Charlie Carroll.

In 1932 he started taking flying lessons from Dave Patterson. After his solo flight in 1934, Elmer flew on weekends, doing aerial exhibitions at the Greensburg Airport and giving sight-seeing tours for one dollar per person. He flew parachute jumpers in his Travel Air on Sunday afternoons. These spectacles brought large, curious crowds. Ashbaugh quickly became a recognizable name among aviation enthusiasts in the area. Seeing the potential for an airport near to his hometown of Harrison City, Elmer thought of building one. In 1935 he did. Originally twenty-five acres, the Harrison City Airport had an 1,800-foot runway that ran parallel to Route 130. The Ashbaugh home was within this twenty-five-acre plot. Elmer later purchased an adjoining farm, increasing the size of his airport to forty acres. He tore down the barn farm and remodeled the house for his family. Elmer often taxied his airplane right up to the front porch, went inside for lunch and took off from his front yard.

Elmer decided his runway was not level enough, and, soon after opening, he made improvements. He graded the property every morning at sunrise, much to the chagrin of neighbors trying to catch a few extra winks of sleep. He built a hanger at the east end of the runway which housed his Travel Air, a Piper Cub and a Piper Trainer. Crowds often gathered just to watch him maneuver his aircraft into the hangers.

Elmer knew many World War I pilots. He must have enjoyed their tales of the Great War and their death-defying feats. One of these men, W.F. Niedernhofer went into business with Elmer in 1936. They purchased a twelve-passenger Ford Tri-Motor with the intention of starting an airline in Florida. Elmer piled his family into the Tri-Motor and headed for the Sunshine State. They are today considered to be the first family to ever move by aircraft. Their airline did not last long, only from November 1936 to February 1937. The Depression kept many people grounded, they had competition from another airline in Florida, and the Tri-Motor consumed a gallon of gas a minute, producing a financial drag on Elmer. Fortunately, Elmer had maintained his airport and garage in Harrison City. He was able to return there with his family.

By 1939, Elmer received a flight instructor's license and began giving flight lessons. When the United States entered World War II, many of his young students went on to become aviators in the war, including his daughter, Eleanor. She soloed at the age of sixteen, becoming one of the youngest pilots in the state. Too young to join the WASPs, Eleanor became a member of the Civil Air Patrol. She was thus able to fill an important role for which the military could not spare pilots.

The war came home to the Ashbaugh family when federal regulations required a twenty-four-hour guard to be posted at all airports. Elmer hired a guard for the daytime, but took care of the night duty himself. He slept in the hangar.

Wartime gas rationing hindered the operation of the

Harrison City Airport and Elmer's garage business. Seeing no choice in the matter, Elmer enlisted in the U.S. Ferry Command at the age of forty-five and ferried aircraft all over the United States. After the war, he returned home to find his airport in disrepair. The months spent away had taken their toll on the runway. Threatened with being shut down for good, Elmer quickly repaired ruts and graded the runway. His airport continued in operation until 1953 when a water line was laid along Route 130 making the forty-acre site ideal for homes. He closed up the airport with an impressive twenty-year record of no accidents or fatalities. Elmer kept his home and a building at the west end of the airport where he operated a gasoline station, garage, storing airplanes on the top floor. Elmer Ashbaugh died in 1985 at the age of eighty-eight, in the same house he used to taxi up to at lunchtime.

Eleanor Ashbaugh continued making headlines as a pilot in the 1940s. In 1946 she entered the Powder Puff Derby. The race went from Bettis Field to Latrobe and back. Eleanor won.

Flying may have been a passion for Eleanor, but her profession was teaching. She started her teaching career in 1953, the fiftieth anniversary of the Wright brothers' flight. She won a national contest on aviation education and flew to Washington D.C. for a ceremony to commemorate the event, where she got to hobnob with such aviation greats as James Doolittle and Chuck Yeager.

Despite her career as a teacher, Eleanor did not want to keep her feet on the ground. In 1985 she got an opportunity to explore both her loves. She applied to get on the "Teacher In Space" program. She completed a fifteen-page application essay that included an experiment to be conducted in space.

Fortunately, she did not get selected for the history-making flight. On January 28, 1986 the Space Shuttle exploded seventy-three seconds after take-off, killing all seven astronauts.

Eleanor Ashbaugh's contributions in the fields of education and aviation are profound. Like her father, she continues to see the possibilities of aviation. She saw this especially in the young people she taught for thirty-six years. Her efforts to educate young minds caused her to co-author the book *Aerospace Projects for the Elementary School*, published by the University of Miami.

Eleanor's father was proud of her achievements. In his later years, as Eleanor worked to get on the Shuttle Flight, he shared her enthusiasm and most likely wished he could go with her into space.

May 24, 1938. Elmer Ashbaugh (right) during National Airmail Week when he flew 500 letters from the Manor, Pennsylvania, post office to Bettis Field. With him are John Weightman, Postmaster at Claridge, and William Smith, Postmaster at Harrison City. *(Courtesy of Jean Loughry).*

ABOVE: Elmer Ashbaugh ready to take off from his Harrison City Airport for Bettis Field, May 24, 1938, during National Airmail Week. *(Courtesy of Jean Loughry).*

LEFT: Eleanor Ashbaugh, Elmer Ashbaugh's daughter, who learned to fly at sixteen. *(Courtesy of Jean Loughry).*

BELOW: The hangar at Harrison City Airport. *(Courtesy of Jean Loughry).*

A SPECIAL PICTORIAL

CURTISS MODEL JN4-B—MILITARY TRACTOR

DUE to the fact that this machine has been widely used for training aviators both here and abroad the JN type is probably the best known of all the Curtiss models.

It has a maximum horizontal speed of 75 miles per hour and a minimum of 43 miles per hour, and will climb 3,000 ft. in ten minutes. Powered with an 8-cylinder, "V" type Curtiss "OX" motor, which develops 90 H. P. at 1400 R. P. M. it consumes slightly more than one-half pound of gasoline per H. P. per hour. It is an economical machine for use in training students or general pleasure flying.

It is comparatively light and for its useful load carrying capacity, is very compact. With a wing span of 43 feet, 7⅜ inches and an overall length of 27 feet 3 inches, it weighs empty only 1,405 pounds but will carry a useful load of 485 pounds. It is equipped with dual control, carries two passengers "tandem," each in a separate cockpit.

ABOVE: Lloyd Santmyer poses with his Waco 10 at J.D. Hill Airport. To the right is Rich's Bar. It served as the airport's "termi-nal" in the early days, and was the site of many festive occasions conducted by the pilots. *(Courtesy of Lloyd Santmyer).*
BELOW: Carl Strickler (left) and "Pop" Cleveland at Bettis Field, August 1927, the time of Charles Lindbergh's reception there. *(Courtesy of Lloyd Santmyer).*

ABOVE: J.D. Hill Airport, June 1928. Russ Brinkley congratulates Joe Crane after another successful parachute jump.
(Courtesy of Lloyd Santmyer).
BELOW: Raymond Elder sits on the cowling of a Ryan monoplane after gassing it up at Peretto's station on the highway at J.D. Hill Airport. Mr. Kefer, owner of the plane, advertised his ice cream and other foods on the fuselage. *(Courtesy of Lloyd Santmyer).*

TIME FLIES

———

KEEP UP WITH TIME

AT THE

AVIATION SCHOOL

ST. VINCENT COLLEGE

LATROBE, PENNSYLVANIA

PHONE LATROBE
410 OR 9982M

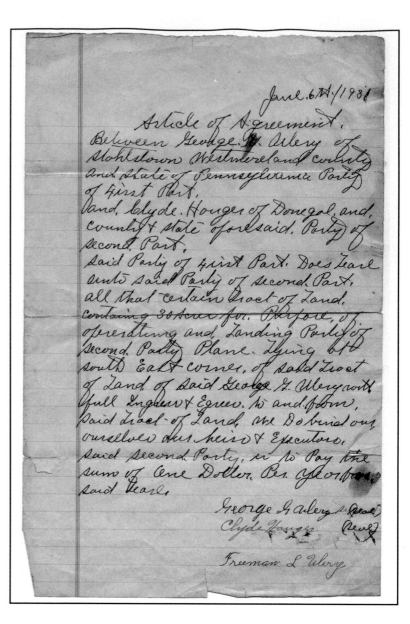

ABOVE LEFT: The front page of Saint Vincent College's brochure advertising its flight school.
(Courtesy of the Saint Vincent Archabbey Archives).
ABOVE RIGHT: The contract between Clyde Hauger and Freeman Ulery for an airport at Donegal, Pennsylvania.
(Courtesy of Clyde Hauger).
BELOW: Two pages from Clyde Hauger's log book. *(Courtesy of Clyde Hauger).*

The front and rear of the post card Charlie Carroll sent to Carl Strickler from Washington, D.C. Carroll was there to welcome Charles Lindbergh back to the United States after the "Lone Eagle" made his historic, non-stop flight across the Atlantic Ocean.

(Courtesy of Anna Mary Topper).

ABOVE: Frank Fox stands nearest this DH-4's number at Longview Flying Field, 1925. The plane was flown for an airshow by Greensburger Lieutenant Alwine. *(Courtesy of Frank Fox).*

BELOW: Lloyd Santmyer took this picture of the Graf Zeppelin. He went up to greet the ship as it passed over Latrobe in the early 1930s. *(Courtesy of Lloyd Santmyer).*

Charlie Carroll (far left) stands next to Lloyd Santmyer under the wing of a Ford Tri-Motor owned by W.H. and Harold I. McAffee of Uniontown, Pennsylvania, at J.D. Hill Airport, ca. 1933-1934. The plane, known as *Mac's Air Palace,* was flown from California by Spud Manning with Tony LeVier (shown tinkering with the mid-engine) flying copilot. The plane barnstormed for a time in the eastern United States. Santmyer relates that LeVier would promote the tri-motor by doing some preliminary stunting in a Travel Air. LeVier stayed with Lou Strickler's family while in Latrobe. *(Courtesy of Lloyd Santmyer).*

Lloyd sits in the cockpit of his airplane. Myrle Baughman, an accomplished pilot, looks on. She was Santmyer's student and wife. She soloed in 1935, on the same day as did Charlie Carroll's wife, Grace. Both women were charter members of the OX5 Club.
(Courtesy of Lloyd Santmyer).

J. D. Hill Airport, ca. 1930-1933. Lloyd Santmyer (in cockpit) poses with three student pilots. LEFT TO RIGHT: Chuck Zito, Cecil Smith, Bobby Mears. *(Courtesy of Lloyd Santmyer).*

Charlie Carroll (second from right) poses with his crew. Latrobe Airport, ca. 1938-1943. *(Courtesy of Josephine Smart).*

Clifford Ball, D. Barr Peat, and Bettis Field

Clifford Ball. *(Courtesy of Ken Scholter).*

D. Barr Peat. *(Courtesy of Carolyn Peat).*

The young man pulled his car to the side of the road when he heard the sound. It was the same kind of sound he had heard in France during the war. He got out of the car and looked up. He saw a flight of Jennies circling overhead. For a moment he thought back to those terrible days in the Argonne when the dawn patrols wheeled overhead scarcely audible amid the constant rumble of artillery fire. During those brief moments when this new weapon of war would appear, he wondered what it was like up there in the spaces of the sky. He watched the Jennies circle closer to the ground. He resolved to meet with the pilots. Perhaps one of them would take him up.

The Jennies landed in a nearby field. He walked towards the machines and waved at the airmen. One of them emerged from a cockpit. He introduced himself and his fellow fliers to the young man. The pilot's name was Eddie Stinson, and his companions were known as the Zephyr Fliers. They were barnstormers. Stinson, offered to take the young man up for a flight.

The year was 1919. The young man was Clifford Ball. He would soon become one of the most influential pioneers of aviation in the area, if not the country.

Clifford Ball was a native Pittsburgher. He got started in the automobile business with a Hudson-Essex dealership in McKeesport. The chance encounter with Eddie Stinson near Dravosburg that afternoon changed the direction of Clifford's life.

He always had a fascination for things mechanical, and the mechanics of aviation was not the least of it.

Clifford had a vision of airports. He imagined them dotting the landscape of rural Pennsylvania, servicing communities much like train stations did. He talked aviation with anyone who would listen, but there were few open ears in those days. One man who did listen because he shared a similar vision was D. Barr Peat. In 1924 the two men began an association that would bring aviation permanently to Pittsburgh.

D. Barr Peat

Like Clifford Ball, D. Barr Peat had a chance encounter with aviation. He was an engineer who worked as a foreman on the Liberty Tunnels in Pittsburgh. One day an airplane made a rough landing in the pasture on his land. The grass was so high the pilot crashed into a tree stump he couldn't see. D. Barr saw the airplane as it came down and ran out to help the pilot. Fortunately, the airman wasn't hurt. He helped the barnstormer fix his aircraft and got him on his way. It was like someone threw a switch in Peat's mind. He thought about building a landing field. He knew his property was not the ideal spot, but perhaps someplace close by would suit his purpose. There was a strip of land owned by a farmer named Harry Neel, Peat's neighbor and friend.

Together, they cleared Neel's land, opened it up and

made it available to any pilots who wanted to land there. D. Barr, along with his friend, William T. Richmond, used the site for air exhibitions and sightseeing. This would be the same field in which Clifford Ball would see Eddie Stinson and his Zephyr Fliers land.

In 1924 and 1925, the pair raised 35,000 dollars. Ball mortgaged practically everything he owned and they borrowed as much as they could. Then, in 1925, they purchased the forty acres above Dravosburg where they started their landing field. With their money, along with funds added by Harry Neel and Clifford's brother, Albert, they erected a hanger and a small machine shop to service the facility. It was an ideal spot, and one that already had a background in aviation.

Pittsburgh-McKeesport Airport

In June 1925, Clifford and D. Barr officially opened their airport, calling it the Pittsburgh-McKeesport Airport. That same year, Clifford started a flying school and Clifford Ball Airlines.

Pittsburgh-McKeesport Airport was only a little over a year in operation when it got a name change. It was rededicated Bettis Field in November 1926 in honor of Cyrus Bettis, a World War I flying ace killed in a flying accident near Bellefonte, Pennsylvania earlier that year. Bettis was a well-known pilot in Pennsylvania and had taken part in the opening ceremonies for the Pittsburgh-McKeesport Airport. Like Charlie Carroll at Longview Flying Field two years later, Clifford and D. Barr were honoring a fallen pioneer by naming their airport after him.

Kelly Air Mail Act

The air exhibitions continued, but the two men knew that their airport had more to offer than just entertainment and diversion. Ball was well connected politically. He knew there were other forces at work that would eventually help in the development of Bettis Field.

In 1922, a few years before the opening of the Pittsburgh-McKeesport Airport, U.S. Representative M. Clyde Kelly, presented the first air mail bill to the House. Later known as the Kelly Air Mail Act, it was signed into law by President Calvin Coolidge on January 17, 1925.

The original purpose of the act was to relieve the government of the responsibility for carrying the mail by air, but it also contained a clause that allowed the fostering of commercial aviation in the United States. The law would have a profound effect; it authorized the Postmaster General to negotiate contracts with private individuals and companies. Ball was awarded Contract Air Mail 11 on March 21, 1926.

Soon after the passing of the act, Clifford established the first privately owned airmail service in Pennsylvania. On April 21, 1927 the first air mail flights landed at Bettis Field. Clifford started out with three Waco 9s. These were christened, *Miss Youngstown, Miss McKeesport* and *Miss Pittsburgh*, now on display at the Pittsburgh International Airport. CAM 11's early pilots were Merle Moltrup, Dewey Noyes, Kenneth "Curley" Lovejoy and Jack Morris; they flew a route from Pittsburgh to Cleveland via Youngstown, Ohio.

Path of the Eagle

One success led to another. Clifford added passenger service to the route in April 1928. The next year saw the passenger service expand. In August 1929 Clifford Ball, Inc. created "Path of the Eagle," a passenger route from Cleveland to Washington D.C.. Around the same time, Ball acquired more aircraft. He bought a Ford Tri-Motor, a successful passenger aircraft. This was not the only reason he bought it. The aircraft's previous owner, W.C. Smith, had given the plane the name "Pennsylvania Airlines," and painted it on the side of the aircraft. This just happened to be the new name of the airline Ball first founded as Clifford Ball Airlines. It was a convenient purchase. Cliff also bought a Fairchild FC-2, a four-passenger monoplane, five New Standard D-27's, and acquired seven Waco 9 biplanes as payment for delinquent storage charges.

It is difficult to imagine in today's world how innovative Clifford Ball's airline was when something like the Air Bus will soon be in flight carrying close to 400 passengers. When Clifford Ball Airlines began, the Waco 9s took off with one passenger, who often had to sit on mail sacks during flight.

Charles Lindbergh's Visit

A major event at Bettis Field occurred on August 3, 1927, when Charles Lindbergh landed at the field in his Ryan monoplane during his 22,000-mile, 82-city official tour. More than 10,000 people greeted him when he landed, and 250,000 more lined his route from Bettis to downtown Pittsburgh, up Bigelow Boulevard to Pitt Stadium in Oakland.

The "Longview Boys," Charlie Carroll, Raymond Elder, Carl Strickler, Joe Crane, and several others from the airport in Latrobe, flew or drove to McKeesport for the festivities.

RIGHT: Cliff Ball (holding papers) stands next to Ken Scholter, taking delivery of mail from a National Air Transport aircraft, Bettis Field, 1920s. *(Courtesy of Ken Scholter)*

BELOW: The office at Bettis Field, 1920s. *(Courtesy of Carolyn Peat).*

Clifford Ball's Miss Pittsburgh over Cleveland, 1928. Pictured above, left and right: "Curley" Lovejoy and Dewey Noyes. *(Courtesy of Frank Fox).*

ABOVE: Ready for a night mail run are **Merle Moltrup** and **Dewey Noyes**. *(Courtesy of the Westmoreland County Airport Authority).*

BOTTOM LEFT: April 21, 1927. Ken Scholter accepts the mailbag for CAM 11s first delivery. *(Courtesy of Ken Scholter)*.

BOTTOM RIGHT: One of Cliff Ball's New Standard D-27s, NC9122. It later found its way to California in 1933 where it was converted into a crop duster. Ball had more of these aircraft types: 9121 (crashed October 1929, with Sievers as pilot); 9123 (crashed November 1933, Melvin Garlow, pilot. 9124, and 9119. *(Courtesy of Ken Scholter).*

Ken Scholter poses with Charles A. Lindbergh, Bettis Field, August 3, 1927, on Lindbergh's official tour with The Spirit of St. Louis to eighty-two cities. *(Courtesy of Ken Scholter).*

LEFT: August 3, 1927. The *Spirit of St. Louis* lands at Bettis Field. "That's me in the white pants!" exclaimed Ken Scholter, when shown the photo. All Ken had to wear were his "grease monkey" clothes, until D. Barr Peat prevailed upon oil-man Sam Brendel to purchase him a new suit of clothes. *(Courtesy of Anna Mary (Strickler) Topper).*

CENTER: The *Spirit of St. Louis* revving for take-off at Bettis Field. (Courtesy of Carolyn Peat).

BOTTOM: The crowd gathers around Lindbergh's Ryan monoplane he landed the plane. *(Courtesy of Carolyn Peat).*

Charles A. Lindbergh in an open touring car with Pittsburgh's Mayor Kline.

RIGHT: Lindbergh strolls toward the offices at Bettis Field.

(Courtesy of Carolyn Peat).

LEFT: "Curley" Lovejoy, "Playboy Pilot," poses with Ken Scholter the day Lindbergh landed. Ken proudly wears the new outfit bought for him for the occasion by Sam Brendel. *(Courtesy of Ken Scholter).*

BOTTOM LEFT: August 3, 1927. Carl Strickler, Charlie Carroll's chief pilot at Longview Flying Field, poses with "Pop" Cleveland.

BOTTOM RIGHT: August 3, 1927. Carl Strickler poses with his wife, Anna Mary, who flew with him to Bettis Field to greet Lindbergh.

ABOVE: August 3, 1927. The crowd at Bettis Field disperses as Lindbergh's motorcade makes its way to Pittsburgh.
(Courtesy of the Westmoreland County Airport Authority).
BELOW: August 3, 1927. A crowd gathers outside a hanger at Bettis Field. A portrait of Lindbergh hangs above the door. Charlie Carroll, wearing a white flying jumper, looks on. *(Courtesy of Anna Mary (Strickler) Topper).*

Green and Gold in the Sky

Courtesy of the Saint Vincent Archabbey Archives.

I t was November 5, 1929. A New Standard Biplane designed by Charles Day had just been delivered to Saint Vincent College. It bore the Approved Type Certificate No. 216 from the National Department of Commerce, and, coincidentally, was painted in the factory livery of green and gold, the colors of the college. The plane was called *The Spirit of Saint Vincent*. Lieutenant Homer Fackler had flown the aircraft from Teterboro Airport, New Jersey, to Bridgeville, PA. Fackler and George Daws brought the plane to Latrobe, landing at Hill Airport around 11 o'clock in the morning. Before he landed, Fackler flipped the plane on its back, did several slow and snap rolls, barrel rolls, loops and stalls.

Later, Lieutenant Jack Bessey was in the cockpit, revving the engine. Archabbot Aurelius B. Stehle, OSB, president of Saint Vincent College, was in the passenger seat, totally fascinated by the machine rumbling around him. Despite his interest, the Archabbot felt some apprehension. He knew pilots had been killed flying in the area. Not long before, Carl Strickler, a well known aviator from Scottdale, was killed near Laughlintown. Interest and fascination, however, were the stronger forces in the Archabbot.

Bessey tapped the Archabbot on the shoulder and gave him the "thumbs up." The Archabbot nodded eagerly. Bessey pushed the throttle forward. The green and gold *Spirit of Saint Vincent* lumbered over the field, gained speed and took flight.

"So this is what it feels like," thought the Archabbot. The biplane gained altitude. The Archabbot marveled at the rolling landscape of Westmoreland County. It was beautiful. He smiled. "This is what we will be teaching," he thought.

Bessey circled the college football field where the Saint Vincent Bearcats and their opponents were waiting. Suddenly, Bessey put the plane into a dive, leveled off, and dropped the game's football to the players.

First Meeting With Archabbot Aurelius

One year before there was a knock at the Archabbot's door. He looked up from his desk. He expected visitors that afternoon. Some people from J.D. Hill airport were coming to propose a new program they wanted to start with the college. He did not know all the details, but he was fascinated with anything that had to do with aviation. "Come in," he said.

Father Alcuin W. Tasch, OSB, the college dean entered. He had with him the *Latrobe Bulletin* publisher, Thomas E. Whiteman, Russell Brinkley, field manager of the J.D. Hill Airport, and Charles Carroll, the airport's owner and founder.

The Archabbot immediately recognized Charlie

from all the times Charlie had landed his old Jenny in the clover field on the campus. During the next few hours the group discussed something totally new in the academic world. They wanted the Hill Airport and Saint Vincent College to establish a joint school for aeronautics. It would be the first of its kind in the world. They made final arrangements. Charlie proposed a new name, Hill Airport at Saint Vincent College, and later applied to Rand-McNally to place it on its aeromaps. Plans fell through, however, when Charlie left the area to work in Florida flying co-pilot to Ed Musick for Pan-Am. Saint Vincent College, however, decided to continue with the program.

Move to Greensburg

In 1930, through association with the Mayer Aircraft Corporation of Bridgeville, Pennsylvania, the Greensburg School of Aviation opened at Main Aviation's Pittsburgh-Greensburg Airport.

The college moved the flight instruction component of the program there. Father Bernard Brinker, O.S.B., would teach ground school courses at the college. Twelve students enrolled in the first class. It was a modest beginning to an innovative program. Flight instructors at the Greensburg Airport included Dick Coulter, Dick Copeland, Norman "Happy" O'Bryan, Dick Laughlin, "Bo" Phelan, E. Henriquez and Bob Trader.

The Great Depression Interferes

But these were the early years of the Great Depression, and expenses for the new program could not be justified. The program was discontinued in 1931, after only two years of operation. This would not, however, be the end of Saint Vincent College's association with aviation. In 1939 the college entered he government's Civil Air Patrol program. Instructors at the Latrobe Airport, now a municipal entity, provided the flight instruction. Charlie Carroll's staff of flight instructors included Cecil Smith, George Allen and Dave Patterson.

The Army Air Corps

Two years later, in May 1941, the United States Army Air Corps recognized the convenience provided by the close proximity of the Latrobe Airport to Saint Vincent College. Here they had an opportunity to both train and educate pilots for military service. The National Aviation Training Association certified Saint Vincent College to teach ground school for glider pilots receiving flight training at the Latrobe Airport. The program was a modified version of the one begun in 1939. It was especially designed for the Army Air Corps Enlisted Reserve. Under the direction of Father Ulric Thaner, O.S.B., the program included courses in mathematics, physics, civil air regulations, navigation, radio and morse code.

Courtesy of Clyde Hauger

In March 1943, by order of the Army Air Force Flying Training Command, Saint Vincent's aviation program expanded to suit the needs of the military. A full compliment of 350 students arrived at the campus. They marched in formation up what is now Monastery Drive. The tunes of the military marching band came with them. If there were doubts before among the Benedictines about the reality of the war, they ended with the last notes of the band. Even the College was going to war.

Roland Heid, O.S.B.

Father Roland Heid, O.S.B. had to postpone his graduate studies and return to Saint Vincent College as soon as possible. The Army wanted to expand the aviation program presently being offered at the college, and the college needed Father Roland to return and instruct the cadets.

Father Roland first arrived at the Saint Vincent College Seminary in 1928, the year Archabbot Aurelius started his aeronautics program. Thrust into the forefront of the college's aircrew training program, Father Roland taught hundreds of cadets over the next eighteen months. Father Roland, Dr. Daniel Nolan and Father Bernard Brinker taught physics to the new cadets. The physics course required four months of study. After the fourth month, the cadets entered one month of flight training.

Father Roland taught four sections of physics, each section at a different level of preparation. Each month, one group of seventy would graduate to flight school, and a new group would come in to take its place. Consequently, Father Roland taught the entire physics course every month. Once the cadets graduated from flight school, Father Roland rarely heard what happened to them. They went off for further training and eventual overseas duty.

In the fall of 1944, with the war winding down, the Army Air Force Flying Training Command ended its program at Saint Vincent College. The college revamped the military program soon after its cessation. Father Michael F. Carmody offered a two-month course in the fundamentals of aviation. The new program put an emphasis on peace-time needs in aviation, new developments in aviation, civil air regulations, aeronautical meteorology, navigation and flight training. One of the texts used in the classes was Russ Brinkley's best-selling *Your Post-War Place in Aviation*.

The 1970s and Vee Neal Aviation

In 1978, to coincide with the seventy-fifth anniversary of the Wright Brothers flight, the college offered ground school courses, with flight school under the direction of Vee Neal Aviation. Once again Father Roland was called upon to teach the prospective pilots. This time he decided to become a student pilot himself. He never went on to get his pilot's license, but when asked how he did on his flights he answers, "Well, I guess I did something right, I'm still here!"

Silver Wings

1978 was a milestone year for Saint Vincent College's association with aviation. That year the college was honored with a memorial plaque by the Silver Wings Fraternity, an international group of aviators who made their first flight more than twenty-five years before.

The fraternity was founded by Russ Brinkley, the former manager of the Hill Airport at Latrobe. Many years before, Russ Brinkley sat down with Archabbot Aurelius B. Stehle, OSB, Charlie Carroll, Thomas E. Whiteman and Father Alcuin W. Tasch, OSB to discuss the possibility of starting an aviation school at Saint Vincent College. The possibility became a reality many times over.

Ruth Frey in 1979. Ruth and her husband, Neal, founded Vee Neal Aviation in 1967. From its beginnings as a flight school and aircraft rental operation, the company became in the 1970s the largest Cessna dealer in the North Eastern U.S. In the 1980s and 1990s the company emerged to the forefront of developments in the aviation industry. *(Courtesy of Ruth Frey).*

RAND. McNALLY & CO.,
AEROMAP DEPT.,
536 S. CLARK ST.,
CHICAGO, ILL.

AIRPORT QUESTIONNAIRE

1. Name of Airport... *Hill Airport at St Vincent College Latrobe Pa*

2. Class: municipal; commercial; government; aero club;

   Commerce Department intermediate; emergency only..........

3. Is field of permanent nature?........................

4. Is field under construction?....If so, when available?........

5. State distance and direction FROM business center of city........

6. State size and shape of field.........................

7. State altitude or elevation of field, if known...............

8. Does field have standard or other markers?................

9. Is surface leveled and improved?........................

10. Are repairs available?........ Fuel?........ Hangars?..........

11. Is telephone available?...............Telegraph?...............

12. Is weather information available at field?....................

13. Does field have standard 24" revolving beacon?................

    Beacon of other type?..........Flood lights?.......

14. Is there a wind indicator at field?........................

15. Name of owner.....................................

    of operator.. *C. B. Carroll*.....................

16. General remarks:...................................

17. Name and location of other airports in your vicinity:..........

*OUR published location and description
of YOUR AIRPORT can only be as good
as the information YOU SEND US.*

Charlie Carroll's application to Rand-McNally requesting that Saint Vincent Aviation Field be listed on their aero map as "J.D. Hill Airport at Saint Vincent College."

(Courtesy of the Saint Vincent Archabbey Archives).

Archabbot Aurelius Stehle, O.S.B.
(Courtesy of the Saint Vincent Archabbey Archives).

Rev. Bernard Brinker, O.S.B.
(Courtesy of the Saint Vincent Archabbey Archives).

Rev. Roland Heid, O.S.B.
(Courtesy of the Saint Vincent Archabbey Archives).

RIGHT: Fr. Alcuin Tasch receives his Silver Wings award from Russ Brinkley [center] as Bob Cheffins, Westmoreland County Airport manager, looks on. *(Courtesy of the Saint Vincent Archabbey Archives).*

BELOW: Army Air Corps cadets line up in front of their Piper Cub at the Latrobe Airport. *(Courtesy of the Saint Vincent Archabbey Archives).*

TOP: 1939. Saint Vincent College Civil Air Patrol student flyers at the Carroll School of Aviation, pose with "Cubby," Charlie Carroll's collie and airport mascot. *(Courtesy of the Saint Vincent Archabbey Archives).*
CENTER: Army cadets at the Latrobe Airport. *(Courtesy of the Saint Vincent Archabbey Archives).*
BOTTOM: Saint Vincent College student pilots at the Westmoreland County Airport, ready to receive instruction from the personnel at Vee Neal Aviation. *(Courtesy of the Saint Vincent Archabbey Archives).*

"Doc" Adams, the Airmail Pick-up System, and All American Aviation

Dr. Lytle Schuyler "Doc" Adams, primarily a dental surgeon, but also an inventor of extraordinary talent, first got the idea of an air mail pick up system in 1923 when he was a real estate agent for the Long Bell Lumber Company in Longview, Washington. Adams needed a road for his Longview clients as much as the town needed one in order to progress. With donations of explosives and heavy equipment from the lumber company, Adams collected volunteer labor from among the townspeople, and together they completed the Ocean Beach Highway. While the road was under construction, Adams took note of how the workers employed grappling hooks attached to tractors to hook and drag away the fallen timber. Why couldn't a similar system be employed on an aircraft for picking up various items, including mail?

W.E. Boeing and Seattle

After the road was finished, Adams moved to Seattle to practice dentistry, having been qualified in that profession since 1905, but he did not forsake his idea of an air pick-up system. In his spare time he built and tested numerous models. In 1925, W.E. Boeing, a man destined to create one of the world's greatest aircraft companies, arrived in Seattle. Boeing bought a small air field, Gorst Field, where he set up a small aircraft factory. Boeing became interested in Doc's ideas and allowed him to use his facilities and staff to develop the ideas for air pick-up. Soon Boeing was ready to test Doc's cumbersome prototype.

Doc acquired an OX5 Travel Air biplane and two young pilots, Clayton Scott and L. Van Rawlings. In August 1928, after rigid and exhaustive tests, Adams conducted the first public demonstrations of his system. With Charles Lindbergh, W.E. Boeing, William P. McCrackin Jr., Chief of Aeronautics of the Department of Commerce, and C.M. Perkins, Seattle postmaster among the observers, Clayton Scott swooped down in the Travel Air and snagged thirty-five pounds of mail. The plane maintained course and speed after the pick-up.

More Demonstrations and Some Financial Backing

Soon after, Adams exhibited his models at the Chicago Post Office. Officials there, duly impressed, submitted favorable recommendations to W. Irving Glover, Second Assistant Postmaster General in Charge of Air Mail. Adams traveled to Washington where he showed his models to Postmaster General Harry S. New, Glover, and an assortment of senators and congressmen.

In September 1928, seeking financial backing, Adams went on to New York where he displayed his models at an aviation show in Grand Central Palace. This time, his model aircraft flew across the room and picked up a small bag of mail. Among the spectators were representatives from the McClure Jones Company, whose directors later helped Adams with financing to demonstrate his model at air shows in Buffalo and Cincinnati. The McClure Jones Company also financed Doc's first companies, the Adams Air Express, an operating company, and Airways Patent Corporation, a patent holding company.

Relieved of financial pressure, Adams refined his system to include in-flight fueling. For subsequent demonstrations, Adams purchased a Travel Air 6000 monoplane. On December 10, 1928, at Hoover Field in Washington, D.C., Mrs. Harry New, the wife of the Postmaster General, christened the plane *The Postmaster General.* Harry New, speaking on the occasion, said:

> This is the last word...for the benefit of air mail....If successful, as we all hope it may be, as it bids fair to be, Dr. Adams will have made a most substantial contribution to the transportation of useful loads through the air.

On December 14, 1928, pilots Don Brown, Captain John O. Donaldson and L. Van Rawlings, operating from Roosevelt Field, Long Island, used Adams' pick-up system to transfer food, letters, oil and fuel. Two men who were watching the demonstration offered Adams contracts. They were Cliff Ball of Bettis Field, owner and president of Clifford Ball Airlines, and P.W. Chapman, president of United States Lines.

Ship-to-Shore Pick-up: The *SS Leviathan*

Chapman, hoping to establish the world's first permanent ship-to-shore service, financed a demonstration on the *SS Leviathan*, flagship of the United States Lines fleet. The same ship was used in a similar demonstration on July 31, 1927, when the first ship-to-shore flight was made by Clarence D. Chamberlin. Chapman treated Adams royally, providing him not only with intensive public relations support, but also with accommodations for his staff.

The caption for this photo from the *New York Evening Journal* reads:

"Bitterly disappointed over the failure of the amphibian to find the *Leviathan* Friday, Dr. Lytle S. Adams, who was aboard the steamer, is busily working on plans to demonstrate his air-mail pick-up invention on the next voyage. Everything on the *Leviathan* is in readiness for the pick-up, the inventor said, and he is confident it will succeed."

(Courtesy of Ed Blend).

Doc's serviceable but unwieldy trap was increased from a width of twenty-one feet to thirty-five feet and placed 100 feet above the water line at the ship's stern.

The first pick-up attempt was scheduled for June 6, 1929. Unfortunately, the Burnelli monoplane which was to be used, crashed at Keyport, New Jersey, on June 5. Adams hurriedly installed his equipment in a Loening amphibian. At 2:00 p.m. on June 6, Lieutenant Commander George R. Pond took off from Newark Municipal Airport, stopped at Roosevelt Field for a wireless test, then flew to New Bedford for refueling. *Leviathan* stood ready off Nantucket Lightship, but the

Loening was struck by lightning. Pond aborted the flight.

The next morning, Pond made another attempt, this time with Adams who was armed with a camera. Adams hung dangerously out of the hole made for the pick-up equipment, a position he assumed would be conducive for a good photo. Pond encouraged him back into the plane. Pond aborted this attempt as well. Dense fog obscured the ship.

Doc arranged still another attempt, this time with two planes, a Fairchild monoplane to make the pick-up, and the Loening to carry a bevy of photographers. At 3:30 p.m., June 12, the Leviathan proceeded in an easterly direction. Adams was on board. Two hours later, Pond, toting a forty-pound bag of mail, climbed into the Fairchild. Both planes took off from Keyport, New Jersey, and reached the liner around 6:50 p.m. Pond circled, swooped down, dropped the bag of mail into the trap, and picked up the ship's mail. They landed at Newark about one hour later.

When he arrived back in the United States, Adams was confident that he would receive a permanent contract, but Chapman's public relations efforts had backfired. The Post Office Department canceled Chapman's contract, charging that his line had used the contract to sell stock in the company, stock that had risen considerably in price during the demonstrations.

Clifford Ball Enters the Picture

Gravely disappointed, Adams transferred his equipment to Youngstown, Ohio, where Truscon Steel was to redesign the trap, hoping to reduce its cost and increase its effectiveness. It was there that Clifford Ball arranged to conduct tests of Adam's equipment. The tests, which began on August 30, 1929, lasted for nearly one month. During this time, Adams reduced the width of his trap apparatus to twenty feet, increased the height, and added a guard rail in the slot to decrease the possibility of the steel cable fraying.

By March 1930, Ball and Adams were ready to demonstrate the system in the nation's capital. From March 6 to March 11, they made nearly 500 successful pick-ups and deliveries for Congress and the Post Office Department. Still, the Post Office Department required a further six months of service testing before it would allow air-mail contractors to use the system. The tests, which began August 4, 1930, were conducted over Ball's C.A.M. 11 route between Pittsburgh and Cleveland, with mail pick-ups at Beaver Falls, New Castle, Pittsburgh, and Youngstown, for delivery to Cleveland. In anticipation, Adams and Ball ordered the building of nine additional traps.

In 1929, Clifford Ball, operator of airmail route C.A.M. 11 between Pittsburgh and Cleveland, tried out Adam's pick-up system. After the Post Office Department agreed to a demonstration of the system, Ball and Adams established pick-up stations in Pennsylvania at New Castle and Beaver Falls. In the photo, Ball poses with the pick-up device, installed on one of his Fairchild FC-2 monoplanes.
(Courtesy of Ed Blend).

The tests lasted two weeks, then the contract was canceled. Ball was pressured to sell his company, and there was no stipulation in the sales agreement concerning Adams. It was not a happy moment for either man. Adams did not venture to negotiate a contract with the new owners, whose company would eventually become Capital Airlines. Over the next year, Adams would become involved in patent infringement lawsuit lodged by a man named John P. Jacobs. Jacobs' claims turned out to be spurious, but the episode drained Adams' resources, and he was left once again to seek financial support for his pick-up system.

Braniff and the Fair in Chicago

It was 1933, and though the Great Depression had begun for the nation and the world, the "Century of Progress" was in full swing in Chicago. The great fair was an opportunity for Adams to once again demonstrate his pick-up system. He began by acquiring two sponsors, the New York Central Railroad and Braniff Airways. Tom Braniff and Adams managed to have the Post Office Department extend Braniff's C.A.M. to the fairgrounds. The government required them to obtain special insurance protection and set in place measures to ensure the public safety.

On September 20, 1934, Trow Sebree, a pilot formerly with Clifford Ball Airlines, and Eddie Gerber, carried 4,000 pieces of mail. They made the trip in six minutes, ten percent of the time it took by mail truck. Though the Chicago pick-ups were thrilling and successful, and though Adams had begun making plans to establish feeder routes in the small towns surrounding Chicago, enthusiasm waned and died along with any plans when the fair closed.

Though disappointment once again clouded Adams'

horizon, something did happen in Chicago that would significantly change the future for him and for his air mail pick-up system. A man named Richard Archbold, who had been making expeditions into the forests of New Guinea to collect bird specimens and small animals for the New York Museum of Natural History, became interested in Adams' system and its potential for picking up and transporting his specimens from the interior of New Guinea to the coast.

The "Goal Posts"

In the spring of 1935, Adams traveled to Archbold's family plantation in Thomasville, Georgia. Together, they tried to redesign the pick-up trap to make it easier for New Guineans to carry and assemble it. It wasn't long before they realized that, even with their modifications, the apparatus would still be too clumsy and complicated. Adams hit upon the idea of using two bamboo poles set apart like goal posts with a loop between, replacing the trap. That way, only the poles and rigging would need to be transported and set-up would be easy. A simple grapple, suspended from the plane, would make the pick-up. At that moment, Adams relegated his cumbersome trap system to history. In less than five years, his "goal post" air mail pick-up system would be servicing 121 communities in the Mid-Atlantic Region of the United States.

Adams Moves to Irwin, PA: Tri-State Aviation

After Thomasville, Adams took up permanent residence in Irwin, Pennsylvania, halfway between Pittsburgh and Latrobe, on a property he purchased during his association with Clifford Ball. In Irwin he established a small field and hanger and began a new round of seeking financial backing for his new system. The new "goal post" apparatus impressed William P. Wilson of Wheeling, West Virginia, president of the Ohio Valley Industrial Corporation and past chairman of the board at Fokker Aircraft. Wilson had been following Adams activities for several years. Through Wilson, Adams gained the confidence of Jennings Randolph of West Virginia's Second Congressional District. Randolph witnessed a demonstration of the pick up system at Morgantown in late 1935, after which he became air mail pick-up's most vocal Washington advocate.

Though Adams welcomed such support, little was done to alleviate his financial situation. Hoping to gain the President's interest, he contacted Eleanor Roosevelt, who passed his letter on to her brother, G. Hall

Roosevelt. Nothing came of the overture. Finally, Adams made contact with Arthur P. Davis, president of Army Engineering Corporation of Brooklyn, New York. Davis, believing that the pick-up system had potential, agreed to lend Adams a substantial amount of money. On May 5, 1937, Adams, along with W. Edgar Leedy, Jr., and Arthur P. Davis, formed two companies, Tri-State Aviation, an operating company, and All American Aviation, a patent holding company. Adams was elected president. Davis became vice-president and board chairman. All American was to engage in air operations involving passengers, freight, mail lines, pleasure flights and industrial flights. Tri-State Aviation at Adams' Irwin Field would replace the work undertaken by Adams Air Express. It would undertake pick-up experiments, and engage in the development and airmail network. In return, Davis received a one-half share in Adams patent for the pick-up apparatus.

Operations in Morgantown

Congressman Randolph, dismayed that existing airlines had largely ignored establishing routes in his constituency, urged Adams and Davis to move operations to Morgantown, which they did do. In 1937, they moved to the new municipal airport in Morgantown, hiring in the process pilot Norman Rintoul and mechanic Vic Yesulaites. The pair flew pick-up experiments and express routes.

Express operations began on September 9, 1937, with Kaufmann's Department Store in Pittsburgh the first customer. Soon, other stores and mail order houses such as Montgomery Ward took advantage of the speedy air shipments. By 1938, Tri-State had three Bellancas and one Stinson servicing Morgantown, Pittsburgh, Charleston, West Virginia, and Baltimore.

Despite some success, sporadic as it was, Adams knew that airmail contracts would be the life's blood of the company. He continued with demonstrations and experiments. One demonstration became the stuff of local legend. On June 3, 1937, a Tri-State pilot, Norman J. ("Happy") O'Bryan, field manager of the airport at Dry Ridge in Greensburg, Pennsylvania made a "special delivery" to members of the House Post Office and Post Roads Committee. Happy swooped down, dropped a container of six quarts of Scotch whiskey, picked up a bag of mail, and climbed into the clouds. History has recorded neither the disposition of the whiskey nor the influence, if any, that it generated.

Less than one week later, at any rate, Pennsylvania congressman Harry Haines introduced H.R. 7448, a bill designed to authorize the postmaster general to receive proposals for experimental airmail to isolated rural areas. After some delay, Congress passed the Experimental Air Mail Act of 1938, and the Post Office Department opened rural airmail pick-up and delivery to bids.

Though Tri-State was in a good position to obtain an experimental airmail contract, finances were still a prob-

Tri-State Aviation's Stinson Reliant 21107 fresh from the factory in 1938. This plane, piloted by Norm Rintoul with Vic Yesulaites as Flight Mechanic, would make the first, officially scheduled All American Aviation airmail drop and pick-up at Latrobe on May 12, 1939. The plane was painted maroon, with blue stripe and gold trim, colors AAA would maintain during the experimental period 1939-1940. Left to Right: Norm Rintoul, Lytle Adams, Vic Yesulaites. *(AAHS Journal).*

lem, despite the capital investment by Arthur Davis. Adams once again approached the Roosevelts. On June 25, 1938, Norman Rintoul and Adams flew to Hyde Park where they spent the evening with Mrs. Roosevelt and her family and friends. Mrs. Roosevelt agreed to let them transport her to a luncheon at a homestead in Arthurdale, West Virginia, just south of Morgantown. The President's wife, through her association with Congressman Randolph, had developed an interest in the mountain folk of West Virginia and in projects involving homesteading and self-help among those who lived in remote and depressed areas. At the evening meal, at breakfast, and during the flight down, Adams explained his system, especially as to how it could service isolated communities with manufactured goods and give them access to distant markets. He must have struck a responsive chord in the First Lady. Accompanying them was New York state trooper, Earl R. Miller, Mrs. Roosevelt's bodyguard and personal friend of the family. Miller promised Adams that he would talk to other members of the Roosevelt family about financial support.

Enter Richard du Pont

After years of frustration, Adams was wary of placing too much hope in his discussions with Mrs. Roosevelt or Miller. Present at the dinner at Hyde Park, however, was the wife of Franklin Roosevelt, Jr., the former Ethel du Pont, of Delaware. She spoke to her cousin, a glider enthusiast and aeronautical pioneer, about Adams system. The cousin expressed an immediate interest. His name was Richard du Pont. The two men met in September 1938.

At last, Adams found the financial backing he had sought for so many years. His association with Richard du Pont, however, would result in his losing control not only of his company, but of his invention as well.

Experimental Routes 1001 and 1002

By December 27, 1938, du Pont signed contracts for air mail pick-up routes 1001 (Philadelphia to Pittsburgh) and 1002 (Pittsburgh, Irwin, Jeannette, Greensburg, Latrobe, Mt. Pleasant, Connellsville, Uniontown, into West Virginia, and return to Pittsburgh). Stinson SR-10C Reliant aircraft with Lycoming 680 engines would make the pick-ups. Norman Rintoul was made chief pilot. In early 1939, the company hired five others: Holger Hoiriis, Camille D. ("Cammy") Vinet, Thomas Kinchelhoe, Gerald E. McGovern, and Jimmy Piersol. Later in the year, Raymond Elder of Scottdale and long-time associate of Charlie Carroll at Latrobe Airport was

hired as a reserve, along with Lloyd Juelson. Pilot requirements were stringent; all were required to have years of experience and thousands of hours in the air. This was little wonder. Not only would they be required to make difficult, low-level pick-ups at high speed, but much of their territory took in the notorious "Hell's Stretch" over the Allegheny Mountains, the graveyard of many regular airmail pilots, and a place of dense fogs and unpredictable weather changes.

Before the pick-ups could begin, changes needed to be made in the pick-up apparatus. Adams was excluded from the process. Some of the changes incorporated elements of other pick-up systems, such as Cabot's. Most were designed and implemented by Vic Yesulaites. Du Pont had serious doubts about Adams' ability to correct problems inherent in the present system. He also considered him to be too emotionally involved in the process to be amenable to change. In this he was correct. Adams' resentment deepened. The final breakdown of the relationship in 1940 is documented in detail in Lewis and Trimble's *The Airway to Everywhere.*

To give its personnel valuable training, All American staged pick-ups and deliveries along its proposed routes. The first occurred at Coatesville, Pennsylvania, March 6, 1939. Other demonstrations took place in Oil City, Warren, Franklin, Corry, and New Kensington.

Latrobe, PA: May 12, 1939

All American's first officially scheduled air mail pick-up took place at Latrobe, Pennsylvania, May 12, 1939, Route 1002.

Norman Rintoul in 1948 at Irwin, PA, the day he performed a human pick-up with Irwin's Bernie Cain as the subject. Rintoul is pictured with All American Aviation Stinson NC2311, the "Black Stinson," or "Black Bess." He later purchased the plane and donated it to the Smithsonian Institute, where it hangs today. Rintoul made the AAA's first official pick-up at Latrobe in 1939, and the last at Jamestown, New York, in 1949.
(Courtesy of Ken Scholter).

There is no known record as to why Latrobe was chosen for the honor, but it is reasonable to assume that Charlie Carroll's promotional abilities and far-reaching friendships had something to do with it.

On May 13, 1940, the government suspended pick-up service, largely because financial returns were disappointing. Yet, the record was impressive. In twelve months of operation All American completed nearly 450,000 miles in the air, made over twenty-thousand pick-ups of eighty-two thousand pounds of mail and air express, all without serious accident.

Permanent Service:
August 12, 1940-July, 1949

In 1940, the Civil Aeronautics Board granted All American Aviation a Certificate of Public Convenience and Necessity. Air Mail Route 49. Eventually, 139 towns and cities would receive direct service. August 12, 1940 saw the inauguration of the permanent service. The experimental year had served a good purpose; all the pilots and mechanics knew their jobs, and there would be few slip ups. There were many refinements to the apparatus, especially to the pick up hook cable and modifications in the height of the pick-up station, which gradually became portable. Power driven units would replace the old hand crank. The wheel pants of the 1939 planes were replaced by wire cutting devices that were supposed to cut through pick-up lines rather than having them get tangled in the wheels. Over the next nine years, the Stinsons would be augmented by the more modern Beechcraft twin-engine D-18C's.

By May 25, 1942 , AAA planes had flown 2,700,000 scheduled miles, made 225,000 pick-ups and deliveries, carried 750,691 pounds of airmail, and 172,801 pounds of air express. Astonishingly, the pilots did it all without damage to equipment or injury to personnel. Leighton Collins, editor of *Air Facts*, speaks of flying with Norm Rintoul, Clyde Hauger and Dave Patterson, and called the AAA system as being comprised of "iron men and SR-10s." The perfect record, however, would soon be tarnished.

On April 12, 1943, Russ Crow encountered a vicious downdraft on Tuscarora mountain and plowed into some scrub oak, severely damaging his aircraft. On October 25, on a flight from Chambersburg to Gettysburg, Tommy Bryan and Flight Mechanic Vic Gasbarro went down on Piney mountain. Both were battered about and the plane was damaged, but the cargo survived. On August 3, 1944, Red Lindemuth and Ralph Monaco crashed and burned at Yorkville, Ohio. This time there were some serious broken bones. The ship was a total loss, and thirty-one sacks of mail were destroyed. On September 29, 1944, Wilson Scott died in a crash at State College, Pennsylvania. It was the first fatality for AAA in 6,000,000 miles of scheduled operation.

The scene above takes place in Jamestown, New York, June 30, 1949, the day of the last AAA airmail drop and pick-up from AAA's northernmost route. "Pop" Oberg, airmail messenger, shares "holding the bag" with Norm Rintoul and Vic Yesulaites. Rintoul and Yesulaite's share one of history's ironies. They were the first in at Latrobe in 1939, and the last out here in 1949. *(Courtesy of Ed Blend).*

In the mid-forties, AAA expanded its interests abroad, organizing its own Brazilian company. Captain Clyde Hauger and Flight Mechanic Raymond Garcia became the operations department of Equipamento All America Aviation S/A, formed in Rio de Janiero. They were to develop short haul transportation through cargo and glider pick-up. AAA also was commended by the US military for its work in air pick-up, glider and human pick-up, and the development of the Brodie system, a portable rig for landing and launching aircraft on a cable.

In the late forties, the company began to move away from airmail pick-up to passenger and conventional air mail service. The old Stinsons were sold off, and the com-pany acquired eleven, twenty-four passenger DC-3s. Passenger operation was headquartered in Washington, D.C., while pick-ups continued out of Pittsburgh. In July 1949, the last airmail pick-up took place in Jamestown, New York. The same pilot and flight mechanic who flew the first pick-up at Latrobe in 1939, made the last. They were Norm Rintoul and Vic Yesulaites.

In 1949, All American Aviation became All American Airways. In 1951, the company became Allegheny Airlines. In 1979, it became USAir. How differently things might have gone but for the persistence of an inventive dentist and his dream.

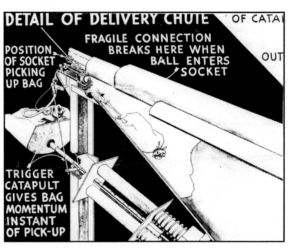

"Doc" Adams sits in his Studebaker next to the Travel Air monoplane he used in pick-up demonstrations and experiments in the-late 1920s. The plane was named *The Postmaster* by Postmaster General Harry S. New on December 18, 1929 in Washington, D.C., and christened by Mrs. New. Adams carried out a successful test of his early chute system at Roosevelt Field, Long Island, a week later. L.V. Rawlins piloted the plane. The same aircraft was used on an endurance flight conducted by Captain John C. Donaldson, former WWI pilot, Rawlins, and Don Brown. Above are two photos of Adam's early chute system, one which was cumbersome and expensive. Officials pose in the "funnel" in March 1930 at Hoover Field. *(Courtesy of Ed Blend).*

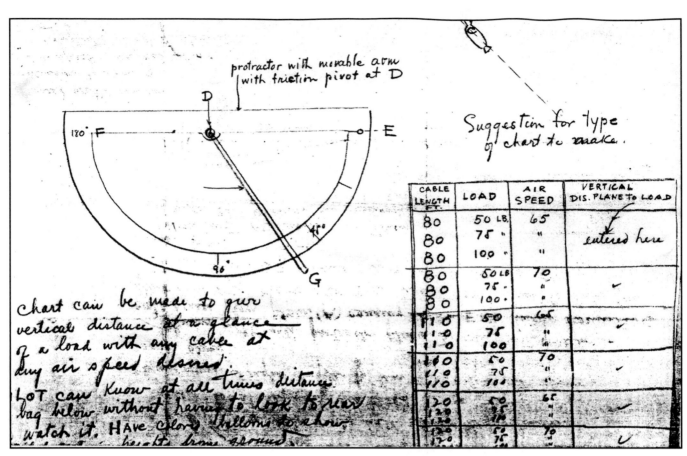

Doc Adams notes and diagrams for the pick-ups. *(Courtesy of Ed Blend).*

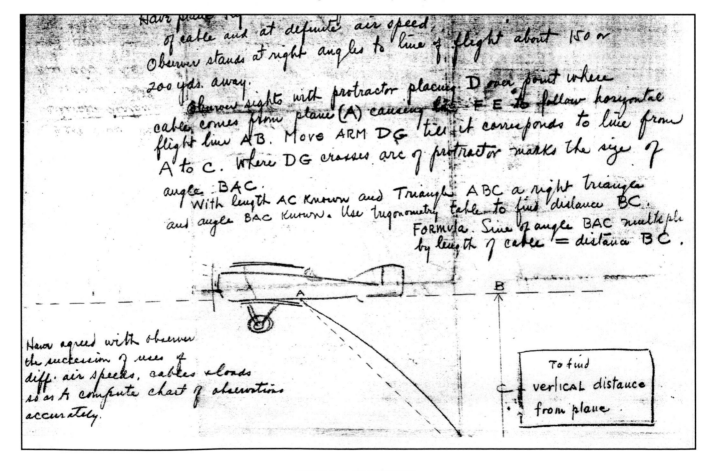

In Their Own Words...

Josephine Smart
Whitney, Pennsylvania
Mail Messenger, Latrobe Airport

Charlie Carroll hired my husband as a mechanic. Charlie got this airmail business and he offered the job of getting the mail bags ready for the pick-up to my husband, Paul. Paul didn't have enough time to handle that on top of his job at the airport, so I got the job. I used to go to Latrobe or the freight office to pick up the mail. I used to take George's and Charlie's boy, Donald into town to pick up the mail. I'd make two trips a day into Latrobe and back. If there was freight that was too big for the airplane to pick up, the pilot would land and pick it up. He could see from the plane if I had freight that was too big for the pick-up. If not, I'd get the bag ready, set it between the two poles and he'd just swoop it up. A few times he would miss picking up the bag, then I'd have to go back and set it up again, but that didn't happen too often. They would drop a bag of mail for me, too. I'd take that into the Latrobe Post Office. They were good pilots. They'd wave at me as they were flying away with the mail.

The bags weren't too heavy. Sometimes we'd have a lot of mail, but it was manageable. The container was weighted on one end. The container was on the ground all the time, so I didn't have to lift it up into place between the two poles. It rested on the ground and then when the plane came down between the poles, the hook on the plane caught hold of the cable attached to the bag and picked it up.

Mail Messenger Josephine Smart readies the mailbag at Latrobe Airport in the early 1940s. She inherited the job from her husband Paul, who was busy with other duties at the field.

BELOW LEFT: Josephine poses between the pick-up poles.
(Courtesy of Josephine Smart).

The first year I did this was 1943. My son was in the service and sometimes I used to wear his coveralls while I was setting the bags up. I drove a Model A Ford. Once or twice I had to dig the car out from under the snow to get out to the airport and set up the mail bags. The mail had to get through! We got watches from the company. Earl Santmyer and I got out watches together. They have pictures of a Stinson making a pick-up on them.

It was exciting to see those planes swoop down and pick the mail up. Once in a while people would gather to watch. Sometimes the pilots would come down to the house and visit us. I never went up in one of the Stinsons.

Kip Barraclough
Pittsburgh, Pennsylvania
Pilot

As a young man, I lived in in Du Bois, PA, and they had a lot of publicity in 1939 about an airmail pick-up coming through the Du Bois airport. I was one of those up there watching that Stinson coming around with that hook. It hit the poles, and it wasn't very successful. Even so, from that day forward, I wanted to fly.

I got hired by All American in February 1943. They gave me an instrument rating in Wilmington, Delaware. I did that for about six months, then went into the military. When the war was over, I came back and started flying for All American. That was in 1946. In my mind, the

On the image: *To my old friend Frank Fox Best Regards "Kip" Barraclough*

Kip Barraclough swoops in for a pick-up at Latrobe, 1948. *(Courtesy of Frank Fox).*

pilots that flew for All American were about the best there was, and I didn't know if I could measure up to what these guys were doing every day. Nobody ever said anything to me do this, do that when the weather's like this they just left you completely alone. I had to learn, more or less, by trial and error. The first time I went out on a run, I was with Roy Weiland, and we were on a West Virginia run, which meant you went from Pittsburgh down to West Newton, Mount Pleasant, Connellsville, Masontown, Fairmont, Clarksburg. Pittsburgh, in those days, was pretty smoky, to put it mildly. We took off from the airport and Roy made a turn, and he headed towards West Newton, and I'm just sitting there beside him. He's talking to me, and suddenly he nods his head, and I hear a noise in the back. The next thing I know, the airplane's up on its side, and we're diving down through this absolutely black hole. There's a couple of little flares down there. We go through the station, pick up the mail, drop off the mail, and I thought, "Holy s–! I could never do this."

By the time we got down to Mount Pleasant, we ran out of smoke. Eventually, I learned how to do what Roy did. It was the greatest flying in the world. You didn't really have any minimum altitude that you had to fly. If

you wanted to fly 100 feet, fine or 200 feet. I rarely went above 300 feet. The only problem you had was if you had an engine failure, you had to work pretty quick to find a place to set it down.

As the days got shorter in the wintertime, they dropped the time that we were allowed to fly from seven o'clock to five o'clock, and in the wintertime, often it was dark before five o'clock. I was on this Harrisburg to Pittsburgh flight, around December 20, 1947 or 1948. We had come through some snow flurries and low-hanging clouds. We got to Johnstown and we had to land because it was Christmastime and they had a lot of stuff to come off. The Stinson didn't have a very good heater, and a really lousy defroster. The only other anti-ice device that we had was a phenol heater and carburetor heat.

We got to Johnstown and they kept putting stuff on, bags and packages and everything. Finally there wasn't room for another package. We took off in a low ceiling. As soon as I got off, I was on instruments. I climbed straight out until I got my bearings for Blairsville. I got to 3200 feet, made a turn, settled down to light a cigarette when the engine blew out. I had no idea where I was. I was somewhere between Johnstown and Blairsville, and there were two ridges there, Chestnut and Laurel. I didn't know whether to go straight ahead and try to get into the valley of Ligonier, or whether to try and go back to Johnstown. I knew there was a strip right along the bridge there, Westmont or a little town that was just developed. I expected to run into the mountain. The flight agent was sitting in the back, and he had the hole open, so I said, "If you see anything, holler and I'll put the flaps on and suck it back, and we'll try to blend as low as we can." All of the sudden, I saw some light on the ground. To my left, I saw a white patch. So, I headed for this patch. Fortunately, the wind was such that we landed on this little knob, a cow pasture. We rolled upside the top of the knob, and then stopped. We found out later that it was four hundred foot drop a hundred feet from where we stopped. I sat there in the airplane, my knees knocking. I didn't want the flight agent to see that my knees were knocking. When I turned around to look at him, his knees were knocking worse than mine. "Let's get the Hell out of here," he said.

Well, we got out, and it was silent except for the wind and our voices. There were lights down in the valley coming toward us. This is what happened, we found out later. We had passed over this little mining town near Johnstown. Some kids who were playing outside went in and told their parents that the mail plane had crashed. One miner there, a Polish guy, took charge of everything. In that day and age, all the miners had safety kits to use in case of a mine accident, and they knew First Aid. This guy organized all these people and they came up this hill in kind of like a snake fashion, which is the way the cows would come up. It was too steep to come up straight. They're shouting, and this guy is leading the way. I said, "We've gotta get the mail, gotta get the mail, gotta get the mail."

So the Polish guy made each of the people grab a bag or parcel, take it down, and put in his truck. We go down to his house and sit down in the kitchen at a round table. He put two water glasses in front of us. He goes to a cabinet and brings his jug of whiskey over. He pours our glasses about a third full and says, "Drink this."

Then I said, "I gotta call the company and tell them we're safe."

He had to find his phone, ring the number, and call Operations. They were looking for us because we declared "May Day" before landing. Everybody then shuts up and listens to where you are. The landing ripped the antennas off, so I couldn't use the radio. Over the phone I told them we were safe, and they said, "Thanks. Well, come on home." The Polish guy puts us in the truck, and pours a little bit more booze out for us. Then down we went, roaring into Johnstown. At the

Johnstown post office, they had a ramp for the trucks. He drives right up to the dock. People are yelling, "No, no, you can't do that!" He yells back, "The Hell I can't! Where's the Postmaster?"

They get the postmaster. In the meantime, Gordo Lang and I get out. We're standing there on the platform, and this guy tells the postmaster, "These are the airmail pilots, and they just crashed on so and so hill. We've got the airmail here, and we've got to get it to Pittsburgh." So the postmaster comes over to shake my hand. He takes one look, then turns to the Polish guy and says, "No wonder they crashed! They're both stewed!"

The Polish guy says, "No, no. I gave them the booze. They needed it!"

The postmaster says, "Well, come on in."

He takes us in his office, reaches down, opens a drawer, pulls out another bottle of whiskey and some paper cups, and we all have another drink. "I always wanted to stop the Broadway Limited, now's my chance," he says. The Broadway Limited went right through Johnstown, like s— through a tin horn. He wanted us to ride down in the mail truck and get the conductor to stop the train. We did. After we explained everything, the postmaster says to the conductor, "You take real good care of these pilots!"

We get on the train, and a porter takes us to a dining car. Then he brought us a drink. By the time we got to Pittsburgh, we were so drunk we could hardly stand up. But we were alive, and that was the important thing. Another time I was on the Huntingdon, West Virginia route, and there was lot of weather. We got down as far as Spencer and started for Charleston, and we started to get some ice. I couldn't continue that way, so I turned around and I headed for a little town called Gallup, where the Kanawha intersects the Ohio. I cut the power off, because we were losing air speed. We were down to about ninety-miles an hour and I had almost full power off, and we were still getting a little bit of ice. So I broke out into the Ohio river, maybe 200-feet above the water.

There was a hill on both sides. I head up the river toward Parkersburg, and a couple of pieces of ice blew off. I knew that I was getting into a condition where I was losing my ice. By the time I got to Parkersburg, the airplane was almost free of ice. I flew right over the old airport. I should have landed right there, but instead I made for the new airport. I was about halfway there when ice started to form everywhere. I knew we couldn't maintain that. I turned. All along the banks of the Ohio, are these little ravines that go down towards the streams. So, I went down one of these ravines and came out by Marietta, made a left turn and started for the airport that

I passed up about ten minutes before, and we were gradually losing altitude, and I had full power on, and I asked Gordo, "Can you swim?"

He says, "No, I can't swim."

I says, "Neither can I, so start throwing mail out."

He tossed a bag out, but we still lost a couple of feet of altitude.

I says, "Gordo, just sit tight." I could see the airport up ahead of me. I had full RPM. We were gradually losing altitude. When we hit, the tail wheel hit a barbed wire fence. I taxied it into the hanger, and when I went to shut the engine off, it wouldn't shut off, it was so hot. There's no way we could get it in if it was hot, so we finally shut the fuel off. I was on F Run most the time Pittsburgh, Irwin, Greensburg, Blairsville, Latrobe, Johnstown, Portage, Holidaysburg, Huntingdon, Mount Union, Lewistown. That run was the roughest! That was Hell's Stretch to the air mail pilots. You would get all kinds of weather on that one.

Downdrafts? We used to put rubber pads on the ceiling to keep from getting our brains beat out! Terrible! At the old airport in Latrobe, Runway 9, on a hill, we had to take off eastbound, uphill, and there used to be a nightclub sitting there, at the crossroads. There were also tension wires, and it was always touch and go whether or not you were going to miss those wires. Sometimes we would opt to take off downwind. When we took off downwind, we got to the end of the runway with our flaps on because we weren't at the speed we wanted to be, and then we'd float down the valley with our flaps up.

There were all those ridges that could get pretty hairy, like Laurel Ridge, or the one between Dubois and Clearfield, or the one between Gettysburg and Chambersburg. Many times it was overcast and foggy. We picked up on what Lloyd Santmyer did. What we'd do is pull out, get a safe altitude, and then time ourselves. Then we'd let down into the valley where the station had to be. The only problem with that is sometimes there would be an unusually strong, sudden wind. And a couple times, I ran into a wind of such power, that it screwed all my timing up. Fortunately, I made it down, and there were trees on both sides of me. It wasn't skill righting me out; it was just pure luck as far as I'm concerned.

When I was a new hire, I came out to do some routes. There was a captain [*the editors agreed with Mr. Barraclough that the captain in question should remain anonymous*] who was supposed to be ready at 6 a.m. for a 7 a.m. departure. I got there at six, and got all the forms made out. It gets to be 6:30, then 6:45

The dispatcher says, "Hey, Kippy, why don't you just go out to the plane. The captain will be there."

I trudge out the gate and go out to our airplane. Lo and behold! The captain was there, hanging on to a strut like a gorilla, two feet on the bottom and one holding on to the top. He's scratching himself and making funny noises.

I thought, "What the Hell is going on?!"

He gets down and says, "Okay, let's get this s—house on the road!"

We go down to West Newton, then down to Mount Pleasant. And when we get to Connellsville (the captain didn't like the station master), the captain says, "His elevator doesn't always go to the top floor. He always gives us funny motions and stuff."

The station master is standing about forty feet to the right of the pick-up station when we came in, and the captain, instead of making the pick-up, goes for the station master. The guy starts running. The captain pulls up and comes back around and releases the mail. The station master's out there lying on the ground. The captain makes the pick-up. Then he comes back around again for the station master. The flight mechanic takes a big wrench, taps the captain fairly smartly on the back of the neck and says, "Why don't you let Kip fly?"

The captain says, "OK." Then he goes to sleep.

We get down to a place called Crafton, the next stop after Clarksburg. At Crafton, the pick-up station was on top of a ridge, where there was a cemetery. It was a small town, and we knew the messengers' cars, and where the post-office was, but the station wasn't set up. So I flew down to where the post-office was and Bernie, the flight mechanic, says, "Hey, there's the messenger's car right there. He a little bit late."

So we kinda flew around, and we waited until the messenger got up to the cemetery. Then he had to run up this hill, and he put up the station. In the meantime, the captain wakes up and says, "Where the Hell are you going? You're costing me time. Why are you circling? We don't circle in this operation!"

I says, "Well the station's not set up."

The captain spots the messenger, winds the RPM as high as it will go, and goes for the poor guy. The mechanic breaks out his wrench again and says, "Hey, that's it. Let Kip fly!"

"OK," he says, and falls asleep.

He slept all the way to Huntingdon. In Huntingdon we had a layover. The captain kept on sleeping. When he woke up, he got some black coffee and a sandwich. After that, he was the nicest man you'd ever want to meet, except when he had some booze in him. When I got back I had a talk with a guy who was like my Rabbi. I told him about the flight with the captain. He asked me not to tell the operations manager because the captain was already on probation for drinking. Anyway, they found out and the captain got suspended. When he came back he was a little cool to me.

One morning around two my brother Kenny calls me. He lived in Du Bois and was city controller, so he was had information on a lot of things.

He says, "Do you know a pilot named – ?"

I says, "Yeah?"

He says, "Well, he's in deep. He checked into the Logan Hotel, went into a bar, and there's this big Lithuanian and a Pole. Big guys. Anyway, your pilot gets into an argument with them and invites them outside. The guy says 'OK,' and goes out the door first. When your pilot gets out, the Pole decks him. Knocks him out." So they called the police and they took him to a doctor. He's got his All American uniform on. What should we do?"

And I said, "For cripes' sake Ken, don't let them arrest him. Get him out of there and let him get on the airplane in the morning and come back to Pittsburgh."

So he got the captain out of jail. The captain flew back to Pittsburgh. He gets out of the plane and nobody saw him for two weeks. He said his sister had died in Minnesota somewhere. He had to go.

When he came back he was sporting this great big black eye.

Vic Gasbarro
Connellsville, Pennsylvania
Flight Engineer

There was a messenger, someone who worked for the postal service and would come out every morning and every night with his mail bags. We would take off from the old county airport in Pittsburgh. Our first stop was Irwin and then Latrobe, and up to Johnstown and clear into Harrisburg, and into Washington D.C. and Philadelphia. The Stinson was modified with a big wedge inside. They had a nylon rope around the drum of this wedge which is about 100-feet long and almost 3/16 inches thick, and at the end of that rope there was a hook that slid down a pole on a small crack. When the man on the ground would put up his station which is two poles with another rope stretched across, attatched to the mail bag on the ground. We would come through there, snag up the rope off of these two poles, drop our mail before we got to that, and then pick up the bag. Inside the airplane, we would hit a switch, and it would guide the mail bag into the airplane. We made a run twice a day. We'd leave at 7:45 and get into Latrobe close to 8:00am. In the evenings we'd get in there around 6:30/6:45. All the airplanes had to be in the airport at 7:00pm.

Vic Gasbarro proudly poses in from of an AAA Stinson. (*Courtesy of Vic Gasbarro*).

AM 49ers ✈ US Air Mail ✈ 1943

The remains of the Stinson in which Vic Gasbarro crashed.

LEFT: Sketch of Vic Gasbarro.
(AAA Newsletter, The Pick-Up, November/December, 1942).

I had a couple of unfortunate situations, one in October of 1943, the 25th. Tommy Bryan and I had just made the pick-up at Chambersburg. Tommy wanted to make the Gettysburg pick-up before we stopped for the day. His instruments weren't working right. A low ceiling and strong winds moved in very fast. Tommy wrote down the time and climbed up. He watched the time until he thought we would clear Piney Mountain. He must have made a mistake, because we went in right on the peak. He tried to pull up at the last minute, but we went through that brush like a lawnmower. We wandered through the woods, until we found a hunter's cabin. I walked those mountains trying to get help. They had the National Guard and everybody else out looking for us. It was raining and cold, and they didn't find us until the morning of the 26th. My forehead was cut, and Tommy broke his foot. Tommy died about a year later in another crash.

I had another incident with pilot Millard Lossing. There was a snowstorm and Millard was using the Juniata River to find the next station. They put some high-tension wires we didn't know about between the hills. We flew right through them and damaged the windshield. The CAA had investigations when there were accidents. We went before the board to explain what happened. After my second one, this inspector said to me, "Vic, you're like a rubber ball. You keep bouncin' back!"

I said, "Well, Tom, I think I'm gonna have to look for other ways and means of making a living!" Anyway, my mother was on my back. She almost had a heart attack from the first wreck I had, and I was the only son she had. I was only twenty-seven years old. She talked me into becoming what they call a designated maintenance inspector. I took that job for awhile, until I got into the insurance business.

Lloyd Santmyer
Greensburg/Ligonier, Pennsylvania
Pilot

Flying the pick-up was the way every one of us pilots wanted to fly full tilt! We had regulations about flying the routes. They called for a 500-foot ceiling with a one-mile visibility. Nobody followed that. You couldn't. Not with what we had to fly over. You'd have nice weather, then get to the mountains, and suddenly it would change. If we followed those regulations the company wouldn't have lasted a year. Sometimes it would be so foggy you couldn't see where the pick-up posts were. Sometimes the ground clerks would put out smudge pots, or else we'd make a two passes. The first one blew away the ground fog so you could see the tops of the pick-up station.

The overcast and fog on those ridges we had to fly

was something. I worked out a system that a lot of the guys used later. I'd find a landmark I knew then climb to an altitude I already worked out, then I'd hold the plane there and keep time on my watch. Then I'd let down through the overcast into the valley. Of course, I practiced all this in good weather! So did the other guys for their ridges and valleys. I'm not too sure how legal all that was, but we kept the schedule!

We had names for the routes. The route from Pittsburgh to Huntington wasn't too bad, because it went right down the Ohio River. We called that "King's Row." Route 49A we called "Slave's Alley," and that one went down into the West Virginia mountains, down around Elkins. There were lots of hills around there, and the weather could change on you in five minutes. Another thing about Slave's Alley was that the hills weren't high enough to do the timing routine, and the pick-up points were closer together down there. So, I'd get between Spencer and Gransville and home in on the hum of the power lines. It was a 60-cycle hum. If you were in a car and your radio was on, you'd get interference. I figure I was pretty close to the top of those lines, maybe fifteen or twenty feet! Of course, I still needed my watch to time the distance between stations. I couldn't see them.

We'd get audiences down below. Sometimes there would be traffic jams at the Jacktown area near Irwin. People used to like to come and watch us pick up the

View of a pick-up point from the flight engineer's seat.
(Courtesy of Clyde Hauger, Jr.)

mail. Sometimes we'd get stuff besides mail in the bags we picked up, things like soda pop and fresh pies. Ray Elder flew the pick-up. He was with Charlie Carroll and Carl Strickler and me at J.D. Hill back in the late 1920s. One day, Raymond spotted a house fire out in Ohio [Gallipolis]. He radioed back to Pittsburgh for them to call back to Ohio for help. Another time he guided an Army pilot to a safe landing at the Allegheny County Airport.

Clyde Hauger, Jr.
Donegal, Pennsylvania
Flight Engineer

It looked organized, but it was really a kind of orderly disorder. There was a lot of excitement to the job. We never knew what was going to happen next. We were all kind of close, like family. The pilots knew their routes like the backs of their hands. We had a raft of regulations like maintaining a certain ceiling and not flying unless there was a one-mile visibility. Now, we had to keep a schedule that was within three minutes of the stop. If we didn't we'd have to file reports when we got back. Nobody liked filing reports. Besides, if we had kept to all of the regulations the mail never would have gotten through.

There were times when those mail bags would have sandwiches and other great food in them. Relatives, friends, or just regular people down below would put that stuff in there.

Orchids To Elder . . .

Sketch of Raymond "Pappy"/"Flying Fire Chief" Elder from AAA's newsletter *The Pick-up*, February and May, 1942, in articles complimenting his "extra-curricular" duties.

(Courtesy of Clyde Hauger, Jr.)

Air Pick-up

A SPECIAL PICTORIAL

"THE AIRWAY TO EVERYWHERE"

Dr. Lytle Adams poses with a New Standard biplane of Clifford Ball Airlines, Inc., a forerunner of Pennsylvania Airlines, Pennsylvania-Central Airlines, and Capital Airlines. In the late 1920s, Ball became briefly interested in the Adams pick-up system. Adams and Ball performed pick-ups at Youngstown, Ohio, in August and September, 1929. Trow Sebree is the pilot.
(Courtesy of Ed Blend).

THE CITY OF YOUNGSTOWN
TOGETHER WITH THE
CHAMBER OF COMMERCE
JOINS DR. LYTLE S. ADAMS AND
CLIFFORD BALL

In extending to you a cordial invitation to visit Youngstown's Municipal Airport and attend the demonstrations of the Adams Air Mail Pick-Up, which will receive its first official application to an Air Mail route, Friday, August 30, 1929. There will be demonstrations daily thereafter to and including September 2, giving visitors to the National Air Races and Aeronautical Exposition at Cleveland the opportunity of seeing this new and important development in this industry.

Letterhead from Adams Air Express, Inc. LEFT: Advertisement of the Youngstown pick-up. ABOVE: The Clifford Ball Airlines New Standard picks up the mail at Youngstown.
(Courtesy of Ed Blend).

BRANIFF
Airways Inc.

USE
U.S. AIR MAIL
ADAMS PICK-UP & DELIVERY
SERVICE

Dr. Lytle S. Adams, Inventor, and Eddie Gerber, Flyer of remarkable Air Mail Service of Braniff Airways, at World's Fair.

Dr. Lytle Adams poses with Braniff pilot Eddie Gerber during pick-ups at the Chicago World's Fair in 1934. Braniff would lose interest in the Adams' system after the fair closed. Adams, however, met Richard Archbold at the fair, a man who would give Adams the idea for the "goal post" pick-up system that would replace his cumbersome and expensive chute. BELOW: Postcard of the Adams/Braniff pick-up at the 1934 Chicago World's Fair. The site is the World's Fair Lagoon. *(Courtesy of Ed Blend).*

USE
U.S. AIR MAIL
ADAMS PICKUP & DELIVERY
DAILY
2.4.6. PM

Photo of Braniff Airways Plane Taking Pouch on Cable After Leaving One at Adams System Device.

LEFT: Advertising poster for the Adams/Braniff pick-up, Chicago World's Fair, 1934. *(Courtesy of Ed Blend).*

BELOW: First cover for the Adams/Braniff pick-up, Chicago World's Fair, 1934. *(Courtesy of Ed Blend).*

ABOVE RIGHT: Fairchild monoplane performs an experimental pick-up from a modified chute. Date unknown, location unknown. Possibly Irwin, Pennsylvania. *(Courtesy of the Westmoreland County Airport Authority).*

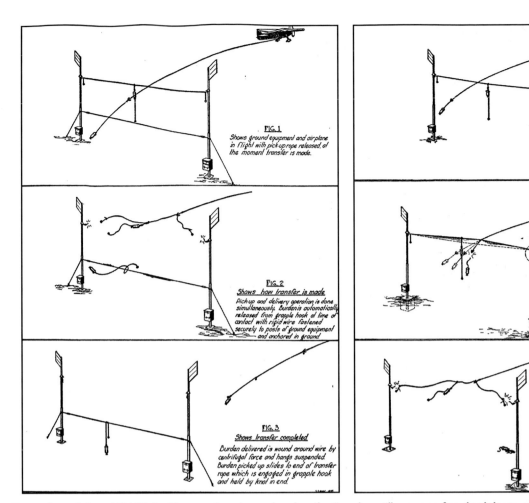

FIG. 1
Shows ground equipment and airplane in flight with pick-up rope released, at the moment transfer is made.

FIG. 2
Shows how transfer is made.
Pick-up and delivery operation is done simultaneously. Burden is automatically released from grapple hook at time of contact with rigid wire fastened securely to posts of ground equipment and anchored in ground.

FIG. 3
Shows transfer completed.
Burden delivered is wound around wire by centrifugal force and hangs suspended. Burden picked up slides to end of transfer rope which is engaged in grapple hook and held by knot in end.

FIG. 1
Shows ground equipment and airplane in flight with pick-up rope released at the moment transfer is to be made.

FIG. 2
Shows how transfer is made.
Burden is automatically released when pick-up line engages the rope on transfer equipment.
In circle is enlarged view showing how transfer rope is fastened to ground equipment by means of break cords. The hoist rope is shown inside the pipe.

FIG. 3
Shows transfer completed.
Pick-up and delivery operation is done simultaneously in approximately one-tenth of a second. The transfer rope slides thru grapple hook and is engaged by knot in end, while burden slides to the end of transfer rope.

Pages from Adams' Tri-State Airways. brochure showing the "goal-post" process for air pick-up. *(Courtesy of Ed Blend).*

LEFT/RIGHT: Pilot Norman Rintoul and Flight Mechanic Vic Yesulaites who made the first officially-scheduled AAA pick-up at Latrobe, May 12, 1939. Their Stinson Reliant NC21107 delivered commemorative covers from Pittsburgh and picked-up commemorative mail bound for Morgantown, West Virginia. Pick-up of actual mail was carried out by Pilot Jimmy Piersoll. Yesulaites was responsible for designing more efficient and safer modifications to the Adams system. Rintoul and Yesulaites made the last AAA pick-up at Jamestown, New York in 1949. *(AAA Brochure, 1930-1940).*

TOP: Norman Rintoul stands in the front row, third from left, with the original All American Aviation airmail pick-up team. In the front row, from the left, as identified by Lloyd Santmyer: Jimmy Piersol, Tommy Kinchelhoe, Rintoul, Holger Horiis, Peg Kiley, James Ray, ——, ——. Back row, left to right: Raymond "Pappy" Elder, Hal Basley, B. Moore, ——, ——, Vic Yesulaites, ——, Bill Burkhardt.

RIGHT: Vic Yesulaites with the mail.

BOTTOM: AAA Stinson Reliants lined up at Allegheny County Airport.

ABOVE: An AAA Stinson Reliant over Latrobe, headed for Chestnut Ridge and "Hell's Stretch." *(AAA 1939-1940 Brochure).*

The first AAA pick-up at Latrobe, May 12, 1939. The caption to this Pittsburgh Sun-Telegraph photo reads : "A plane dropping a bag of mail, seen in midair, and at the same time picking up another bag suspended between two 34-foot poles. The scene is at Latrobe Airport, where the first regular pick-up air service was inaugurated yesterday. Among hundreds present was Richard C. DuPont, president of All American Aviation, Inc., which has the pick-up contract. *(Courtesy of Ed Blend).*

Commemorative postmarks published when other Pennsylvania towns were added to the AAA route system in the experimental year **1939-1940.** *(Courtesy of Ed Blend).*

LEFT: The headline and caption on this Pittsburgh Press photo of May 12, 1939 reads: "Postal Service Passes Another Milestone." "Pilot James E. Piersol and Postmaster Steve Bodkin inaugurate world's first airmail pick-up service." Piersol made the the pick-up of regular mail at Latrobe, May 12, 1939. *(Courtesy of Ed Blend).*

TOP: Ed Blend, of Irwin, Pennsylvania, poses with an AAA mail canister he restored. *(Courtesy of Ed Blend).*

BOTTOM: Outside the North Hanger at Latrobe, the early 1940s. Before and during a pick-up.
(Courtesy of the Westmoreland County Airport Authority).

May 12, 1939, Latrobe, Pennsylvania. Charlie Carroll readies the mail bag for All American Aviation's first officially-scheduled airmail pick-up as Mrs. Carroll and Richard DuPont, president of AAA, look on. *(Courtesy of the Latrobe Historical Society).*

Norm Rintoul lines-up AAA Stinson NC21107 for the first pick-up at Latrobe. *(Courtesy of the Latrobe Historical Society).*

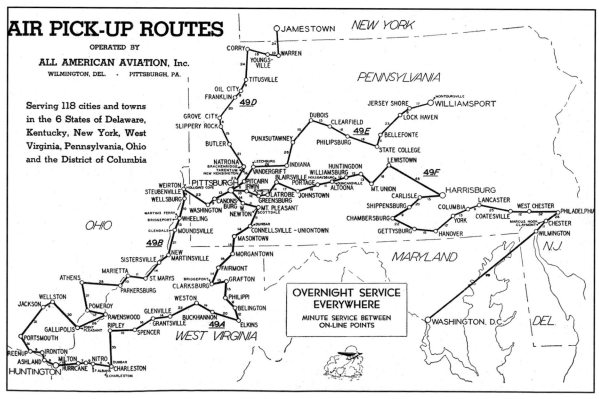

AIR PICK-UP ROUTES

OPERATED BY

ALL AMERICAN AVIATION, Inc.

WILMINGTON, DEL. · PITTSBURGH, PA.

Serving 118 cities and towns
in the 6 States of Delaware,
Kentucky, New York, West
Virginia, Pennsylvania, Ohio
and the District of Columbia

OVERNIGHT SERVICE
EVERYWHERE

MINUTE SERVICE BETWEEN
ON-LINE POINTS

ABOVE: Postage stamp designed by Clyde Hauger to honor Richard DuPont, who was killed testing gliders for the U.S. military.

LEFT: An AAA cartoon concerning Pilot Dave Patterson, an avid hunter.

BELOW: A New Yorker Magazine cartoon. Often called "The Treetop Line," AAA pick-up planes sometimes belonged to the "Clothesline Line."
(All courtesy of Clyde Hauger).

As indicated above, the season is at hand and Dave Patterson has packed his rod for his annual bear-hunting sojourn to the deep woods. With rationing and rugs the way they are—we wish him luck!

Christmas
1942...

Over a greatly improved and expanded Air Pick-up System, now serving 115 communities, in 6 states,

ALL AMERICAN AVIATION, INC.

sends sincere wishes for a

Merry Christmas
and a
Happy New Year

Preview
OF THE FUTURE . . .

Of immediate importance to our present war effort and with a bright post-war future in the transportation of mail, freight and passengers, is the Glider Pick-up System, developed during 1942 by All American Aviation in cooperation with the Army Air Forces.

An adaptation of the Air Mail Pick-up System it permits loaded gliders to be picked up, from the ground, and towed by an airplane in full flight.

Clyde Hauger

All American Aviation greeting cards showing the development of the company's services over the years. The Stinsons were supplemented and replaced by Twin Beechcraft and Douglas DC-3s. The company also experimented with human pick-up, designed to rescue Army Air Force pilots downed in enemy territory, and glider pick-ups. *(Courtesy of Clyde Hauger).*

IRWIN CELEBRATES
125th
ANNIVERSARY

50th ANNIVERSARY
Adams Non-Stop Air Mail Pick-Up
First Regular Pick-Up Irwin, PA
Home of the Inventor

Dr. Lytle S. Adams
RD 5
Irwin, Pa

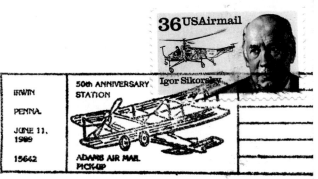

36 USAirmail

Igor Sikorsky

IRWIN
PENNA.

JUNE 11, 1989

15642

50th ANNIVERSARY
STATION

ADAMS AIR MAIL
PICK-UP

Judy Blend
802 8th Ave.
Irwin, Pa.
15642

50th
ANNIVERSARY

1939 - USAIR - 1989

Samuel P. Langley
Aviation Pioneer

45

USAirmail

LATROBE,
MAY
12
1989
USPO

Celebrating the
50th Anniversary Inauguration
of Air-Mail Pickup Service.
The A.M. 49'ERs

ABOVE: 50th Anniversary commemoratives of air-mail pick-ups. *(Courtesy of Clyde Hauger).*

LEFT: This Stinson Reliant made a forced landing in a Blairsville cow pasture sometime in 1943.
(Courtesy of Ronald Jasper).

To Ken
From
Bernie Cain
1949

The Kids Loved the AAA Pilots

Slippery Rock
May 5, 194?

Dear Pilot,
I am the little girl who worte you your letter on Saturday.
We will send our pictures on the our evening pick-up

yours truly
Second Grade
Here is a 1¢ stamp.

Please circle the pick-up several times, if you see us watching from below.
Can you pick up some "dummy" bags so we will be sure, to see, just how you do it?
Please answer our letter by Wednesday.
We are, very anxious to take the trip and hope it is a nice day.
Your friends,
Seecond Grade

Second Grade
Slippery Rock, Pa.
April 3, 194?

Dear Clyde Hauger,
We have been studying about mail for a long time. We have found it very interesting. We want to, go out, to the mass, pick up on Wednesday, if it is a nice day.
May, we ask you some questions?
1. Where do you live?
2. Do you have children?
3. How many, men are on your plane?
4. How long have you been a pilot?
5. How many trips a day do you make?
6. How many hours a day do you work?
7. How far do you travel?
8. How many sacks will your plane hold?

ABOVE: Clyde Hauger and Ray Garcia (left) were chosen to staff the operations department of AAA's Brazilian subsidiary. For several months, they trained Brazilian pilots in Rio de Janiero to perform the pick-up, while developing pick-up routes in Brazil. *(Courtesy of Clyde Hauger).*

BELOW: Clyde Hauger comes in out of the clouds in his Stinson and lines up for a pick-up at Latrobe. *(Courtesy of Clyde Hauger).*

The Naugle Mercury:
The Model T of the Sky

The Naugle Mercury was a step forward in light commercial aircraft design. Powered only with a modest 4 cylinder, 75-horse-power, Lycoming engine, the Mercury achieved speeds over 140 miles per hour. Similarly powered aircraft of the day reached only 100 miles per hour before the Mercury's flight. The Naugle Mercury attained the greater speeds through light construction and improved aerodynamics. Designed to be fast, light-weight, strong, easy-to- handle, safe (it was reputed to be spin-proof) and inexpensive, the Mercury was "everyman's" aircraft. It was called the "Model T of the Sky" after Henry Ford's reliable and inexpensive automobile. Like the Model T, there were hopes of the Mercury one day supplanting the automobile as a dominant mode of private travel.

Such innovations in a light aircraft should be well-known, but they are not. Outside of a few of the older local pilots and people in the aviation industry, not much is known about the Naugle Mercury. Like many unique designs in aeronautics, the Naugle Mercury seems to have faded away with time and technology.

The Mercury's developers were two brothers from Ligonier, Richard C. and Harry Naugle, both highly skilled aeronautical engineers. Richard graduated from the Massachusetts Institute of Technology and Harry attended Culver Military Academy, Leigh University and Parks Air College. Richard was associated with numerous engineering companies (Piper, Fairchild, Waterman, McDonnell and Laister-Kaufman) before branching off with his brother. The brothers started their Latrobe-based Naugle Aircraft Corporation with backing from Al Williams and Richard King Mellon, setting up shop in a an abandoned factory once owned by the Vanadium-Alloys Steel Company building. Richard Naugle became president of the corporation, Glenn Cook, secretary-treasurer, and Harry Naugle, vice-president. The board of directors consisted of Richard Naugle, Cook and Harry Naugle. Later, James H. Rogers, president of Greensburg's First National Bank, and Ben Kerr, president of the Railway and Industrial Engineering Company of Greensburg, came onto the board.

Having been in the design stages for years, the idea for the Naugle Mercury took shape in December 1939. That year Richard Naugle applied for a patent on the wing construction for the Mercury aircraft. The model submitted to the patent office employed a novel wing spar and rib construction that improved wing strength and provided a method of fabrication and assembly that was practical and economical. But it was the performance in relation to the small engine of the Mercury that made it stand out.

During the Mercury's construction, there was much speculation about its flight characteristics. World War II had just begun in Europe and the military took an interest in what the Naugle brothers were doing. The brothers hoped to land a military contract for the Naugle Mercury as a trainer. In fact, Harry Naugle was already in the Army and stationed at Langley Field, Virginia at the time when the Mercury was ready to fly. It is possible he promoted the benefits of the airplane to the military.

A week of test flights took place at the Latrobe Airport sometime in 1940. Latrobe's Lou Strickler put the Mercury through its paces. Strickler achieved a speed of 142 miles per hour. The previous record for a plane powered with a 75-horse power engine was only 118 miles per hour. After a successful series of test flights, the Naugles went ahead with plans to produce more airplanes.

Supplies of aluminum and other materials needed to begin construction were not assured; national defense came first. Even though the United States was not yet at war, the possibility of being dragged into another European conflict loomed larger every day. Supplies of aluminum were eventually approved and construction began on a second Mercury. During the original flight tests the brothers discovered that the design did not have to be as strong and heavy as previously thought. Minor improvements were made to the second Mercury with an expectation of speeds exceeding160 miles per hour.

The Naugles made final refinements of their aircraft at the Latrobe Airport, and were working on the plane's major flaw—a disturbing flutter of the tail—when World War II intervened.

Soon after the test flights, the Japanese bombed Pearl Harbor. Richard Naugle went on to serve at Wright Field with the Air Service Command. Richard, along with his financial backers Richard Mellon and Al Williams (who had been called up and was a major in the Army), had plans to continue with post-war production of the Mercury, but the war changed these plans, like it did to many other things.

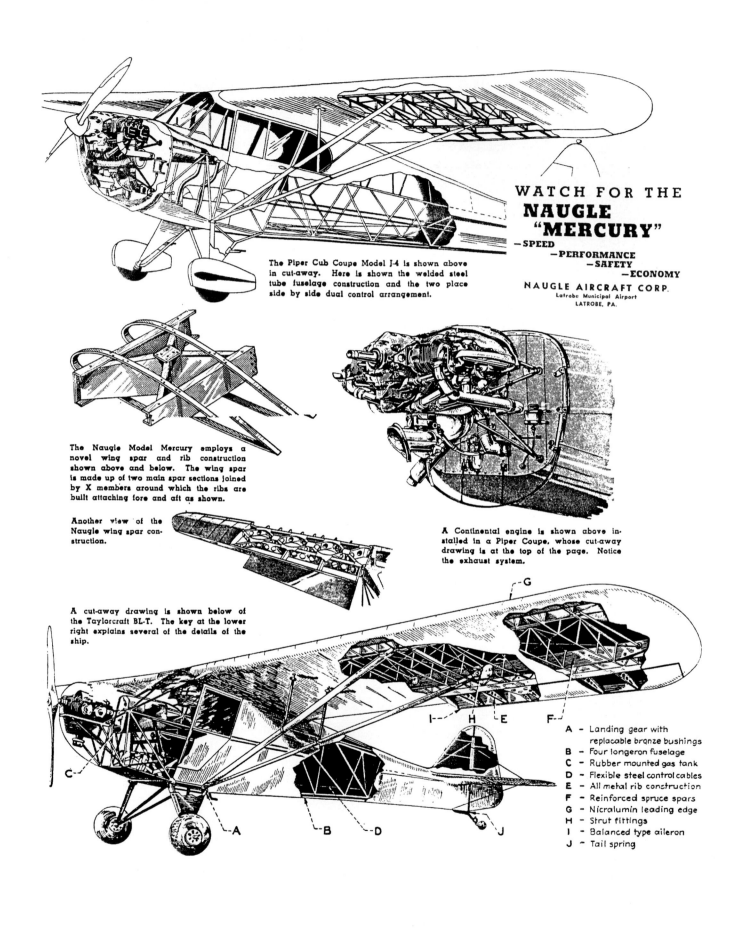

The Piper Cub Coupe Model J-4 is shown above in cut-away. Here is shown the welded steel tube fuselage construction and the two place side by side dual control arrangement.

The Naugle Model Mercury employs a novel wing spar and rib construction shown above and below. The wing spar is made up of two main spar sections joined by X members around which the ribs are built attaching fore and aft as shown.

Another view of the Naugle wing spar construction.

A Continental engine is shown above installed in a Piper Coupe, whose cut-away drawing is at the top of the page. Notice the exhaust system.

A cut-away drawing is shown below of the Taylorcraft BL-T. The key at the lower right explains several of the details of the ship.

A – Landing gear with replacable bronze bushings
B – Four longeron fuselage
C – Rubber mounted gas tank
D – Flexible steel control cables
E – All metal rib construction
F – Reinforced spruce spars
G – Nicralumin leading edge
H – Strut fittings
I – Balanced type aileron
J – Tail spring

OX5 Club of America

An OX5 engine from the 1917 Curtiss catalogue.
(Courtesy of Ken Scholter).

A way of life has made us brothers.
Let none now tread the road alone.
Let's seek out and share with others
All the friends we once have known.

Care not for temples not for creed
One thing alone holds us firm and fast,
The mem'ries the OX gave us,
A precious heritage from a golden past.

The OX5 Club of America, with the OX5 Club of Pennsylvania as the parent organization, was founded on the afternoon of Saturday, August 27, 1955, at the Latrobe Airport. In June 1955, Charlie Carroll presented to the Aero Club of Pittsburgh his idea for a reunion of Pennsylvania aviators who flew behind the OX5 engine between the years 1918 and the outbreak of World War II. The idea for the formation of the OX5 Club arose earlier at the Latrobe Airport in a conversation between Charlie and Lloyd Santmyer. Lloyd Santmyer is the one who actually came up with the name "OX5 Club." Earl Metzler was at the Latrobe Airport that day and confirmed the substance of the conversation when he was interviewed.

For years afterward, John "Juny" Trunk, who was president of the organization in the 1960s, pointed out that Lloyd never got proper credit for his role in the formation of the club. Lloyd initially recruited many members from the Aero Club of Pittsburgh, and continued recruiting many new members for years after the OX5 Club's founding.

With some strong motivation from "Juny," he, Lloyd Santmyer and George Markley traveled to the old Elder farm in Juny's pick-up truck and retrieved the OX5 engine from Raymond Elder's "Canuck" that Raymond cracked up years before and Raymond's dad chopped up for firewood. Juny cleaned up the engine and got Johnny Evans to have a display case made for it by the fellows at the Duquesne Beer Shop. The engine went on display at the Latrobe Airport, where it remained for many years. Then Gene Lakin sent the engine down to Pittsburgh to be cleaned. Then it was put on display at the Pittsburgh International Airport where it remains. Just recently, the OX5 Club agreed to return it to the Arnold Palmer Regional Airport for ten-year renewable periods. Few disagree that Latrobe is the right place for it.

Lloyd Santmyer describes the day when Charlie Carroll and he developed the idea of a club that would honor the "early-bird" aviators:

Charlie and I had the idea of starting that OX5 Club. We said we were gonna put our original office over there at the airport and hang a propeller above the door and have a place for the old-time flyers to congregate, a place for them to come and visit. So I said, 'We should call it the OX5 Club.' Anybody who flew an OX5 here would be qualified to be a member, because it was the Curtiss OX5 that flew all these commercial airplanes, all these biplanes, and the old-fashioned planes. So I said, 'Yeah! Let's call it the OX5 Club!'

So we talked to guys from the Aero-Club, and to Clyde Hauger, Ray Elder, and Dave Patterson, and some of those fellas, and we thought we could have an air meet and get a bunch of guys in. They all said, 'Yeah! Why don't we do it?!'

So Charlie got on the phone and called Cliff Ball. Right away, Cliff was all for it, because he was the one who started the first airmail here.

There was a well-known fella that used to fly across here on those early mail flights and passenger flights out of Pittsburgh named Sam Bigony. Cliff called him. He was all for it. And we got Russ Brinkley, who was in Harrisburg at the time. He became first president of the thing. More than a hundred came to that first meeting. We didn't expect that many, but they came.

And they did come, more than 250 pilots, aviation pioneers, wives, family and friends. The event was officially called "The First Annual Pennsylvania Aviation Reunion." They represented thousands of years of flying experience. The White House and Pennsylvania Governor, George M. Leader, sent best wishes. Later in the festivities, 100 of them became charter members of the OX5 Club. The organizing committee was comprised of Charlie Carroll, Sam Bigony, Clifford Ball, Blanche Noyes, Ken Scholter, John Kratzer, Henry Noll, Oscar Hostetter, Ralph McClarren, Earl Southee, Don Rose, John MacFarlane, William T. Piper, Joe Field, Roy Clark, John Bartow, Ed Chadderton, and Wesley Price, with Russ Brinkley as chairman.

Hundreds of others witnessed an air show at the Latrobe Airport, a show that included fly-bys of World War II Corsair fighter planes, Sabre Jets, Air National Guard fighter planes, civilian demonstrations of commercial, experimental and unusual aircraft, helicopter stunt flying, and a parachute jump by the perennial Otto Hoover, of New Alexandria, Pennsylvania, one the nation's oldest jumpers. Hoover had participated in air shows for thirty-three years, and this was his 3,019th jump. Dr. Lynn Bollinger, of the Massachusetts Institute of Technology flew the Helio Courier; Charlie Carroll took up his OX5 Challenger; Guy Miller demonstrated the Bell helicopter; Earl Metzler gave a demonstration of his Wings With Springs. Father Edmund Cuneo, O.S.B., of Saint Vincent College, blessed the ceremonies.

Charlie Carroll hosted the event, and the group held a twelve-hour formal program and dinner at the nearby Mission Inn. Dozens of planes flew singly and in formation over the inn's outdoor patio. Then the organizing committee honored several of the participants with awards.

They named William T. Piper, who fathered the Piper Aircraft Corporation, "Mr. Pennsylvania Aviation of All Time," and John "Reds" MacFarlane "Mr. Pennsylvania Aviation of 1955." Piper, known in aviation circles as "The Henry Ford of Aviation," also received the Edward Chadderton Award, presented to him by Chadderton himself, owner of the Sharon Airport in Pennsylvania. In addition, MacFarlane received the Pennsylvania Aviation Trades Association Award, presented to him by Oscar Hostetter, of York, Pennsylvania, president of the Association.

Russ Brinkley presented awards of his own invention. The "Oldest Active Pilot Award" went to Harry M. Jones, of Washington, D.C., flying for forty-three years, and George Scragg, flying for forty-six years. Russ gave the "Pilot Who Flew the Greatest Distance to Attend the Reunion Award" to Harrison Doyle, of Washington, D.C. Charlie Carroll took honors for owning a 1927 Challenger aircraft, "Miss Tydol," the oldest OX5 aircraft still parked at Latrobe Airport.

The organizing committee also honored Doctor and Mrs. D. E. Strickler, parents of Lou Strickler; Brigadier General Laurin Faurot, commander of the Air National Guard, and Charles "Red" Gahagan, a regular at the Latrobe Airport who was engaged in experimental work with helicopters there. Colonel John Morris from the Civil Aeronautics Administration outlined the purposes of the OX5 Club, which was to be formalized at a later date. The program ended with an Aviation Ball at the Mission Inn. Jimmy Brunelli and his orchestra provided the music.

A highlight of the festivities was the selection of a "Miss Sky Queen" chosen from eleven models from the Earl Wheeler Charm School. The judges for the contest were selected "on the spot" by Russ Brinkley from among the veteran airmen. Norma Small won the contest, and was presented with a bouquet of roses by Semon H. Stupakoff, president of the Greater Latrobe Chamber of Commerce.

The official mascot for the OX5 induction ceremony was "Billy," a white goat owned by John Rich, Jr. The official song for the event was "Wait Till You Get Them Up in the Air, Boys," by Albert von Tilzer and Lew Brown.

Little had changed since the old days. Russ Brinkley reported that attendance would have been much greater had it not been for the fog over Chestnut Ridge that turned several airmen away.

In 1959, Charlie Carroll retired and left the airport he had managed for thirty-five years. On the last day of the year, a Saturday night, the old-timers honored him with a dinner at the Jacktown Hotel in Irwin, Pennsylvania. One-hundred-and-fifty people showed up.

Those who remained with him in life were all there: Al Litzenberger, Joe Fields, Joe Reedy, Lloyd Santmyer, Dave Patterson, Herb Morrison, "Red" Gahagan, D. Barr Peat, Earl Metzler, Johnnie Evans, Kenny Scholter, Sam Bigony, Cliff Ball, and "Reds" MacFarlane.

Three groups planned his tribute: the WESPEN Group of the OX5 Club; the Westmoreland Aviation Association, which included B. Patrick Costello and Arnold Palmer; the Aero Club of Pittsburgh. Sam Bigony outlined Charlie's contributions to the OX5 Club of America; "Reds" MacFarlane talked about "Charlie, The Fixed-Base Operator;" Colonel John P. Morris reviewed Charlie's role in the United States' Military Training Program; Ralph Sloan spoke of Charlie's place in local aviation activities.

Charlie posed for a picture with Lloyd Santmyer, Al Litzenberger, Frank Fox, and "Curley" Korb.

They ended the ceremony with "Auld Lang Syne."

In 1959, Charlie moved to 708 Pearl Street, Sarasota, Florida with his wife, Grace, and his fourteen-year-old son, Don. In 1962, the OX5 Club of America honored Charlie with its Distinguished Service Award. At the awards ceremony, organization president E. A. "Pete" Goff said:

It is with the greatest possible pleasure that I call Charlie Carroll up here to receive an exceptional award.

Charlie was the instigator of the original meeting that resulted in the formation of the OX5 Club. As one of the original board members, he served for five years, during which time he expended limitless time and energy in the interest of the organization.

Charlie is still recruiting members and supplying assistance and counsel in untiring efforts to assure our success. It is doubtful that any other member has so taken the welfare of the Club to heart or contributed more to its success. There are four members of the Carroll family who are OX5ers: Mrs. Grace Carroll, Charlie, and two sons.

Charlie, you're a grand guy and I can't think of anything more appropriate than presenting you with this plaque in recognition of your efforts. The plaque reads: 'In grateful recognition of his wise leadership, devoted service, and unselfish efforts on behalf of our organization.'

Best of luck to you, old timer. I'll see you at then next reunion.

In 1965, the OX5 Club held its tenth anniversary in Latrobe. Charlie Carroll was the guest of honor.

In 1970, a few years before Charlie's death, they formed the OX5 Aviation Pioneers Hall of Fame. Inexplicably, Charlie was not elected to it.

On May 12, 1989, Westmoreland County Airport held a reunion of OX5'ers and All American Aviation 49'ers. It was the fiftieth anniversary of the airmail pick-up at old Latrobe Airport. After the ceremony, they placed a plaque in the terminal building honoring the first 100 charter members of the OX5 Club. The plaque states that the OX5 Club was started by Charles Carroll and Sam Bigony. Before time erases all memory of the original events, let this history show that the idea for the OX5 Club came from Charlie Carroll and Lloyd Santmyer.

Charles "Red" Gahagan sits on the wing of Charlie Carroll's OX5 Challenger *Miss Tydol* around the time of the founding of the OX5 Club. Charlie steadies the club mascot "Billy." Charlie's son, Donald, is in the cockpit. Charlie's plane took the prize for "oldest aircraft" at the Latrobe Airport. At the time of his retirement, Charlie sold the plane to Frank Fox. (*Courtesy of Frank Fox*).

PROGRAM

WELCOME TO LATROBE .... Charles B. Carroll, Host

Introducing:

MASTER OF CEREMONIES .... Russ Brinkley, WHP-TV

CROWNING OF PENNSYLVANIA SKY QUEEN OF 1955
Direction of Mr. Earl Wheeler

AVIATION AND THE PRESS .... W. Lowrie Kay, Editor, Latrobe Bulletin

PENNSYLVANIA AVIATION .... John W. MacFarlane

AWARD: MR. PENNSYLVANIA AVIATION OF ALL TIME
Direction of Mr. Oscar Hostetter

AWARD: MR. PENNSYLVANIA OF 1955
Allegheny Airlines Flight To National Air Races

INTRODUCTIONS .... Responses by honored guests

AWARDS: To oldest pilot present. Owner of oldest airplane on field. Pilot
who came the greatest distance to attend the reunion.

----------★----------

OFFICIAL ORGANIZATION

Mother Chapter of the National OX5 Club. Membership open to every
pilot who ever flew behind the famous Curtiss engine of World War One
vintage.

INITIATION TEAM UNDER DIRECTION OF SAM BIGONY

----------★----------

INTERLUDE

For reunion with old friends and meeting newcomers to aviation.

----------★----------

FLYING - DEMONSTRATIONS - STATIC

Dr. Lynn Bollinger, M.I.T., flying the Helio Courier
C. B. Carroll and his 1927 OX5 Challenger.
Guy Miller of Pittsburgh, flying the Bell Helicopter
Earl G. Metzler, flying Wings with Springs.
Ball Airlines Firth OX5 WACO 9.

----------★----------

GRAND FINALE

9:30 P.M.

AVIATION BALL:—MISSION INN BALLROOM

Music by

JIMMY BRUNELLI and His Orchestra

PROGRAM

12:00 Noon:—Fly-in and registration.

1:00 P.M.:—Aviation Banquet. Mission Inn.

STAR SPANGLED BANNER

SILENT TRIBUTE TO DEPARTED AIRMEN

INVOCATION:—Rev. Edmund Cuneo, O.S.B.

OFFICIAL SONG

WAIT TILL YOU GET THEM UP IN THE AIR BOYS
by Albert Von Tilzer & Lew Brown

REUNION COMMITTEE

Clifford I. Ball	John W. Macfarlane
Blanche W. Noyes	William T. Piper, Sr.
Kenneth Scholter	Samuel Bigony
John B. Kratzer	Joe Field
Henry Noll	Roy W. Clark
Oscar Hostetter	John Bartow
Ralph McClarren	Ed Chadderton
Earl Southee	C. B. Carroll
Don Rose	Wesley Price

Russ Brinkley, Chairman

Semon H. Stupakoff, President, Greater Latrobe Chamber of Commerce.

Press Host: W. Lowrie Kay, Editor, Latrobe Bulletin

Radio & Television: Joe Harper, WHP-TV

Public Relations: William Laughlin and John Hasson.

Secretary: Grace Carroll

First Officers and the First One Hundred

President, Russell Brinkley
1st Vice President, John P. Morris
2nd Vice President, Blanche Noyes

3rd Vice President, Asa Roundtree
Secretary, Clifford Ball
Treasurer, Charles B. Carroll

Albright, Harry S.	Donnelly, Hugh J.	Myers, Gilbert K.
Alexander, Menges	Doughty, Stewart E.	Neely, Honorable Wm. H.
Allen, George W.	Doyle, Harrison	Noyes, Blanche
Andress, Vincent T.	Elder, Raymond	O'Connor, Walter
Arthurs, Addison E.	Ensley, Chester K.	Oat, Frank, Jr.
Backenstoe, G.S., M.D.	Evans, Johnny	Patterson, David
Ball, Clifford	Field, Joe	Peat, D. Barr
Barbour, B.K.	Fitch, Milan W.	Peters, Ralph B.
Barclay, W. Buril	Fox, Frank M.	Peterson, Paul
Bartow, John B.	Fradel, John F.	Pilley, Frank E.
Booth, W.W.	Gahagan, Charles	Piper, William T.
Bower, A.R.	Gingell, Thomas	Planck, Charles E.
Bradley, James C.	Goff, E.A., Jr.	Post, M. Wilford, Jr.
Breene, Dan A.	Hahn, Colonel B.C.	Ricker, Joseph P.
Brooke, Pat, Sr.	Hancock, Robert H.	Russell, Howard J.
Brooke, Pat, Jr.	Jones, Harry M.	Santmyer, Myrtle
Brown, Nancy	Keck, Stanley	Santmyer, Lloyd
Brown, Douglas, Jr.	Keffer, Walter M.	Seiler, Arthur J.
Buehl, Ernest H.	Kratzer, Jack	Sheffer, Helen
Burke, S.L.	Kratzer, Blair S.	Slavin, Kenneth P.
Burroughs, W.E.	Laedlein, Robert	Smith, Russell K.
Caldwell, Paul C.	Lease, Kenneth	Smith, J. Wesley
Carroll, Kenneth E.	Litzenberger, Carl	Stefanik, Emil
Carroll, James P.	Litzenberger, Al	Stitley, Arthur E.
Carroll, Charles B.	Lossing, Millard	Stockdale, Floyd W.
Carroll, Grace S.	Lutz, Sherm	Strouss, Harry D.
Chambers, Joseph W.	MacFarlane, John W.	Thomas, T. Foster
Clark, Leroy W.	Martin, Willis H.	Thomas, W.S., Jr.
Corbin, George	McMullen, A.B.	Trunk, John E., Sr.
Covey, Bernard	Moltrup, Merle	Voelter, Karl E.
Crane, Joe	Moore, O.A.	Weiland, Leroy C.
Culbertson, Bill	Morris, John P.	Wetovich, Charles W.
Davis, Harry	Morrison, Herbert O.	
Dell, Thomas H.	Murphy, W.J.B.	

1965: The OX5 Club Tenth Anniversary -
Don Riggs Remembers

Ten years after Charlie Carroll, Lloyd Santmyer, Russ Brinkley, Sam Bigony, Clifford Ball and others met at the Mission Inn in Latrobe on the day the OX5 Club was formed, they all got together again and had a party at Latrobe Airport, the airport Charlie Carroll nurtured for so many years. In 1955, Charlie had been the host. This time he was an honored guest. And what a party!

Corporate and retired airline pilots, mechanics and just plain friends of old-timers descended on the grassy part of the airport that manager Paul Bradley had carefully divided with a snow fence. The crowd could get close enough to smell the castor oil but be safe from the propwash of both the Nieuport 28 and the Fokker D-VII. Yes! World War I fighter planes! And not re-creations. Both were originals direct from Old Rhinebeck Aerodrome in Upstate New York. They were there in honor of local World War I pilots who were members of OX5. There was also a 1910 Thomas Brothers Pusher powered with the old V-8 OX5 engine. That one was pre-World War I. You should have seen the Gypsy trucks that hauled all those pieces of flying relics (soft, thin mattresses and clothesline galore!)

The inspiration to bring Cole Palen and his Old Rhinebeck Aerodrome Flying Circus to Latrobe came from Jim Fisher, VP of Public Relations at the very-aware Pittsburgh Institute of Aeronautics. P.I.A. had always been a true friend of OX5 and didn't mind the expense. In fact, the next year the school brought Palen and Dave Fox back to Pittsburgh to do a real-history dogfight over the Allegheny County Fair.

It was a lousy day to fly, especially for those old "rag-and-tube" creations with tail skids and no brakes. The wind speed was about thirty miles per hour with gusts. It was far too windy to fly the old pusher, so they recruited some wing walkers and just taxied the old ship around a bit just to hear the engine, the ubiquitous OX5-V8-water-cooled-single-magnetoed-mill that weighed 360 pounds and put out ninety horse power maybe.

The engine was a wonderful example of advanced technology and practical design for its time. Designed by Glen Curtiss, the OX5 powered the famous Curtiss Jenny of primary training fame. You could buy an Army surplus JN4D with an "oh-by-five" engine for five hundred dollars or less back in the 1920s. Lindbergh did. So did Charlie Carroll and other intrepid airmen from Scottdale, Latrobe, Greensburg, Mt. Pleasant, Ligonier and beyond. "EVERYBODY" had a Jenny with a five-gallon gas can, a grease gun, extra rags, a flying helmet, goggles and a dirty, white scarf, sometimes even a couple extra engines. Jodhpurs, boots, and leather coat were optional. Everybody also had hairy stories of a leaky water pump shorting out the magneto over Chestnut Ridge, or maybe throwing a pin from a rocker arm right through the windshield over Pleasant Unity, Pennsylvania. It's a fact that Raymond Elder and Jim Carroll did just that in the late 1920s.

Back to that sunny-but-windy day in 1965. Cole Palen had just taxied the French Nieuport up close to the fence so we could see everything, including the famous "Hat in the Ring" insignia of Captain Eddie Rickenbacker, and the "guns" mounted on the sides of the fuselage. The guns were a piece of pipe with a glow plug on one end which ignited propane fed from a handyman canister. It sounded like a machine-gun where half the shells were duds. But it WORKED, and it was VERY CLEVER. Just like Palen.

One of his Old Rhinebeck Kids spun the Le Rhone rotary engine and Cole was off! ACROSS the runway, right into the stiff wind! RAT-TAT-TAT. RAT-TAT-TAT! Suddenly he was Snoopy chasing the Bosch. Now comes the German Fokker D-VII with the Mercedes straight eight out front. Dave Fox also takes off across the runway and joins Cole in a friendly dogfight. Call it a puppy fight. The crowd loved it! Dave and Cole made passes over the guests that would give an FAA Safety Monitor fits today. Close! But now came the time to land.

Fox in the Fokker tries it first, crosswind on a hard runway with no tail wheel and no brakes. It's a skid. He needs quick, violent rudder action to keep it straight until he can get over on the grass and dig in. He makes it, and everyone says, "Whew."

Now it's Cole's turn. (How do you say "chicken out" in French?) Palen makes one pass and flies out of sight. About ten minutes later we hear, faintly, "Those Magnificent Men in Their Flying Machines." Here comes Cole with a bunch of helpers pushing the plane, tail held high, across Route 981 and into the airport. He had landed safely in some lady's cow pasture, and was bringing the plane home by hand! We never knew where the music came from.

What a party for the tenth anniversary of an organi-

zation started in Latrobe that grew quickly to over one-hundred-thousand members nationwide. The camraderie was rampant, the remembrances exciting, and everyone who attended, even the wives, had a great time!

The "capper" for the day, however, was flown in a DC-3 by "Curley" Korb, retired chief pilot for Westinghouse. It the spirit of those below, Korb dove the plane down to pick up speed and, just as he got to the crowd, rolled the left wing down, stood on the right rudder, and HELD IT for what is called a "Knife-Edge Pass." Beside him, helping with the rudder, was his new boss, a young wealthy Texan who owned the airplane and who had a grin as big as Curley's. They rolled the old "3" level and headed for Texas. Those rascals! Korb, of course, was an OX5er. Of course!

ABOVE: Bob Hancock, Carolyn Peat, and D. Barr Peat at the OX5 Club's tenth anniversary, Latrobe, 1965.

LEFT: Paul Garber of the Smithsonian (holding microphone), Charlie Carroll, Clifford Ball, and Pete Goff, National President of the OX 5 Club, pose with a plaque commemorating the tenth anniversary of the founding of the OX5 Club at Latrobe on August 27, 1955.

BELOW: Cole Palen, Bob Hancock, Charlie Carroll, and Cliff Ball pose with Palen's Thomas Brothers pusher at the OX5 Club's tenth anniversary. *(All photos courtesy of Carolyn Peat).*

A SPECIAL PICTORIAL

STMORELAND COUNTY
airshow
SECOND ANNUAL
AIR SHOW
WESTMORELAND COUNTY AIRSHOW
Westmoreland County Airshow
September 27 and 28, 1980
Blue Angels
U.S NAVY
154986
6

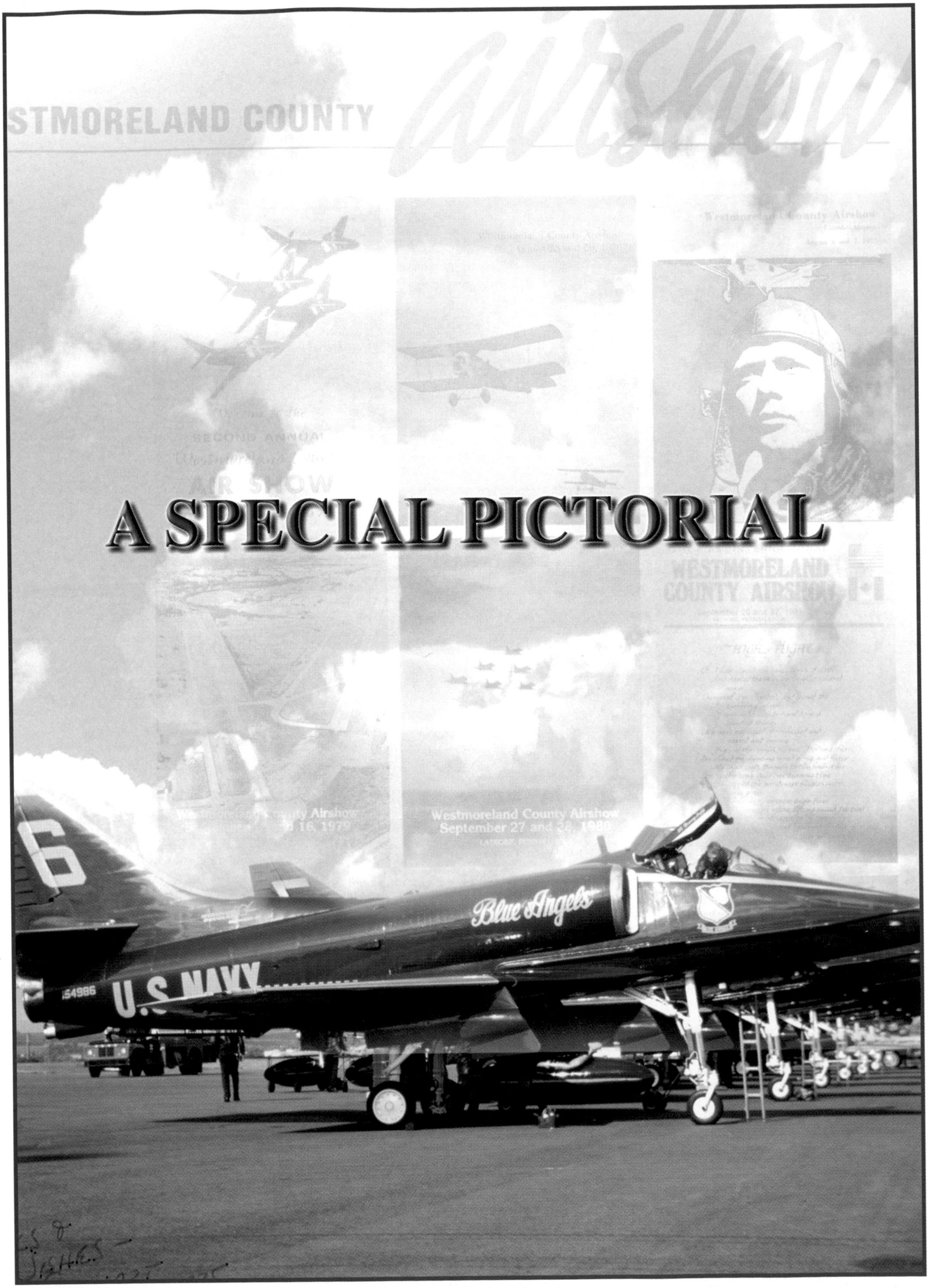

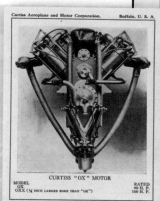

Pages from the Curtiss catalogue of 1917
and the EagleRock catalogue of 1927.

Scottdale school children wrote this card in 1928 after Carl Strickler's funeral. "Red" Grahagan, flying Charlie Carroll's plane, dropped flowerstreamers along the funeral route.

These are flowers dropped by Carrols airplane on the grave of Carl Strickler Nov. 28, 1928 our well educated aviator. He was killed # in a wreck on the Ligonier Mts.

Jim asenner my first school teacher gave me this card Anna Geary

A collection of airmail first covers, air mail pick-up first covers, an All American Aviation logo. At the top left is the cover of AAA's first brochure, published in 1939. The bottom cover is from the late 1940s.

Clyde Hauger (right) with fellow AAA pilots, ca. 1940s. The photo was taken from 8mm home movie film.

Old Blue painted in one of the several mid-1940s AAA livery. The 1939 colors were cherry maroon with navy stripes and gold trim.

Fabric from an AAA Stinson Reliant

1989 Airshow "Red Shirt" volunteers pose with Old Blue.

Representative Westmoreland County Airshow brochure covers and admission tickets.

Arnold Palmer with his Cessna Citation 10. The picture below is the Arnold Palmer Regional Airport as it looks today.

The Westmoreland County Airshow

It was 1981. They pulled the station wagon into a field above the airport. A young boy about seven years old and his father got out of the car. The boy looked up at the sky as if waiting for a miracle. He had a pair of binoculars around his neck. They seemed ridiculously large compared to his thin frame, but he held them firmly in both hands. Periodically, he stared through them at the sky and at points on the horizon with all the importance of a general viewing enemy positions.

While the boy played with the binoculars, his father unpacked a cooler from the trunk of the station wagon.

The boy asked his father a question.

"Are the Flying Tigers going to be here, too?"

His father grinned.

"I don't know. We'll have to wait and see," he responded.

"Here, have this," he said to his son.

He handed him a carton of orange juice.

At that moment, beyond the slope of the hill, there came a sound that seemed to emanate from everywhere. The boy felt the sound rising up out of the ground and into his chest. It almost frightened him. The boy turned and looked in the direction of the sound. He dropped his orange juice. He recognized the sound as it got louder. He had heard it going over his house many times before, but he had never heard it this close before. It was what he had been waiting for.

Over the rise of the hill three airplanes roared into view, suddenly appearing as if willed there by the boy's enthusiasm. They seemed so low to the ground he felt he should duck. One was a brilliant yellow and the two flanking it were silver. The aircraft banked to the left and headed towards the horizon like huge, growling birds.

The boy remembered the binoculars in his excitement and hurriedly peeked through them at the now distant aircraft. This was the closest he had ever been to airplanes. He would get a lot closer as the day progressed. Over the hill lay the Westmoreland County Airport. This was the boy's first air show.

That day I would see aircraft up close that I had only seen in books or admired in the old World War II movies. John Wayne in *The Flying Tigers* was a personal favorite of mine while I was growing up. The first air show I attended featured a vintage P-40 Warhawk with the shark mouth painted under the engine cowling. I thought "The Duke" himself was going to spring out of the cockpit of that monster, swagger over to me and give me a ride in his war bird.

In 1981, the Confederate Air Force flew its vintage planes and re-enacted the bombing of Pearl Harbor, minus the battleships of course. The pyrotechnic display put on to simulate that horrific attack awed me. A life-long interest in World War II aviation followed. The glamour and dash of the World War II fighter pilot kept my younger self glued to books on aviation and clouded my days with dreams of flight. However, as I grew up, I realized the closest I would ever come to that era would be to talk with the men and women who were there or see the airplanes they flew. I have since done both and feel very privileged to have had those opportunities.

I see air shows as one of the living manifestations of childhood dreams. Where else could a person go and see airplanes from nearly all the decades of flight take to the air once more? But when did these living dreams come to life? One could argue the very first air show ever was when Orville and Wilbur Wright made their first successful, powered flight on December 17, 1903. Soon after this flight the possibilities of flight began to expand in the minds of the public who watched in awe the aircraft and the pilots who flew them.

One man in particular began to experiment with how airplanes handled turns, dives and other more dramatic maneuvers. This was Glenn Curtiss, of Curtiss Jenny fame. He and pilots like Lincoln Beachey began to do "stunt flying." According to Johnny Evans:

> Glenn Curtiss popularized early flying exhibitions in a craft of his own invention, the Curtiss Flying Machine known as the 'June Bug.' In 1906 and 1907 he built more aircraft and began to teach others to fly. From this the Curtiss Exhibition Team was created. A pilot from the Curtiss Team would sometimes travel one hundred miles with an airplane in a box car of a train to perform at a County Fair. Much like today's Blue Angels or Thunderbirds, these early pioneers would put on flight demonstrations to thrill and ignite the imagination of the audience.

World War I, despite all of its fruitless slaughter, was a stage for great advancements in aviation. The dogfights that took place over the Western Front throughout the war furthered ideas of what airplanes and pilots could and could not do. Acrobatics and daredevil maneuvers were not exhibitionism for these men. It was staying alive. Who could turn the tightest or roll out of an attack the fastest, lived. However, knowledge gained through conflict migrated to peacetime aerial demonstrations. A whole new generation of pilots with tremendous experience were coming out of the military into civilian life. Many of them still wanted to fly. The Golden Age of the barnstormers was about to begin.

Glenn Curtiss had designed a magnificent aircraft shortly before the United States entry into World War I. This was the Curtiss Jenny, the workhorse of the fledgling United States Army Air Service in the Great War. Used as a trainer, the Jenny proved to be a rugged and easy to handle aircraft. At the end of hostilities, the Army wanted to unload its surplus Jennies. Taking advantage of the growing interest in aviation, the Army offered them for sale to the general public. The Jenny became synonymous with barnstormers. The pilots returning from the war who could not keep their feet on the ground bought these aircraft up as did numerous other civilians, Charlie Carroll being one of them.

Throughout the country, aerial parades, air circuses and air shows drew crowds. The barnstormers were the kings of the sky at these events. They would take people up in their Jennies and give them a look at the world below. Wingwalkers, parachutists and other stunt fliers thrilled those who never dared leave the ground and inspired those who had.

Air shows have been a part of the airport at Latrobe ever since 1925, when Charlie Carroll and his gang of daredevils thrilled and inspired the populace of Latrobe and the surrounding environs with their acrobatic displays and air races. These were well-attended and well-publicized gatherings. However, air shows at the airport that we know today did not officially begin until 1974, the year of my birth.

The first air show was organized by the Westmoreland County Airport Authority. Leonard Bughman, chairman of the Airport Authority, and James Cavalier, airport manager, were instrumental in putting it together.

The purpose of the first show was twofold. First, the airport was backed by tax money. By providing a service to area residents and stimulating the economy with jobs and income, these same residents had a right to tour the airport and know how it functioned. The second reason for the air show was the same as when the early barnstormers hopped from town to town, and that was to give people a chance to see airplanes up close and be a witness to the advances in aviation technology. Perhaps there was a third reason—publicity for the airport.

The airport had grown considerably in the previous ten years. It was considered a sophisticated, first rate facility by many pilots who stopped to refuel. It was time all the hard work was shown off to everyone, and an air show seemed the best way to do this.

The first air show in 1974 brought together more than 15,000 area residents. The success of this event made the members of the Westmoreland County Airport Authority look more closely at the possibilities air shows could offer to the community and the airport.

The 1975 show was even bigger. Military pilots parked airplanes, and flew many of them. Household names like The Blue Angels, the Navy's Flying Demonstration Team, made their first appearance at the annual air show. Names that would become regulars at the air shows over the years included: Clancy Speal and his Pitts Special, Bob Hoover and his Mustang and later on his sleek, twin-engine Areo-Commander Shrike. All of the pilots, parachutists and aircraft thrilled crowds with their acrobatic skills, courage and maneuverability. It was and still is a place for families to gather and witness what was once thought impossible—flight.

Don Riggs was the master of ceremonies for the first seventeen air shows at the airport. His memories of these events are vivid, and Riggs waxes poetic about them. Of the first air show in 1974, he says:

> How about as nice and friendly an air show as we could possibly put together? How about honoring the aviation-pioneer OX5 Club that Charlie Carroll and friends started in 1955? How about inviting every aviation organization to participate? Let's make it a big, happy party with only a three-dollar admission and free parking. Then everybody will know about the new airport and will have had an exciting time there. And so they did. And grabbed a tiger by the tail! Today, pilots and aviation performers who meet every year at the International Council of Air Shows want to come to Latrobe. The hospitality at Latrobe has become renowned throughout this organization. The enormous crowds don't hurt either.

—*David Wilmes*

Don Riggs, first airshow emcee.
(Courtesy of Westmoreland County Airport Authority).

Damien at the Airshow: 1975

It was just past three o'clock in the afternoon. A nine-year-old boy wiped the sweat off of his brow. It was hot for late September. He had been waiting all day. He let go of his father's hand, and pushed through the crowds to the front, until it seemed as through there were mere inches between him and the runway. Half-thrilled, half-scared, he wouldn't have to wait any longer. This was the moment.

Carefully clipped from the pages of a magazine, a photograph clung to the bedroom wall, taped just above Damien's bed. A diamond of A-4F Skyhawk II's, their crisp navy bodies branded with gold, seemed less than a breath apart on the azure slice of sky. As they hung suspended in their paper rectangle, Damien thought of them as some kind of dream, unreal, disbelieving that the planes could stay so close without collision. He tried to make the diamond with the model planes he and his father had built—a shiny blue F4U Corsair, a Curtiss P-40, a Japanese Zero. He measured the distance between the wings with his fingers, but the bellies brushed against the cockpits no matter how hard he tried to keep them apart.

The magazine was worn from constant reading and re-reading. The team consisted of six men, young fighter pilots, volunteers, who practiced thousands of hours just for a chance to make that diamond. Six planes, beautiful Skyhawks, screaming from just above the treetops, all the way to 60,000 feet. Damien had always wondered how the clouds looked from up above, wondered if they were soft to the touch. He decided that the Blue Angels had to know this. One day he would know. One day he would dance in the clouds.

Damien's father touched his head, and hoisted him up onto his shoulders, just as the Blue Angels started their ascent. They flew towards the crowd, closer and closer, in absolute silence. Only after they had gone by did Damien hear the shriek of the engines. Then, they were up again, six Angels abreast in a line, curved effortlessly into a loop, trailing garlands of smoke behind to mark the path. Next, a lone plane coasted inches from the ground, then shot skyward, like a Roman candle, barreling into a spin. Suddenly, four planes locked into the diamond, their wings breathlessly threaded together, like the dance of four giant marionettes, guided by the hands of one master. Finally, all six planes stacked like cards into a triangle–the Delta. They looped together, curving like a single brush stroke, and then swooped up into a roll, a twisting drill of blue, with a funnel of smoke spurting behind, from the earth to the sky.

It was over all too quickly. Damien brushed the dust from his face as his father helped him down. As his father led him toward the autograph booth, Damien turned his head, unable to take his eyes off of the planes, off of the ground controller who saluted each pilot as he stepped out of the cockpit. He let go of his father and turned around. Damien, standing at attention, raised the edge of his hand to his forehead, paused, and brought it down again, in salute. *[Today, Damien Wissolik is a pilot in East Africa].*

Once again . . .
DON RIGGS -- "The Voice of the Westmoreland County Airshow

We are enthusiastic to have Channel Eleven's all-pro man-about-television call all the action for the seventh Westmoreland County Airshow. An accomplished pilot, Don belongs to the Aero Club of Pittsburgh, the Experimental Aircraft Association and many other aviation-related organizations. He has helped create the highly successful Westmoreland County Airshow, and has served as its announcer since 1973. Don's career in broadcasting began in Columbus, Ohio, while he was majoring in music at Capital University. He was a disc jockey for WHKC, then a singer/announcer/puppeteer and part-time Santa Claus for WBNS-TV. He came to Pittsburgh in 1960 to co-host the popular "Daybreak" program with Marcy Lynn and Johnny Costa. It ran on KDKA-TV for seven years. So did "Safari," which Don hosted and produced as "B'wanna Don."

Presently, Don is producer and host of WPXI's early morning talk show, "Starting Today." This half hour program airs at 6:30 A.M., and features local and national guests discussing subjects of current interest to TV viewers in the tri-state area.

Before joining Channel 11, Riggs produced and hosted several programs for WQED-TV and the Public Broadcasting System. His "Close-Up" series achieved the highest audience rating of any locally-produced cultural series in Public Broadcasting in 1969. For PBS (then NET), Don produced "Pittsburgh: A Festival of Folk," which received Golden Quill and AFTRA Awards for excellence and was selected by the U.S. Information Agency for worldwide distribution.

In 1975, Channel 11 received a Freedom Foundation Award for "On Final Forever," a nostalgic look at how a B-25 bomber was laid to rest in a Washington County, Pa. cemetery. This documentary, (which Don claims is his favorite so far), also won the 1975 James Steibig Memorial Trophy from the Aviation/Space Writers Association, this organization's top national award for excellence in aviation writing. Don and his wife, Joan, have four children. The Riggs family resides in Mt. Lebanon.

DON RIGGS
"The Voice of the Westmoreland County Airshow"

BOB CHEFFINS
Airport Manager & Airshow Coordinator

AND . . . once again the star performer nobody gets to see -- BOB CHEFFINS

In the air or on the ground at the Westmoreland County Airshow, the man behind the scenes is Bob Cheffins. Since 1976 when he became airport manager at Latrobe, Bob Cheffins has been quietly and efficiently directing the extensive daily operations at the airport, always working to develop new and better services. And when it comes to putting together an exciting and memorable annual Airshow, Bob Cheffins is the star! We said it before and we'll say it again with Bob behind the controls the shows keep getting better each year.

This page was a favorite in several airshow booklets. *(Courtesy of the Westmoreland County Airport Authority).*

TOP: 1989 Air Show. Volunteers and Latrobe Hospital Aid Society members pose with *Old Blue*, the Stinson Reliant used that year to commemorate the air mail pick-up.
LEFT CENTER: ca. mid-1970s. Jim Cavalier, airport manager, (top row, left) poses with Lenny Bughman and the Airshow Hospital Aid Society.
RIGHT CENTER: 1992 airshow. Congressman John Murtha (left) and Bruno Ferrari. Murtha is instrumental in bringing military pilots and aircraft to the airshows.
BOTTOM LEFT: 1998 airshow. The **organizers** *(Courtesy of the Westmoreland County Airport Authority).*

An airshow crowd gravitates to a military transport. *(Courtesy of the Westmoreland County Airport Authority).*

When Don Riggs announces an airshow, everybody looks up. *(Courtesy of the Westmoreland County Authority).*

TOP: The late Dan Speal of New Alexandria, Pennsylvania. BOTTOM: Dan's son Clarence ("Clancy"). Both father and son were renowned and beloved stunt pilots at the airshow. They were among the best in their profession. To the sorrow of all who knew him and watched him perform, forty-three-year-old Clancy was killed in a crash at the Pittsburgh Regatta when his Pitts Special suffered structural failure. *(Courtesy of the Westmoreland County Airport Authority).*

In Their Own Words...

James Carroll

I was in high school when Dad opened the airport at the Kerr farm. I drove the truck back from Scottdale with lumber and stuff to build hangars. I was brought up in airplanes. I remember I went over to Uniontown one time with Dad and some men to see a race at the speedway. Dad liked to go there because he had a chance to look over the race cars. He was a real mechanic. A little white plane came in and landed in the infield and Dad was all eyes. That did it for Dad. Then he got hold of someone in Pittsburgh to get a surplus Jenny. He bought one, but had to go to New York to get it. It was 1919, and he and Torrance Overholt flew it back. They got as far as New Jersey when the engine developed magneto problems. They landed in a field and ran into a fence. Dad had to send back to Scottdale to get a truck to haul the plane back. Torrance was a World War I pilot, and he took that plane up for stunts over Scottdale. He and Dad started a flying club there.

Truth is, Dad never had any lessons, except a couple from Torrance. He kept his plane out a Felger's farm in Scottdale. One day, Dad got the motor going and was taxiing around Felger's big field. A big wind came and picked him up. Before he knew it, he was flying. Oh, he didn't intend to fly that day!

I was ten when I had my first flight. There was a fair down near Scottdale. Overholt took me up. It was a World War I plane. I did it just to fly. When I got my license, I could take up a plane from Dad's field anytime I wanted to, as long as I put in gas. One day a guy said to me, "I'd like to go over to Uniontown to see my brother. Could you fly me over in the plane that you're allowed to use out there?"

I was working at an ice cream store in Latrobe. I was the manager, so I could take off whenever I wanted. I told the guy, "How about tomorrow?"

Next day, we took off and we went over to Uniontown, and the field over there was right along the mountains. When we came in to land, I said "What the hell is going on here?!"

The wind was like a hurricane. We didn't have that kind of wind in Latrobe, even though it was the same mountain. We got down and onto the long runway and I was pretty much going sideways because of the wind. I remembered my early training about keeping your rudder turned so that your tail wouldn't be blown backwards. I had it under control. I had the left wing down because I was running along opposite the mountain, and we started to drift. I kept the power on. We were headed down the runway and all of a sudden the left wing came up and the left wheels underneath the fuselage were on the ground. Then the left wheel came off the ground, I realized it was because the plane was tilted. So I told Kenny to jump out and grab a hold of the end of that wing, but don't let us get blown away. So he jumped out and ran out and grabbed a hold of the wing before it was lifted off the ground. He held on up to the hangar. We cut up to the hangar and the guy there said, "Who the Hell are you and what are you doing landing in the crosswind? Did you see our new runway?!"

I said, "I didn't see a new runway. I used to come in right by the mountain."

He said, "Oh, we have a new runway. Why didn't you use it."

I said, "How come Latrobe never got a notice that you had a new runway?"

He shut up real quick because he was in violation for running an operation like that and not telling other airport operators. He realized right away that he was in trouble.

Kenny called his brother, but his brother wasn't home, so we got in the plane, cranked it up and went out over the new "runway." All it was was a big, grassy field.

Marcia Nair
Latrobe, Pennsylvania

Charlie Carroll was my father's brother. Dad always took us out to the airport on Sundays. Charlie was always so busy. Even his daughter Dorothy said I hardly ever saw him, he was so busy with the airport.

I was born in Scottdale. For a while we lived in Florida. Dad couldn't find enough work and my brother developed asthma and we moved back to this area and settled in Greensburg. Then we started going back to the airport.

Once, in the summer time, Charlie took me up in an open-cockpit airplane. I don't know if it was a Jenny, but

I'm thinking it was. It was 1928, when I was about eight. I was scared, but now when I think of that airplane I'm more frightened! Children rarely know fear. We flew around the landing field. I'm surprised my mom and dad let me do it. At that time, flying was a thing for men. Women rarely had a part in it. Although, I never felt left out, I think I just accepted the fact that it was something for the boys.

Thomas E. Smith
Greensburg, PA

In the 1930s, when I was a young boy in the village of Carbon, "Happy" O'Bryan used to fly over Greensburg and the surrounding area on Sunday afternoons, playing music over a loudspeaker on his plane an announcing airplane rides and other events. He played "Deep Purple" by Gene Austin.

Also in the 1930s, there was airmail pick-up at the Carbon airstrip located on the hill that is now between Greensburg Central Catholic High School and St. Paul's Church.

Joe Boerio
Latrobe, PA

In the early 1920s, I was in grade school at Loyalhanna School, Derry Township. We heard that there was a plane landing in McChesneytown. I was too late to see the plane, but it landed on a large, open field a little beyond Latrobe's Sylvan Avenue out toward McChesneytown and between East Main and Walnut Streets. Later on this became a football field for independent football.

In the middle twenties, there was a landing field at what was referred to as Toner Farm. That would be the area within the loop of the Loyalhanna Creek as it winds from First Bridge (Lymer Street at Latrobe Brewery) to Second Bridge.

Eleanor Johnson Kenny
Crabtree, PA

In the Fall of 1932, Oscar D. Johnson was the night watchman at J.D. Hill Airport. During the Summer of 1933, Oscar had a stand located at the corner of Route 30 and 981 on airport property. He sold ground chicken

sandwiches with gravy and lots of caramel corn. Otto Hoover parachuted every Sunday, and the kids held signs on Route 30 east and west advertising it. Lots of cars filled with families stopped to watch it. The signs read "Parachute Jump in One Hour;" Parachute Jump in One-Half Hour;" "Parachute Jump in Fifteen Minutes."

Joseph D. Assini
Greensburg, PA

I was a youngster fourteen years old in 1939, before World War II began. The New Alexandria Airport used to be one-mile out off old Route 22 (William Penn Highway) from New Alex, where I lived.

I remember pushing planes out of the hangar and gassing them up to be flown by the pilots. My friend, Jim Wandless, and I used to do all this work for one dollar a day, mostly because we liked the planes.

We liked Sundays the best because that is when Otto Hoover used to parachute. Jim and I would hold up signs on Old Route 22 that would say "Parachute Jump in Fifteen Minutes," but it would usually take him an hour to get ready.

Before he went up, Otto would wait for fifty or sixty people to gather. Then he would mount a step ladder and make a speech. "I can spell my name the same way backwards and forwards. O-T-T-O. If this chute doesn't open, I will take it back and get a new one!"

He would then ask for a donation from the people. He kept an eye on me and Jim while we collected the change. Otto told us to shake our heads "yes" if we got twenty-five cents from anyone. Then he would say, "Thank you!" If someone gave only ten or fifteen cents Otto would say, "Much obliged." We usually collected about twenty dollars. We got paid twenty-five cents.

One day, while we were at the gas station where the planes got gas, the owner came out and told us, "Hey, the Japanese just bombed Pearl Harbor!" We had never heard of the place.

Robert Fisher
Greensburg, PA
(Air Traffic Controller, Pittsburgh-Greensburg Airport)

I was the first air traffic controller in Greensburg in 1929. There were three of us when it opened, there were so many planes. They only let us out there one at a time for two hours at a time. Then, they would take us in for a rest.

They gave us each a pole. It was fairly long, with two great-big flags on it, red and white. The planes would be flying around up there. If the runway wasn't clear, we'd hold up a red flag. They listened! If everything was clear, we'd hold up a white. Then we'd get down out of the way, because they'd come right in. Then things died down after about two weeks, and the pilots could take care of themselves. Of course, there was no night flying there at the time.

When it got slack, they'd give us a ride in a Ford Tri-Motor. They'd load all the airport workers in that plane. That was my first flight. Later, I went up in the Taylorcrafts and the Wacos.

"Happy" O'Bryan would go up an stunt. One day he forgot to take one of the seats out of a Waco, and when he turned upside down, the seat fell out! I found it, and took it up to him. "Thanks," he said. I knew I lost it somewhere."

Mansel Negley
Greensburg, PA

My first experience with an airplane was when word got out that there was going to be an airplane coming into Salzburg Extension. There was a little field in there. The pilot was going to haul passengers. Children rode for free. I went down with my dad, my aunt, and my sister. It was just a little biplane and it was only a dollar or two for each passenger, and they gave you a pretty good ride. I really loved the experience. If an airplane flew over any of the towns, people would get so excited and come running out of their houses to see the plane.

Otto Hoover would parachute jump at all the little airports. He sometimes had a monkey that would make the jumps with him.

A guy named Cecil E. Davis had an American Eagle biplane that he finally took over to the Latrobe Airport. Davis bought a little Aeronca. They were dangerous airplanes. They had very little lift, and Davis and the airport mechanic and Davis' student, Andy Sivak, from Westmoreland Homesteads, went up in that plane on a really humid day. About five or six miles from the airport, the plane wasn't climbing at all. He couldn't get more than about 1,000 feet, and instead of nosing it down to get a little speed, like we were all taught to do later, he hit the rudder pedal to make a turn, went into a power spin, and hit the ground nose-first. They both got killed. They were both only twenty-seven.

I was flying one day, and a similar thing happened. I had a nurse in my plane, and I took her for a ride, and I was making my final approach at the Leechburg Airport. The runway was across the river. There was also a steel

mill with the open hearths. We always got updrafts there, but never any downdrafts. While I was leveling out, the airplane got hit by a downdraft and just settled. So, I opened the throttle and nosed-down. About twenty feet from the ground, I pulled up, and went in for a landing.

The nurse laughed. "Boy-O-Boy," she said. "What you did out there. Do you do that often?"

I said, "Oh, Yeah. I do that occasionally just to give someone a thrill."

"Boy, that was really good. I enjoyed that! Next time we go for a ride, I want you to do that again"

The poor girl! She didn't know that that was my only method of survival. Had I not learned how to do that, both of us would have been dead!

I learned to fly around 1939. I fell in love with a girl, and asked her to marry me. She dumped me, instead. I never found out why. Anyway, I got lonesome and started to think about flying. On August 9, 1939, I took my first lesson at Latrobe Airport from George Allen. George was the chauffeur for the Rogers family. Eventually, he would teach young Fred Rogers to fly. George and I got along pretty well. As a matter of fact, I started landing and taking off in my first hour of instruction. Charlie Carroll gave me a little instruction, too. As a matter of fact, Charlie was the last one to give me flight instruction. That was December 25, 1939. After that, I went over to Leechburg Airport an soloed from there.

I managed to save a little money to buy a used Piper Cub E-240, license number 15312. That was in 1940. I soloed on that. I liked that little plane. I made a forced landing in it once, when I went back to visit the guys at the Latrobe Airport. That plane just had a skid on the tail, and I had to always land it in the sod. It was like a pig-on-ice on any other kind of surface.

I enjoyed years of flying. But I finally gave it up. The actor, Jimmy Stewart, had a plane just like mine. He wrote to me once and said, "I, like you, have given up flying. I miss it, and I know you do, too."

One time I taught a ten-year-old kid to fly. Of course, that wasn't to be known then, but now it's too late to do anything about it.

Mrs. Norman J. Micher
Belle Vernon, PA

My husband Bernard worked for Mr. Carroll at the Latrobe Airport. He swept out the hangar, cut grass, painted all the fence posts around the airport, and set the mail bag for pick-up by the Stinson Reliant.

One time, around 1945, there was a storm pouring rain, thunder and lightning and a two-engined airliner made a landing. The actress Zazu Pitts got off the plane!

Then a P-47 Thunderbolt fighter plane landed, and when he came to the intersection of the runways the pilot thought he was at the end. He slammed on the brakes and the plane flipped over and caught fire. The rain put out the fire, and the pilot was not hurt.

Bob Downs
Murrysville, PA

In 1945 through 1948 I pedaled my bicycle the three miles from my home in Latrobe to the airport where airport manager Charlie Carroll allowed me to be around the airplanes. He employed me as a mechanic and go-fer. I worked full time in summer and part time in the spring and fall while I was in high school. I made thirty cents an hour for two years, then fifty cents!

Paul Smart was the mechanic and was assisted by Tom Rankin. I washed down the engines while they did repairs. I held the J-3 cowling, while they riveted patches on the incessant cracks. I rode the mower that they pulled with an old Ford dump truck. Gasoline fuel was scarce, so they resorted to running the truck on dry-cleaning fluid. After several days, I developed severe nausea and headaches and left one day at noon, pedaling my way home. I painted the office and sold airplane rides. I was happy because I was around planes.

Airplane tail wheels wore down and had to be replaced. Tom discovered that we could roll the wheel on the hangar floor where the usual taper on the worn tire caused the wheel to roll in large circles. The game was to see how long the wheel would roll before it collided with a wheel of a hangared airplane. One day Tom took aim on a barrel and rolled the wheel with a lot of force and cried out, "Bowling!" The wheel hit the barrel and bounced far into the air. It descended through the wing of Charlie's prized Waco. Tom had a cloth patch on the hole and was almost ready to put the color coat on when Charlie walked up and asked, "What happened, Tom?"

Then there was the day Tom decided to get rid of the old paint thinner and other flammable materials that had accumulated. We put the material into a fifty-five-gallon drum located some distance behind the hangar. Then Tom and I took turns flipping big kitchen matches at the barrel from what we thought was a safe distance. One of us finally flipped a match onto the rim of the barrel and it dropped inside. You should have seen the genie that was unleashed! A huge ball of rolling black smoke interlaced with orange flame when up into the sky as we ran away. Meanwhile, Charlie was eating his lunch a short distance away in his home in Lawson Heights. He hap-pened to glance out his kitchen window. All he could see was the hangar and the ball of fire. He made the trip to the airport in record time. He ran up and asked, "What the Hell are you doing, Tom?"

We used to burn the grass off the airport periodically. Spreading a line of gasoline, we torched it and controlled the fire line by beating the fire with brooms. We were covered with soot at the end of the day. Soon, I found out that the best way to clean up was to stop at Murphy's Hole in the Loyalhanna Creek. I carried soap, and was able to get home without being yelled at for getting the bathtub dirty. But the farmer across the road from the airport, where Big Lots is now, yelled at Charlie because the smoke from the fires made his milk go bad.

We didn't have an electric pump for fuel. We turned a crank connected to a gear that engaged and lifted a rack. This pumped the fuel up into the hose. A large, clock-like dial with a big pointer indicated how much fuel had been pumped. Only five gallons could be pumped before it had to be reset. This wasn't so bad when refueling a Cub or and Aeronca or a T-Craft. It wasn't my lucky day when three, old, dirty yellow Navy N3N biplanes with their comparatively huge, empty tanks landed for fuel.

There was an annex attached to the back of the hangar. At one end was the shop-parts room. At the other end was a classroom. Adjacent to the classroom was the rest room, the ceiling of which contained a 200-gallon rain-storage tank. This was the only water for the field. It definitely was not drinkable, even on the hottest day. It was used for toilets and airplane washing. The furnace room was in a sunken center section of the building. Above the furnace room was a small, one-room apartment with a bed and coal-burning stove used for cooking and heating. Bill (I don't remember his last name) lived there. He was an airport guard of a sort. He made his rounds walking with crutches. He was friendly to all persons, and the airport dog, "Cubby," a Collie, was his friend.

One day, "Cubby" learned a valuable lesson. Paul Smart transferred the air mail from the Latrobe Post Office to the airmail pick-up site. Usually his wife did the driving, and Paul set up the poles. "Cubby" was very protective of the mail bags. He ran circles around them, and didn't let anyone come near. Finally, "Cubby" got in the way of a bag that was being picked up and got picked up with it, or was thrown by it. He survived, but for several weeks hobbled around. He also kept his distance from the bags after that.

Once there was a severe storm at Allegheny County Airport. Three airplanes were diverted to Latrobe. The Stinson Reliant air mail pick-up plane landed first. It was the most vulnerable to weather. A military Douglas C-47 loaded with troops was next. Then a Republic P-47 made its run. As it passed over the end of the runway, the storm hit and the plane disappeared from sight. I will always remember seeing the fighter's red wing-tip light just before it disappeared. A short time later, there was a flash and a noise where the airplane should have been. People ran toward the flash and noise, some of them carrying fire extinguishers. A few of the more level-headed drove to the site in cars or the old Ford truck. It was a scene from a Marx Brothers movie! The pilot thought he had reached the end of the runway and spiked the brakes, putting the plane on its nose. He emerged unscathed. What excitement for a high school kid!

Tom and Paul were practical jokers. One of their tricks was to wait until I was jockeying a plane (they were all fabric covered) into position in the hangar. One of them would sneak up behind me and rip a sheet of newspaper. Oh! The sinking feeling as I thought I had ripped a hole in the airplane!

One day, while I was stocking parts into the bins, Paul's wife drove up to the door with the mail sack. Paul proceeded to tell her about a B-25 bomber that flew into the side of the Empire State Building. I was rolling in the aisle as Paul embellished his story. A short time later, I found out that this was not one of his jokes. It really did happen!

One day the manager of the New Alexandria airport flew in to talk to Charlie. The conversation turned to birds in the ceiling of the hangar at New Alex. Charlie said that he didn't have a problem with that at Latrobe; he just shot them. That sounded like a good idea to the New Alex manager. A few weeks later, he came back and unhappily described to Charlie the leaks in his hangar roof. It turned out that his hangar had a thin, metal roof, while Charlie's was made of thick wood and covered with roof paper.

To me, at that time, any pilot was a super-special person; they could fly. A flight instructor was next to God. One of Charlie's instructors was George Allen. I liked George; he talked flying with me. Some forty-five years later, I found out that George was the first black commercial pilot in Pennsylvania. He was still flying in the Toledo area, well into his eighties. Kenny Walters was another instructor. Kenny was spit and polish. He wore riding pants, leather leggings, and he had a thin mustache, must like Smilin' Jack in the comic strips. Kenny's brother Skip took for an occasional ride in his two-cylinder, house-trim green Aeronca.

I had heard about Lou Strickler. The guys told me he did all kinds of things with an airplane, like how he used to go out to Keystone Lake and drag the wheels of his air-

plane in the water, to impress his girl or somebody, or how he dropped a roll of toilet paper from his plane. It would drop like a streamer, and Lou would cut through the streamer as many times as he could before the roll hit the ground. One day, a glistening, brand-new Beech Stagger Wing landed, and out climbed Lou Strickler himself. He was ferrying the plane through for somebody from the factory, and he stopped by to visit the guys. The next morning he moved this beautiful plane out, started it up, and moved down the runway for his usual takeoff roll. He never lifted the tail. He just did a three-point rise, and immediately did a steep, climbing turn. He had a lot of power in that plane. I never saw a plane take off like that. It impressed the heck out of me!

Latrobe used to have a non-precision instrument approach radio on field for instrument landings in bad weather. It was decommissioned and another station on the mountain near Seven Springs was assigned the same 108.2 frequency. A pilot without the latest charts, thinking he was clear of the mountains, let down toward the station and was killed.

One time the state, or somebody, wanted to provide an emergency lighting system for the airport. Charlie was the recipient of four dozen six-volt, batter-operated lanterns like the trouble lights used on highways. We were to put them on cars or trucks. If someone had to make a night landing, we would drive the vehicles out to the side of the runway and provide some sort of landing light. I'm not sure whether or not they could even be seen from the air. I'm not even sure if they ever got used. I just remember storing them, and Charlie shaking his head and saying, "I don't know what the Hell we're going to do with those!"

The hangar at Latrobe held a great number of aircraft because of the way the "tail-draggers" were stacked. The planes were pushed nose-first into the hangar. Then the tails were lifted, using a handle on the fuselage near the tail. At a certain height, the planes became nose-heavy, so we used a pole with a hook on the end. This helped control the easing down of the nose. The horizontal prop was eased into a sort of low sawhorse with padded slots that took the prop. By standing the planes almost on their noses, we could store many planes. We always hoped the guy in the back of the hangar didn't want to use his plane!

The old bike of mine saw a lot of miles on the road and on the grass at the airport. I carried several "monkey links" to repair the frequent chain breakage. I also kept a spare front axle at the house. The half-moons in the Morrow coaster brake also were subject to frequent breakage, so I kept a spare set at the house.

In those days, I dreamed of flying. I couldn't afford

ABOVE: "Cubby," Charlie Carroll's collie dog and airport mascot. Cubby knew the times when the pick-up pilots were due over the field. He considered himself to be "Protector of the Mailbags." *(Courtesy of the Saint Vincent Archabbey Archives).*

LEFT: Bob Downs, ca. 1945 at the Latrobe Airport. *(Courtesy of the Micher family).*

BELOW: Pilot Bob Downs today, posing with his Piper aircraft at the landing strip in Bouquet. *(Courtesy of Bob Downs).*

ABOVE: O.C. Harrold's Taylorcraft at the Latrobe Airport, 1947. Harrold developed the dangerous habit of smoking cigars while in flight. *(Courtesy of Bob Downs).*

BELOW: Skip Walters, brother of Kenny Walters, flight instructor at Latrobe Airport, 1947. Skip was the proud owner of a two-cylinder, bright-green Aeronca K. *(Courtesy of Bob Downs).*

ABOVE: 1947. The Consolidated BT-14 Valiant that made a forced landing on the Mellon family's Rolling Rock estate. The staff at the Latrobe Airport built a cradle into the bed of the airport's 1929 Ford dump truck, obtained the necessary permits, then towed the damaged plane back to the airport where it was repaired. *(Courtesy of Bob Downs).*

LEFT: Paul Smart, mechanic at Latrobe Airport in the 1940s, gasses up a plane. Paul helped Charlie to handle the mail for the pick-ups, then handed the job over to his wife, Josephine. *(Courtesy of Josephine Smart).*

it. Later, I received a degree in mechanical engineering from Carnegie-Mellon and became a mechanical design engineer (now retired), a pilot, and an airplane owner. Today, I keep my small plane at Arnold Palmer Regional Airport. Many years ago I became a flight and ground instructor. The FAA named me Flight Instructor of the Year 1999 for the Allegheny Flight Standards Office. It all began for me at the Latrobe Airport!

Don Riggs
Pittsburgh, PA

John Trunk Jr. is an important name in the history of OX5, simply because he was the Pennsylvania president, and in 1960, Channel 2 had committed Paul Long to go to Clarion and emcee a banquet that John Trunk had put together honoring bold airmail pilots, government airmail pilots, like Terry Smith and Jack Knight, people like that who were still alive. He felt that we should honor them simply because Clarion, Pennsylvania was an airmail stop, and emergency field for an airmail, and it was the base for a big search for one of the airmail planes that went down in the 1920s, so Johnny had always been an airmail fan he was an aviation nut, and a wild man, too, by the way. The things those guys did to airplanes in those days! He's the guy who provided the motivation to go down to Scottdale and resurrect Elder's old OX5 engine.

Paul Long couldn't make it, so the station said, "Riggs, would you go?"

And I said, "Yeah." I'm the short man on the totem pole. I was just a new guy in those days, and so I called Trunk, and Trunk said, "Okay, I want you to do the banquet, if Paul can't do it, you'll do it fine, but, caveat, I want you to come up with your wife and stay a day and a night, and the next day we'll do the banquet."

And I said, "Oh, okay." And I did. And we went up, and he put me in the breakfast nook, and he filled me with the aviation history of Clarion county for a whole day, and then he filled me the next day with the exploits and the achievements of the people, one by one, right down the list: "This guy invented the system where you buzz the field and turned on the lights; this guy invented the first weather information that you could see, like three lights on the hangar. One white light meant, so-so. Red light meant the weather was terrible. Green light meant go ahead."

Then he told me the story of an airmail pilot. He parks his plane and gets into a little Thomas Morse Scout, spins the prop, and starts off. But there's no wings on the plane. It was just a fuselage. Then he drives the thing down to the barbershop in Clarion. Underneath the doormat is a key. He opens the door, goes in, gets in the barber's chair and goes to sleep. That was standard procedure in Clarion. Can you see that? That old fuselage taxiing down the main street in Clarion! God! Those guys! They were a bunch.

Anyway, that's the beginning of my involvement with OX5. Then, in 1963, I made a movie called *The Seat of Your Pants*. It featured OX5ers, old-timers flying antique airplanes, and kids pulling their own homebuilts. And it was a good little film, honoring Clarion, the first municipally owned airport in America.

Juny Trunk died in 1966, hauling a staff photographer in the back seat of a J-3. The photographer had a speed graphic camera. Juny took off, and the engine coughed or something, and the photographer leaned forward with the camera, and forced the stick forward. The plane crashed. The photographer walked away from it for a minute, but he died about two hours later from internal injuries. That's what killed my friend John Trunk.

My association with Latrobe began in 1960s. I knew Jim Cavalier. I went out and shot some film of Jim and Dave Fox in their homebuilt airplane. That's why Cavalier knew to call me when they were ready to do an airshow, because I had done other air shows in the area. The first really modern one at Latrobe was in 1974.

We had a reunion of the OX5 Club in Latrobe in 1965. Jim Fisher of the Pittsburgh Institute of Aeronautics said, "I'll tell you what, I think it's worth it to honor these guys, we'll bring Cole Palen and his old World War I group down to Latrobe from his place in Rhinebeck, New York. We'll fly these for the old-timers and the World War I pilots." And he did.

Charlie Carroll was there. The guys just loved Charlie, and Charlie's sons were there. It was more a party for Charlie than it was a party hosted by Charlie, as he had done ten years previously, at the founding.

The Mellon family did a lot for the airport in Latrobe. Alan Scaife and Prosser and R.K. One day, R.K. Mellon and Lenny Bughman were out on the field when a jet landed. The pilot had to burn rubber to get the plane stopped because the runway was so short.

R.K. said to Bughman, "Is that normal?"

And Bughman said, "No sir, that's not! But he had to do that to get the airplane stopped, the runway's so short."

And R. Kay said, "Well, that's dangerous! Can we extend that?

Bughman answered, "Not unless you tunnel under Rt. 981!"

R.K. said, "Give me some figures. look into what we have to do to make a longer runway, to make it safer."

That's how a lot of the airport expansion started in the early 1970s.

Don Kane
Greensburg, PA

I graduated from high school, got a job at Sears and Roebuck, and like any young kid I was looking for something to do. Students from Greensburg going out to Saint Vincent would hitchhike from in front of the YMCA. I used to come out to Saint Vincent a lot, and the airport was right near there. During World War II, we used to build a lot of models and things, so I got interested in flying. I started taking lessons.

At the time, it was expensive; ten dollars an hour for dual, and probably seven-fifty if you went solo. I never told my folks I was taking flying lessons. I was the last of six, so you had to be careful what you said. You'd have not only your mom and dad on your back, but also five siblings older than you.

I learned to fly in a J-3 Cub. My instructor was Babe Krinock. It had no radio, no starter, and you propped it by hand. Sometimes those planes would not start, then suddenly kick in. A lot of pilots lost a digit or worse when that happened. The plane had no lights, no electrical sys-tem, no fuel gauge, and weighed only six hundred pounds. I had my first lesson in an hour on February 11, 1954, and I soloed on May 10, 1954. The first time you see that stick, and the instructor is not in the plane with you. . .wow!

The day I soloed, we were landing the opposite way, which I never did. That's upsetting to find something different. I came in and touched down. The J-3 was a tail-wheel airplane. It was tricky to land. I made a heck of a big bounce. I decided to salvage the landing. I pushed the power in. Babe was standing off the runway, watching. This time I paid more attention to what I was doing, and the landing was good. Nowadays, I think they have a tradition where they take the shirt that you're wearing, put the date on it, cut a patch out, put it in the office or wherever took your lessons. It wasn't anything like that in those days. I didn't take classes. It was just me and Babe.

Gene McDonald
Latrobe, Pennsylvania

I was a boy when they had the J. D. Hill Airport at Latrobe. They'd have parachute jumps and so forth. Charlie Carroll leased the land from the Kerr family.

The WPA, during the Great Depression did a major

IDENTIFICATION

Pilot's Name DON KANE

Street Address 40 PARK

City and State GREENSBURG, PA.

Telephone No. 1834-J

Log Book No. _____ From _____ To _____

Certificate Numbers PRIVATE 4/C, 1292703

Types of Certificates

Ratings Held _____

KANE DONALD R AF 13 519 134

IN CASE OF EMERGENCY NOTIFY

Name MRS ANNA M. KANE Relationship MOTHER

Street No. 40 PARK City and State GREENSBURG PA. Phone 1834-J

Or _____

First page of Don Kane's pilot's log. *(Courtesy of Don Kane).*

project with Latrobe and Charlie Carroll to improve the airport. They built a double-cross runway. They also built the main north hanger out of concrete block. Prior to that it was just a small building where they housed planes and offices. In 1939, the air mail pick-up made the airport doubly famous.

My involvement with the airport started in the early 1950s. Jim Underwood, an industrialist from Latrobe, was very interested in getting the county airport located here. Back in 1935, Latrobe made an agreement with the Kerr family that they could buy the Kerr property for $1.00 with the proviso that, at the end of fifteen years, the land could be purchased for about $22, 500.00.

There was a gentleman named Clinton Burns, an heir of the Kerrs, and Underwood worked through him. Underwood convinced Latrobe Borough council to buy the site of the airport. That was a major feat. It might sound that it was a little selfish on his part, but really, he was from the generation interested in the growth of Latrobe. He saw a real growth possibility in that little twenty-three acre one-man operation.

I came out of law school in 1949. In 1951, I became associated with Attorney John Lightcap, who was associated with Latrobe Borough. Underwood had contacted the Westmoreland County Commissioners and the Mellon family, especially Alan Scaife.

Underwood's team negotiated with the commissioners. He told them that Latrobe would contribute to the effort if the county would use the airport as the county airport. At the time, the county was looking over in the New Kensington area as a possible site.

Underwood was a good leader and a good salesperson, so the county accepted, and the borough handed over the airport site to Westmoreland County. Then, Underwood, Scaife, Bruno Ferrari and others suggested that an airport authority be formed under the provisions of the Pennsylvania Municipalities Authorities Act so that the commissioners wouldn't have to worry about it on a day-to-day basis. They formed the Tri-City Airport Authority consisting of Latrobe, Greensburg and Jeannette and five members. They made a gentleman's agreement that at least the majority of the members had to come from the Greensburg, Latrobe, Ligonier. That made it easier to get a quorum. Later the name was changed to the Westmoreland County Airport Authority.

I got a call one morning from Jim Underwood. "Gene," he said, "how would you like to be the solicitor for the airport authority?"

I said, "What airport authority?"

He said, "The Tri-City Municipal Airport Authority."

I said, "I'm interested."

I didn't know the meaning of navigation or airports,

but I said I'd do it. That was in 1951, and I'm still with it after fifty years!

We got engineers to lay out a plan. Our earliest engineers were predecessors to the now-international firm of Michael Baker. They came out, took a look, and gave us a quote on doing a master plan. I traveled to Washington with the engineer and learned the ropes on Capitol Hill and the Civil Aeronautics Board, the predecessor of the Federal Aviation Administration.

We were trying to find out how to bring in commercial aviation. We learned early on that that was going to be a most difficult thing to do. Underwood flew us to places like Jamestown, New York, and Philadelphia, and Richmond, Virginia, where there would be hearings of different types and you could make applications with the CAB. We worked to get funding for improvements. We worked on getting commercial service. We're still working on that.

We got to be well known in Congress, in the different transportation departments, and by the FAA. We learned the avenues of fund raising.

Our first major project was to eliminate the those old WPA runways, and put in totally new ones. To do that we had to acquire more land. We called that Project Number One, but we still didn't know where we were going to get the money. We knew that there was money available from the federal government for grants of fifty-percent of the cost of land acquisition. We needed a master plan and survey showing where the runway was, where it was to be, and how much land we needed. We needed land to construct the runway, supporting facilities, and navigation needles. In addition to land, we needed lighting.

When we started, Mr. Mellon was influential in getting help from the state. State authorities made a very substantial grant to the airport authority to acquire the land and the navigation easements for that first major project. We made a proposal and they accepted it. We condemned parts of farms, and this without money in the bank! I wouldn't recommend that today. At the time I believed that just with the offer of a grant, the money would be there when we needed it.

Usually, we negotiated successfully with the farmers, and never had a court trial. My theory was to figure what land was going to be worth five to ten years down the road and pay that amount. I said to the authority, "If we can acquire any piece of land that we need within the price or less than what we prospectively think it will be worth ten to fifteen years from now, do it. Don't spend it on litigation fees, do it. In the long run, we'll be ahead."

They accepted my theory. We offered reasonable prices, and we got all that we needed to build the runway, and then we negotiated and got lights for the runway.

We discovered that a 3,600-foot runway wasn't going to be enough. We didn't have enough room on the south end of it, and we needed those navigation easements. Then we designed an overrun, which meant that heavier aircraft could come in and land on the regular runway, and they'd have 800 feet more of safety area. The overrun extended the runway to 4,400.

Bruno Ferrari was very active in the construction business, and he wanted every project we had, but we had to competitively bid it. He bid, and he got the work. It was years before anybody would beat him on a price. Why? Well, he just took a loss in order to get that work. He was interested in the welfare of the project.

We had our application into the Pennsylvania Bureau of Aviation and the FAA. Bruno went ahead and started construction, but the authority said to him, "We don't have the money to pay you. We need to get the money."

"That's all right. I'll take a note!"

We signed off on a note, would you believe!

Then we changed engineers from Baker to Simpson. We kept filing for project after project. By this time the county commissioners knew what we had gotten into. We completed the first land-acquisition project, and we didn't have to ask the county commissioners for any money at all.

Gene McDonald. (Courtesy of Westmoreland County Airport Authority).

Alan Scaife suddenly died around 1958. When we opened the Tri-City Municipal Airport in October 1958, his daughter Cordelia cut the ribbon in his honor. The county commissioners appointed a man by the name of Leonard Bughman in his place. He was very close to Mr. Mellon. He was also a famous World War II pilot, and prisoner of war. At the time he was working for Gulf Oil in Pittsburgh. Lenny became an active advocate for the airport. This was also the time of Congressman John Dent's tenure in Harrisburg. He eventually became a U.S. Congressman. Through his seniority he became very active in helping the airport get the funds it needed.

It became apparent that the way we had built the runway restricted us. We couldn't extend it any more than we had without going across Route 981, which would have meant a major change in the location of the highway.

So, we had the engineers design the runway that we now have, the long runway called "523." We needed it if we wanted to be a commercial reliever airport. That meant that, under the definitions of the FAA, you had to have to have specific facilities that would accept large plans, or even if you wanted to apply for more money. So, with the funds that we had, and again, with the help of contributions from others, the authority authorized the engineers to design the location of a runway that would give us maximum prevailing-wind coverage. We got that done with the help of Mr. Mellon and others in Pennsylvania. Mr. Mellon even had Bughman get estimates of what it would cost to move Rt. 981 or tunnel it underneath the runway!

So now we're on land acquisition Project Number Two. By this time, instead of fifty percent grant money from the federal government for land acquisition and navigation easements, federal funding had risen to the point where it was on the basis of ninety percent and ten percent. That meant we had to come up with only ten percent of the cost. It also meant another master plan!

We got what we needed, plus we had some money left to use as seed money. Then the authority made another basic decision. We talked about all these farms that we'd have to condemn. We decided to take whole farms rather than pieces of them. If we could touch a piece of land, and if we could justify it, we'd condemn the whole farm. I forget how many farms we condemned, but we had forty-seven separate condemnations of land in that area, small parts of farms, and so forth. We litigated only eight cases. We settled all the rest, which was an economic feat, although sometimes we got criticized for paying too much. But we used our old theory of thinking ahead of what it's going to cost us ten, fifteen years from now.

Eventually, we had more than 1,000 acres. We didn't

need that much, but airport dreams aren't built on short runways. We dreamed of one day having a 10,000-foot runway. FAA wouldn't quite let us go full way.

We had a farm at the southwestern end of that runway that we wanted to acquire, because with that, we would have enough land to actually build a 10,000-foot runway without ever leaving our own land. They wouldn't consider that an eligible part of our land acquisition.

We had gone to the bond market to raise the money for the land acquisition project and the major runway project. We allocated so much of that to land acquisition to cover the ten-percent cost and whatever. This master plan came to fruition in that 1966-68 era. Those were the days of high interest, and our bond money was earning great interest. We built a new control tower out of our earnings on the bond issue, and we did it with own money.

By this time, Mr. Mellon had died, but his widow still remained very interested in the airport. Through her knowing Lenny Bughman, and flying in and out of the airport, she raised some questions about a control tower, and Lenny was interested in getting a control tower for the safety factor alone.

In those days, somebody had developed solid-state circuitry. They had put all the instrumentation in this mobile home. They slanted the roof, and it looked like an elongated, narrow control tower. Mrs. Mellon bought it for us.It cost twenty-five-thousand dollars. We didn't know where we were going to put it, and the engineers said that it would go very well on Mr. Ferrari's land at that end of the airport. They designed the ironwork, put it up, and lifted this mobile home, set it down, and we had our control tower. That was the first solid-state circuitry control tower in a mobile home anywhere in the eastern United States.

Our major runway got completed in the 1970s, without complication. We bought the land the FAA wouldn't allow us to buy. Today the runway is 7,000 feet. Its length and strength allows it to take a Boeing 727.

Once that runway was built, we knew we needed an approach landing system. We got funding for that. There was an outer marker, a middle marker, and an inner marker. Now we're modifying that and improving it, and we've just applied for and received a grant for an entirely new approach lighting system, which will be coming on stream a few years from now. [*Editor's note: Mr. McDonald's interview was conducted in 1999*].

We get a lot of questions like, "What are you doing, or why haven't you done it yet, or why haven't you gotten commercial service?"

Well, commercial service is a tough nut to crack. The airlines basically control it. We worked very hard in order to get commuter service, and we have had several.

In the early days, we had a commuter that came in but it failed, and then Neal Frey, who is the founder of Vee Neal Aviation, started his airline, and then they sold that out to an operation in Erie, and then they gave it up.

We continued to work with everybody that we could. US Air was really interested in coming in, primarily because one of the vice-presidents of US Air was a gentleman by the name of Bruce Jenkins who was born and raised in Bradenville. We became good friends with him. With Bruce's help, and the help of many others, the Chamber of Commerce, Kennametal, Latrobe Steel, local industry, the county commissioners banded together with Larry Larese's county planning group. Bruce helped us get US Air Express, now owned by Mesa Airlines.

"Use it, or lose it," was their attitude.

That still is the expression today. The service has grown from three round trips a day to six or seven. Each time they close the Parkway from Pittsburgh, it gives a boost to the commuter service. Do we want more than that?

Yes!

The airport during the Gene Lakin's tenure has blossomed. Arnold Palmer, grants from the state, the help of our state legislators, Jess Stairs, Joe Petrarca and Senator Alan Kukovich, have advanced our cause. Other legislators have been very helpful, even though the airport may be on the other end of the county, out of their districts.

Our present US Congressman, John Murtha, never loses a beat. He learned the congressional ropes from the knee of the master, John Dent. John Murtha has helped us get grants for our master projects. Our air shows wouldn't be what they are without his influence with the military and their jet performance teams.

For the future, I see the possibility of the runway being extended at least another 1,500 feet to 8,500 feet. It's 100-feet wide now, so I don't see any widening being required. It's what's required for commercial traffic, and the air freight carriers like United Parcel Service. Do I see it going to 10,000 feet? Yes, if we become a major commercial hub, and I don't think we'll do that. We'll continue to be an airport like we are now, a regional airport, one that serves a region and feeds to the major hubs. I think within five to ten years we will see a change, but I think it will come sooner.

In The News: 1919-2001

Local Pop Calls
(Mt. Pleasant Journal,
October 9, 1919)

A low-flying aeroplane passed over the East End northbound Friday afternoon. It landed in a field on the Isaac Horner farm east of town and was joined there soon after by a second flyer, both pilots having been compelled to come down from the clouds for more gasoline.

The machines quickly drew a crowd of hundreds of people. Mr, Horner wanted to take a fly and would have gone along to the Somerset county fair, but the operator couldn't promise that he'd get back by Sunday and "Uncle Isaac" would run no chance of missing church.

Air Exhibition at Latrobe
(Latrobe Bulletin,
October 19, 1919).

At 11:40 a.m., a Curtiss Jenny, en route from Berlin, Somerset County, landed at the newly named Saint Vincent Aviation Field. The plane made a "splendid landing" on the field, and the two occupants, Jack Webster and R.R. Deckert, went to the Archabbey where they enjoyed lunch. After lunch, the aviators returned to the plane where 1,000 people had gathered to see the "workings" of the plane. The plane was owned by W. L. Kreps of Youngstown, Ohio, and was one of two he owned and used for aerial exhibitions. After lunch, the fliers took off, did several stunts over the field, and made their way to East Liberty in Pittsburgh.

Latrobe Aircraft Company Sponsors Exhibition
(Latrobe Bulletin, August, 1920)

The Latrobe Aircraft Company on Depot Street, Latrobe, sponsored flights for the locals. The planes landed and took off on a plot of land on Latrobe's South Side, in the neighborhood of No. 1 School House..

Lieutenant Jack Grow
(Latrobe Bulletin, Tuesday, July 27 and August 14, 1920)

Lieutenant Jack Grow, a former government flying instructor, who was at this time an employee of the Irwin Aircraft Corporation, brought his Curtiss Jenny to Latrobe and gave fifteen minute flights to interested townsfolk. V. J. Rogers, of Weldon Street and a friend of the pilot, was the first passenger. Grow hoped to take his aircraft to Idlewild Park on August 26th, the day of the Latrobe Community Picnic, where he planned to sell flights to the picnickers. Plans for the even were formulated by M. W. Saxman, Jim Hughes, W.S. Jones, John Stader, Clark Dalton, Ralph Anderson, Ed Yealy, Fred Underwood, H.E.Frampton, Joe Harkness,, Roy Eiseman and Ralph Conrad.

Daring Stunts Done By Local Pilot
(Scottdale Independent Observer, Thursday, September 2, 1920)

Piloted by Lieutenant Torrence Overholt of this place, and witnessed by hundreds of people thronged on the grounds above the hangar at East Home Place, the new Curtiss airplane of the Scottdale Aerial Club made its trial flight over the town at five o'clock Sunday afternoon. Spectators began to gather on the hills around North Chestnut Street and on the lawns of homes near there about 3 o'clock, but owing to some engine trouble the flight was delayed several hours. Finally, when the plane began gradually to rise into the air a cheer from the enthusiastic crowd of men, women and children, rent the air. It was with a feeling of awe, and one big thrill that they watched for the first time a Scottdale plane, driven by a daring young Scottdale aviator, do a series of stunts, the tail spin, falling leaf, loop the loops, etc., above town at a height of several thousand feet.

On the first flight, the plane carried only Mr. Overholt. The second ascent, about a half hour later, Earl Loucks, of Hawkeye, made the flight with him, and on the last successful trip into the clouds, Frank Kenney, of this place, was the thrilled passenger.

The first young lady passenger to make the flight was Miss Florence Copley, of this place. At probably one of the greatest heights by which Lieutenant Overholt has so far taken passengers, Miss Copley experienced the thrill of looping the loop five times. She can be commended on the so-called nerve which she possesses.

Flights will be made by Lieutenant Overholt during the three days of the Fireman's Fair at Loucks park, beginning today, and if all goes well the plane will be seen soaring in the clouds again.

Old Quiet Observer Comes to Town

(Scottdale Independent Observer.
Thursday, September 2, 1920)

An old quiet observer comes to town and arrives just in time to attend the first evening of the Scottdale Fireman's Social Outing being held at Loucks Park. . . .

"Howdy, Joe, howdy. . . .I allows to Mandy that I would like to see one of them aryplanes or just about bust, and she said, 'Get out o'hare quick and take no chances!' "What's that?"

"That? Why that is just the aeroplane warming up for the grip around town. Get your glasses wiped off, Q.O."

Pulling out his red bandanna kerchief, Q.O. gets busy just as the plane comes low across Loucks Park.

"By cracky, she's bigger'n a big eagle, haint't she now? My what a fuss! Sounds like the battle of Gettysburg all over again, except it's much worse. There she goes, up, up, up! Now what's wrong! She's fallin', by Jiminy, she's fallin'! No she ain't nuther. She's going up again. Didja see that? She turned clear over, and no buddy fell out. By gumps. I wish Mandy could have seen this! There she comes again. Now she is coming down! Look out! Well, what do you know about that? Fell over four times and then lit right out again. Well, that is some bird!"

Carl Strickler and Jerry Elder take an ax to Raymond's rebuilt Canuck Jenny after they crashed the plane on Christner's field in Scottdale, Pensylvania. *(Courtesy of Anna Mary Topper).*

Two Boys Injured in Aeroplane Wreck

(Scottdale Independent Observer,
Thursday, May 21, 1925).

Tuesday evening Carl Strickler and Raymond Elder were flying over Scottdale in the aeroplane that they had recently built when the control refused to work and the boys were forced to land in the Christner field west of town. Strickler was piloting the machine and was about 100- feet in the air when the control refused to work. He circled over Scottdale and managed to keep just above the trees until he reached the Christner field. Here he made a drop of thirty-five feet, the front of the plane burying itself in the soft mud. Neither Strickler nor Elder were seriously injured. Strickler was in the rear seat and when the plane struck the ground was thrown about ten-feet clear and with the exception of a few bruises was all right yesterday. Elder, who was in the front seat, was struck with the gasoline tank and was injured about the head. He was taken to the home of this parents, Mr. and Mrs. Jerry Elder near Scottdale, and Doctor Arthur Waide was called to attend him. For a short time he was unconscious and, while he was stiff and sore yesterday, he seemed to have had a loss of memory from the accident, arguing with Strickler and members of the family that the plane had not been wrecked.

Yesterday morning, Jerry Elder, father of the injured boy, with Strickler, went to the Christner field and dismantled the plane, hauling it in.

It was miraculous that neither of the young men in the plane were killed. [*Editor's note: Ray Elder rescued the engine and stored it in the family sheep shed. More than three decades later John Trunk, Lloyd Santmyer and George Markley retrieved the OX5 engine and brought it back to Latrobe as a trophy for the OX5 Club. Then, it was placed on display at the Greater Pittsburgh Airport. In 1973, Johnny Evans brought it back to Latrobe where the OX5 Club was founded. It was sent back to Pittsburgh in the late 1980s for repair and then placed on display at the Pittsburgh International Airport. The motor was returned to the Arnold Palmer Regional Airport in 2001, where it will remain on display for renewable ten-year periods*].

LONGVIEW FLYING FIELD

Eight Miles East Of Greensburg

Each Sunday afternoon at 3:30 and 6:30 o'clock there will be an exhibition in flying.

Passenger Flights $5.00 A Trip

"King" Joe Le Boeuf, a former lieutenant with the British Royal Flying Corps will leap from the wings of the plane and make a drop in a parachute and many other stunts. Something different every Sunday.

(Courtesy of Scottdale Independent Observer).

King Joe Le Boeuf At Flying Field
(Scottdale Independent Observer, July 30, 1925).

On Sunday, August 2, at Longview Flying Field, exhibitions if flying will be given. Joe Le Boeuf, a former lieutenant with the British Royal Flying Corps, will leap from the wings of a plane and make a drop to earth in a parachute. Le Boeuf will also do other stunts. His machine will be piloted by E. C. "Pop" Cleveland, of Mayer Field, Bridgeville, who taught Eric Nelson, one of the World's Flyers.

New Parachute Artist Engaged Longview Field
(Scottdale Independent Observer, May 21, 1926)

According to Charlie Carroll, of this place, one of the owners of the Longview Flying Field, announces that Joseph Crane, of Detroit, pictured in Sunday newspaper sections as the only living man to drop from an airplane in a parachute, is to give such an exhibition at the Lincoln Highway field east of Greensburg this Sunday afternoon at 3:30 without fail.

Crane, who is an ex-army parachute jumper, drops the dizzy height of 2250 feet before opening his parachute. He is not the "King Joe" scheduled for the opening of the base ball season here and who failed to appear, but an entirely different personage.

This daredevil of the air who has had all kinds of offers to do movie stunts, but prefers to be a "lone lance" has performed on flying fields and at special occasions all over the United States. A syndicated press has sent out a full page of illustrations to chains of newspapers for magazine

Joe Crane, barnstorming parachutist of the 1920s and 1930s at J.D. Hill Airport. He was the founder of the National Parachute Jumpers-Riggers Association, which later became the Parachute Club of America, which evolved into the United States Parachute Association.

(Courtesy of Anna Mary Topper).

sections, in which it tells of Crane's unique exploits and experiences with the public. A record breaking crowd is expected at the Flying Field Sunday afternoon.

Drops 1400 Feet of Sure Death, Parachute Opens

(*Scottdale Independent Observer.* June 21, 1926)

"Why not?" was the calm interrogation of Joe Crane, 23-year-old parachute wonder, lying on a cot in the Latrobe hospital, after his parachute failed to open for 1400 feet and finally at the last 100 feet opened and cheated death of another victim, at the Longview Flying Field at 6:45 last evening, when asked if he "ever expected to do stunt work again."

Charlie Carroll, manager and one of the owners of the Longview Flying Field . . . had a thrill all of his own last evening when in the presence of thousands of Memorial Day

spectators his stunt artist, Joe Crane, launched himself from the airplane piloted by Bob Clohecy . . . and at the expected point when the parachute should have opened and brought his performer gracefully to the ground it failed to function and he with a few others of the great assemblage, realized that there was an apparent death scheduled in a few minutes.

"Charlie," in talking over the telephone this a.m. from the flying field said that "when the parachute finally did open at 100 feet from the ground, and he found Crane a very much alive man, he had that grand and glorious feeling as expressed by the cartoon." The injured man was immediately rushed to the Latrobe hospital where it was found that is sole injuries consisted of a cut above the eye and two stove ankles, swollen, but not broken.

Mr. Crane was scheduled to appear in Michigan next Sunday, and this engagement only will be broken as a result of the accident as he expects to continue to do his sensational parachute jumping at Longview as soon as he can again navigate on his injured ankles.

First Annual Air Races To Be Staged Saturday

(*Scottdale Independent Observer.* Tuesday, October 5, 1926).

The First Annual Air Races at the Longview Flying Field and possibly the first similar event conducted in Western Pennsylvania will take place at the Longview Flying Field this Saturday afternoon beginning at one o'clock.

Real air races with twenty different planes participating, in an aerial triangular course marked off by miniature balloons similar to that floating at the North Side Service Station, will give Westmoreland County a new thrill that will put auto racing into the shade.

The course will be fifteen miles and the planes will fly close to the ground in order to get the atmospheric conditions conducive to speed. As a preliminary to the new speed event, it is possible that the airmen, driving the twenty or more planes will fly over Greensburg and adjacent territory to the flying field.

Planes from Hagerstown, Maryland, Altoona, Bridgeville, Aspinwall, Punxsutawny, Brownsville, Beaver and

This is a piece of the PARACHUTE used by JOE CRANE MAY 31, 1926

(Courtesy of Clyde Hauger, Jr.).

Air Races

20 AIRPLANES PARTICIPATING 20

FIRST ANNUAL AIR RACES AT

LONGVIEW FLYING FIELD

Eight miles East of Greensburg, on the Lincoln Highway

TOMORROW

Starting at 1 P. M.

3 AIR RACES---25, 50 and 100 Miles Triangular Course, Marked by Miniature Balloons

DEAD STICK LANDINGS

(Planes shut off engines from 1,000 feet and glide to given point. Nearest landing plane to receive prize.)

PLANES PARTICIPATING are from Hagerstown, Md.; Altoona, Bridgeville, Aspinwall, Brownsville, Punxsutawney and Beaver.

BOXING BOUTS
Orchestra, Vocal Numbers and Other Attractions
REFRESHMENTS ON GROUND

LONGVIEW FLYING FIELD

(Courtesy of Scottdale Independent Observer).

other points will be present and compete for the trophies.

The "dead-stick landing," a new aerial contest will also be staged. This event includes planes soaring to an altitude of 1,000 feet and stopping the engine and gliding to the ground where a special spot is marked out and the plane coming nearest to this goal wins the prize.

Saturday afternoon will be a gala day at the popular Flying Field, eight miles east of Greensburg, on the Lincoln Highway, when an admission fee of fifty cents will be charged for adults and twenty-five cents for children. Parking space is free.

Boxing bouts, vocal numbers by Waide Weaver of Scottdale, orchestra, parachute dropping, etc., will add to the attraction at which fully 10,000 people are expected.

A banquet will be tendered the

flyers at the Mountain View hotel Friday evening, the day before the aerial races, at which time the kings of the air will be given due homage. Many of the men participating are army fliers. Several pursuit planes will be present from Washington.

Fourth Accident Results in Death of Girl

(Scottdale Independent Observer, Tuesday, March 15, 1927).

The series of mishaps which have followed the aeronautic experiences of local civilian aviator Carl Strickler has ended in the death Saturday afternoon of Miss Pauline Reynolds, a twenty-one-year-old daughter of Mr. and Mrs. B.E. Reynolds of Market Street, while Strickler has again escaped with slight injuries.

Carl Strickler, licensed aviator of the Longview Flying Field, who lives at Hawkeye and has had varied experiences in the building and flying of airplanes in this neighborhood, had just reconstructed a new airplane and prior to the fatality had been giving lessons in flying to Rayburn Jordon, a brother-in-law of Miss Reynolds.

Part of Saturday morning was devoted to flying with Jordon. At 11:30, Strickler had as his passenger, Pete Lutman, of this place, and the plane apparently was in good condition.

The first trip after lunch was at 1:45.

Mr. and Mrs. Rayburn Jordon, Mrs. Jordon's brother, B.E. Reynolds, Jr., Pauline and Strickler, were grouped about the plane when the question came up as to who would be the first passenger in the afternoon. Mrs. Jordon had intended going up, but conceded to her sister, Pauline. The plane arose to an altitude of possibly 700 feet, and was up about three minutes when the pilot started to make his landing.

The aviator suddenly found his control out of commission. Miss Reynolds sat in the front cockpit with a hand on each side of the plane. Strickler asked her if she was afraid and she replied, "No."

The plane then went into a nose-dive, landing in a pit-hole close to the Elder farm. The shock threw Strickler a considerable distance of the machine, but Miss Reynolds is believed to have caught one foot in the bottom of the plane and, when it hit, was held in the cockpit.

Miss Reynolds was rushed to the office of Dr. W.H. Fetter, and then to the Memorial Hospital in Mr. Jordon's car, and did not die until reaching that institution, contrary to reports that she had died en route. Her neck was broken, skull fractured, arm broken, and suffered many contusions to the body

This photo of Lindbergh at Bettis Field was found in the collection belonging to Clyde Hauger, Jr., and was taken either by his father or Lloyd Santmyer.

(Courtesy of Clyde Hauger, Jr.).

When the few spectators had covered the intervening mile to the scene of the accident, they found Strickler some distance from the plane, staggering about in a dazed manner, while Miss Reynolds was crumpled up in the wrecked plane.

Flying Field Is Proving Popular With Motorists
(*Scottdale Independent Observer*, May 31, 1927).

The Longview Flying Field is now going full tilt on the Lincoln Highway east of Greensburg, with three airplanes in daily use and parachute-drop exhibitions by a former army expert.

Motorists from all parts of the United States are daily visitors at the Longview Flying Field, and much attention is being attracted to Westmoreland County through motorists who witness the modern, aviation-field activities, hundreds of passing tourists becoming air passengers.

Not only is the Longview Flying Field under ownership and management of a Scottdale man, but local boys, qualified aviators, are pilots of the three airplanes that skim along the huge field and soar aloft with passengers from time to time. Charles Carroll, owner; Raymond Elder and Carl Strickler are the regular pilots, and with the latest safety passenger planes and perfect landing field there is practically no danger to the many passengers who enjoy the latest thrill of a "trip to the clouds."

Longview Boys to Fly to Reception of Colonel Lindbergh
(*Scottdale Independent Observer*, August 2, 1927)

Four airplanes from Longview Flying Field under the leadership of Charles Carroll, owner and manager, will fly in formation over Greensburg and this vicinity enroute to Bettis Flying Field, McKeesport, this Wednesday morning, leaving Longview at 11 o'clock, to participate in the reception to Colonel Charles Lindbergh, Wednesday afternoon and Thursday. Those piloting the planes will be: Charles Carroll, civilian; Lieutenant Robert Clohecy, ex-army; Raymond Elder, civilian; Carl Strickler, civilian.

Each plane will have one or two passengers, not definitely decided upon at this time. The pilots will be photographed with other flying men and Colonel Lindbergh.

The air hero will land at Bettis Field at two o'clock Wednesday afternoon. His plane will be roped off with 400 policemen to keep the crowds back. He will then be rushed to Pittsburg by automobile and take part in the program as outlined for Wednesday and Thursday morning in the Pittsburgh papers.

The parachute men, Joe Crane and Mickey DeBurger, of Longview, were both in the Independent Observer office today at noon and explained that they had been called upon to fill a rather distinct place at the big reception to Lindbergh.

Crane has been asked to jump directly after the arrival of Colonel Lindbergh and just after his departure Thursday morning to help hold the crowd to the Bettis Field and avoid a jam of humanity and automobiles. De Burger will also make jumps during the two days.

Will Scottdale be Selected as Site for Airport
(*Scottdale Independent Observer*, Tuesday, August 30, 1927)

Since Scottdale men, C.B. Carroll and others, have been the pioneers in aeronautics in Westmoreland County, and J.D. Hill, a Scottdale boy, is expected to hop off any minute for a non-stop air trip to Rome, under international limelight for publicity, the question arises as to whether Scottdale will not eventually be chosen as an airport and landing field location.

The proximity of Scottdale to the Yough river and the fact that air men prefer to follow river courses, with the additional inducement that an airplane can cut off a considerable distance in this route by flying over Scottdale, still keeping the trail of the Yough, is very much in favor of Scottdale as an airport. The increased interest in airports in the United States arouses the question.

More than 1,000 airports and intermediate fields will dot the United States from coast to coast and from Canada to the Gulf of Mexico by the end of 1927, according to the aeronautics branch of the Department of Commerce.

A survey just completed by the Air Information Division shows 865 permanent fields now in use, with 187 cities definitely considering the establishment of municipal airports. Of present fields, 207 are municipally owned. Chambers of Commerce, business clubs and other civic organizations are cooperating in the effort to build up a complete airway and airport system, it is stated.

Many authorities are urging permanent construction for airport buildings and especially for fields and runways. Planes for projected passenger lines, such as the Ford line between Chicago and Los Angeles, and seven or eight ton freight planes will require rigid landing surfaces. Turf and cinders, it is claimed, will not stand the wear.

Captain Donald E. Keyhoe, flying aide to Colonel Lindbergh on his tour of 75cities, recommends runways of concrete 100 feet wide, and Commander Richard E. Byrd, U.S.N., suggests that entire fields be of concrete, particularly since this permits landing and taking off regardless of weather conditions

[Editor's note: Unfortunately for Scottdale, airfields situated near major roads and railroad junctions would prove to be more viable sites for airports, a fact which Charlie Carroll realized when he founded his airfield in Latrobe].

Not the Log of the "Sally Ann" But A Modern Airplane

(*Scottdale Independent Observer*, September 13, 1927)

Raymond Elder, of this place, pilot at Longview Flying Field made a quick trip to Beaver Falls the other day with parachute jumper Lewis DeBurgeer keeping "log" of the trip.

When it comes to speed note the difference in chronicling is a matter of minutes, not hours:

5:14 p.m.-Left Longview, flying wide.

5:24 p.m.-Greensburg, open climb, 2,000 feet.

5:25 p.m.-Throttle motor, getting bumps, bad fog ahead.

5:27 p.m.-Making straight to McKeesport.

5:28 p.m.-Jeannette on the right, Grapeville under us.

5:31 p.m.-Adamsburg, all is well. Motor cut down.

5:32 p.m.-Can see tank at Irwin.

5:34 p.m.-Irwin to our right about one and a half miles; a little cross wind from the right. Wind going south.

5:35 p.m.-River to our left about two miles, must be Youghiogheny.

5:39 p.m.-Flying at 2,500 feet. Can't see a damned thing. Fog.

5:42 p.m.-Trafford, Pitcairn, Wilmerding, off to the NW.

5:46 p.m.-Bettis Field. Air time, 32 minutes.

5:57 p.m.-Can see Bridgeville smoke.

5:59 p.m.-Strong headwind,

ground speed only 55 miles per hour.

6:03 p.m.-Headwind getting stronger.

6:14 p.m.- 100 out.

6:19 Can see Big Beaver River.

6:20 Over field, Beaver Falls, can see car in field.

6:31 Landed

6:32 Stopped motor

6:40 Start motor and at 6:43 take off and start on homeward air trip.

The plane arrived back at Longview at exactly 7:45 the same evening

This will give prospective air flyers an idea of the overhead perspective. No traffic cops. No bad roads. No nothin' except watch the ground doesn't fly up and hit you.

Local Aviators to Hop Off From Denver, Colorado

(*Scottdale Independent Observer*, September 13, 1927)

Raymond Elder and Carl Strickler, of this place, pilots of the Longview Flying Field, will "hop off" from Denver, Colorado, next Tuesday, September 29, in an Eagle Rock, single-motor airplane for an overland trip to Longview on the Lincoln Highway, east of Greensburg.

The plane will be a brand new one made by the Alexander-Eagle Rock Company of the Biplane type. It will be the first demonstrator plane whereby Longview Flying Field, under the direction of Charles Carroll, will become an airplane sales center, Mr. Carroll being agent for the Eagle Rock biplane.

Elder and Strickler will alternate flying the new plane to Pennsylvania from Colorado. The machine has the new principle of high lift wings and a pay load capacity of 800 pounds, with two passenger and pilot accommodations.

En route the plane will stop at Kansas City, Missouri; Indiana, Indiana; Columbus and Zanesville, Ohio and Bettis Field, McKeesport, from where the arrival will be telephoned to Longview....

Carroll, Elder, Strickler Will Try for Aerial Honors
(Scottdale Independent Observer, Friday, October 7, 1927)

Three Scottdale air pilots are entered in the air races scheduled for Longview Flying Field tomorrow and Sunday. The events begin at one o'clock each afternoon preceded by an air parade over surrounding towns.

With such competitors as Captain E.W. Day, with a Woodson plane, of Pittsburg; Lieutenant Jack Morris, Eaglerock plane, of Pittsburgh; Jack Smith, Ryan plane, of Bridgeville; George Autland, Eaglerock plane, of Pittsburgh; Lieutenant F. J. Ambrose, Eaglerock plane, of Pittsburg; Colonel D. I. Lamb, Waco 10 plane, of Bettis Field, McKeesport; Lieutenant W.H. Emory, Travel Air plane, of Bradford, three local pilots, Charlie Carroll, Raymond Elder and Carl Strickler will compete for air honors.

The events at Longview will be unique in the annals of racing in this section and the prospects are that the automobile and horse racing crowds will be but a drop in the bucked as compared to that at Longview. The air courses will be so laid out that there will be no danger to the many thousands of spectators expected present for the second annual event, much larger than the one of last summer at Longview Flying Field . . . .

There will also be parachute jumping, wing walking on airplanes aloft, and other air stunts to keep up a continual thrill for the two afternoons.

Saturday evening will witness a banquet of aviators in the new Masonic Building at Latrobe at 8 o'clock.

Of special interest will be the presence of many other planes, two Ryans, and an M-1 monoplane, the twin to that of Lindbergh's in appearance, from the Bridgeville field.

The fact that a Scottdale man is owner of the Longview Field, Charles B. Carroll, should draw a large crowd from Scottdale, to say nothing of the three pilots who will participate.

Wrecked Plane Not C.B. Carroll's As First Reported
(Scottdale Independent Observer, December 2, 1927).

The report published in Connellsville newspapers yesterday that an airplane belonging to Charles Carroll of Longview Flying Field had been wrecked by the high wind of Wednesday evening is all in error. The plane wrecked was that of an unknown pilot flying East. Carroll's planes are all intact in hangars today.

Wednesday, Mr. Carroll and Carl Strickler flew to Uniontown to take pictures of the wrecked plane in the mountains in which two army pilots were killed this week. En route at Matthew's Field, along the Connellsville-Uniontown road, the Longview crew came across the strange aviator and his plane and advised him to put his plane under cover or "tack" it down with ropes to avoid the heavy wind then blowing up.

The strange flyer evidently failed to take heed for his plane was practically demolished by the strong gale which caused havoc in many sections of Westmoreland and Fayette counties.

List 5 Flying Fields in County
(Scottdale Independent Observer, March 21, 1928)

By June 1, five aviation fields will be operating regularly within Westmoreland county, according to a recent survey made by Russ Brinkley, of the Longview Flying Field. These fields are located at Latrobe, Scottdale, Donegal, Mt. Pleasant, and New Kensington.

There are 12 pilots in the county and 15 planes. Of the planes, only four are new production jobs. Six are rebuilt army planes, and the others specially built machines.

On January 1, there were 32 students listed at the different fields, and two of these were women. Two Westmoreland men were listed as professional parachute jumpers and three others were listed as capable mechanics.

At present there is not an aeronautical organization active, although a chapter of the National Aeronautical Association is being organized in Latrobe.

To Drop Watch From Clouds
(Greensburg Morning Review, Monday, May 28, 1928)

Did you ever see it raining watches?

Well, if you happen to be along Main Street between Otterman and Second streets about 12:45 tomorrow afternoon, you may find a watch

dropping at your feet and better still, it will be yours.

DeMay Brothers, Pennsylvania Avenue jewelers, have planned this unique demonstration. Clyde Hauger, aviator from Longview Flying Field, flying at a height of 1,000 feet, will drop a Bruner Master Built Wrist Watch to the street below.

The purpose of this demonstration is to prove that this make of watch will withstand any severe shock and that it will keep time as accurately after, as it did before the drop.

The finder of the watch will turn it over to Mayor Yont for examination, and after it has been on display in DeMay Brothers store for two weeks, can have either this watch or a duplicate selected from the regular stock free of charge.

Many Planes Coming Saturday
*(Latrobe Bulletin,
May 31, 1928.
By columnist Russ Brinkley)*

All the way from Seward to Bettis Field, the Los Angeles was escorted by two Latrobe Flyers.

Carl Strickler and Russ Brinkley, flying in one of the planes from the local field, flew to Seward to meet the big dirigible and blazed the way for it over Derry and Latrobe. They did stunts all the way.

At Bettis Field they made arrangements for several additional planes to come to Latrobe, Saturday and Sunday, for the big air meet which is to mark the dedication of the field as Hill Airport.

George F. Bischop, a former friend of the late J.D. Hill, is flying here from Forth Worth, Texas for the dedication.

An American Eagle plane, from Sharon, carrying Robert Mason and his mechanic J. P. Reed, already has arrived at the field.

The big monoplane which passed over Latrobe yesterday morning is to be used to carry mail between Cleveland and Pittsburgh. It was en route from the Fairchild factory, at New York, and was flown by Pilot Dewey Noyes, with Clifford Ball as a passenger. It is to be here for the air meet, Saturday and Sunday.

Due to the fact that so many inquiries have been received from outsiders concerning the aviators' banquet to be held at the Mountain View Hotel, it has been decided to make it a public affair instead of for fliers and their friends only. Preparations are being made to care

I NEVER GET ENOUGH

STUNT FLYERS

(Greensburg Morning Review, Monday, May 28, 1928)

for 200 guests and the following program has been adopted: Master of Ceremonies: Clifford L. Ball, air-mail contractor from Bettis Field, McKeesport. Toastmaster: Russ Brinkley, field manager of Hill Airport. Feature Address: Wesley L. Smith, manager of the National Air Transport, eastern division, air-mail service, who will speak on Commercial Aviation. Responses from the following: C.P. Mayer, of Bridgeville, the first man to operate and airport in this part of the state; Frank Hill, brother of the late pilot in whose name the field is being dedicated; C.B. Carroll, operator of Hill Airport; Carl G. Strickler, chief pilot and instructor of the Carroll School of Aviation.

Hill Airport Dedication Ceremony is Appropriate: Huge Crowd at Field Yesterday

(*Latrobe Bulletin*, June 4, 1928).

It is now the Hill Airport, it's complete title being The Hill Airport at Saint Vincent College, Latrobe, Pa . . . The Rt. Rev. Aurelius Stehle, O.S.B., Archabbot of Saint Vincent College . . . made a brief address, his presence marking the new relationship between Saint Vincent College and the airport, with the field having been adopted by the college as a training place for students in aviation.

Between 10,000 and 15,000 persons jammed one side of the field and threatened to cover the entire field, but for the vigilance of the police and attendants. Over 500 cars were parked in the field and fully 1,000 more were in the strings which stretched along both sides of the neighboring roads.

The race for the Curtiss production planes was the first event on the program. Of the ten entries listed, only four passed the inspection of government officials, and these planes were piloted by C.B. Carroll, Carl Strickler, Ray Elder and J.D. Jones.

J.D. Jones, of Lancaster, Pa., nosed out Carroll by barely fifty yards, after five laps of strenuous competition. Elder took the lead in the first lap with Strickler a close second, Jones following in third place and Carroll trailing the field because of a bad start. In the second lap the positions began to change. Jones went into the lead by passing both Strickler and Elder. But Jones failed to hold his lead as Carroll came up fast in the second lap and took the lead as the third lap ended. Jones regained the lead in the fourth lap and held it to the end. Elder finished in third place, with Strickler trailing the field.

The high-speed race with only three entries did not offer much competition and Dewey Noyes, Pittsburgh-Cleveland air-mail pilot, roared down the home stretch two-thirds of a lap ahead of Carl Strickler. Noyes piloted a six-cylinder Pitcairn plane, which averaged around 110 mph for the fifty-mile race. Strickler piloted an Eaglerock to second place two laps ahead of an American Eagle, piloted by Ray Elder.

Between races the big wing-walking stunt was offered to the public. A new dare-devil was introduced in the person of Russell J. Brinkley.

"Daredevil" Brown of Kansas City made two successful drops in his parachute during the afternoon. On both occasions he landed on the field to the north of Hill Airport, as a jumper can no longer land on the airport itself, by a ruling of the Department of Commerce.

Plane Makes Forced Landing On A Hillside
(Latrobe Bulletin,
June 4, 1928)

The only near-accident to occur in connection with the big doings at the Hill Airport, occurred Saturday afternoon, when a big, four-passenger monoplane, owned by Clifford Ball was forced down, by lack of fuel, on a hillside of the Ferguson farm, near the airport.

None of the four occupants of the plane suffered injuries of any kind, and the plane itself escaped damage, except for a fitting on the fuselage, which was broken, and which put the big ship out of commission for the time being. One of the department of commerce officials present at the field, said he had never witnessed a better landing, under the circumstances. Dewey Noyes was at the controls and was responsible for the avoidance of an accident in the high wind which prevailed.

The failure of the fuel supply was due to the fact that only one of the two feed pipes had been opened at the time, and the motor suddenly stopped. The other supply line was turned on at once, but not in time to get back into flight.

Mr. Ball was one of the passengers. A niece of the late J.D. Hill was another, and Carl Strickler's father was the third.

Many Planes Coming Here For Meet
(Greensburg Morning Review,
June 21, 1928).

From acceptances being received for Greensburg's great air meet, to be held on the George R. McNary farm, on the New Alexandria road, next Tuesday afternoon, this city and surrounding country will have an opportunity to witness a larger variety of planes than has seldom been gathered together in one spot.

It is apparent that Western Pennsylvania and other pilots have been pleased to receive the invitations from Greensburg and while all acceptances have not yet been received, enough are on hand to assure a most successful afternoon.

Charles L. Semans, of Uniontown, will be present with his Ryan monoplane, which is a duplication of that of Col. Lindbergh's, now in the Smithsonian Institution in Washington. Capt. Voss, of Rogers Field, will bring his new Curtiss "Hawk", an official army pursuit plane and one which has been seldom seen except at government fields. Two army training planes will accompany Capt. Voss.

Clifford Ball, of Bettis Field, will drive over here in his five passenger Fairchild cabin monoplane, which is the largest airplane ever to visit Greensburg.

William A. Gardner, of the Gardner Sign Co., Pittsburgh, will bring his new Eagle Rock and his new Lincoln-Paige while C. W. Beckman, of Mount Oliver, will also be present in his plane.

Additional invitations are being issued and an attempt is being made to have one of the Ford all metal planes used by the Stout representatives present while Assistant Attorney General

Thomas G. Taylor, of this city, member of the Pennsylvania Aeronautical Commission, is hopeful that a

squadron of United States army fliers from Middletown will be present. Other members of the commission are also expected that day.

Charles Stanko, of the William Penn Flying Field, at New Alexandria, will also be present.

Weather Not Expected to Delay Meet
(Greensburg Morning Review,
June 26, 1928).

The whine and drone of airplanes during this afternoon forecast somewhat the activity which may be Greensburg's within a very few months if contemplated plans arising from the special air demonstration scheduled here today materialize.

While threatening weather prevailed during most of the morning hours, the disturbance was purely local, according to weather observers and every indication was given that the meet will go along during the day as scheduled.

The landing field on the George R. McNary farm, on the New Alexandria Road, was in good condition this morning, despite the inclement weather. The field was being marked early this afternoon for the landing of the planes and also for the parking of automobiles.

But the western Pennsylvania airmen who will put on the aerial demonstration this afternoon are Thomas J. Hilliard, president of the Waverly Oil Works of Pittsburgh; William M. Gardner, president of the Gardner Sign Company of Pittsburgh who will have two planes in the meet; C. W. Beckman, president of the Beckman Chevrolet company of Pittsburgh; Charles L.. Secans of Burgess field, Uniontown; Captain Thomas S. Voss, executive officer of the 324th Observation squadron, Rogers field, Pittsburgh, who has entered three planes;

Clifford A. Ball, air mail contractor of Bettis field, McKeesport; D. Barr Peat, manager of Bettis field, McKeesport; Kenneth "Curley" Lovejoy, air mail pilot of Bettis field, McKeesport; John P. Morris, Morris Flying School, Rogers field, Aspinwall; Col. Harry C. Fray, Jr., Pittsburgh; C. P. Mayer of Mayer Aircraft corporation, Bridgeville; Walter Stewart, Freeport; James D. Condon, Pittsburgh; and C. B. Carroll of the Hill airport, who will enter two planes.

Air Pilot Knocked Out by Bolt
(*Latrobe Bulletin*, July 5, 1928)

Robert Parnell, chief pilot at the Hill Airport was unconscious for half an hour after being stunned by a lightning bolt at the flying field yesterday. He was standing by his plane, preparing to place a rubber blanket over the motor to protect it from the downpour.

A bolt of lightning crashed to the earth a short distance from him, and the pilot was so seriously stunned, that he was rendered unconscious, and did not recover his senses for half and hour. A physician was summoned and Mr. Parnell was revived. He had sufficiently recovered in the afternoon that he was able to pilot his plane.

With Blacksnake as Passenger, Legless Flyer Flies East
(*Latrobe Bulletin,* July 12, 1928)

With a blacksnake mascot as the only other passenger, "Dinger" Daugherty, New Martinsville, West Virginia flyer, hopped off from the Hill Airport this morning at 9:50 o'clock, with Roosevelt Field, New York, as his destination. His snake-ship was presented to the aviator by an admirer and has been fed on bread and milk for the past few days.

It was a perfect day for the flight, with a bright sun shining, which forecast good visibility in the mountains, which always present a menace, even to the best flyers.

Quite a large number of spectators, mostly Shriners, en route to Idlewild Park, who had parked their machines along the road to witness the hop-off, saw the "West Virginian" speed across the field, her engine roaring, then rise gently into the air.

It was not long till they had lost sight of the plane as it disappeared into the bright sun to the east.

Departing from a field named in honor of a flyer [*J.D. Hill*] who had given his life in an attempt to link the United States and Rome by air, Daugherty was bound on a journey with a similar end in view. Once at New York, he intends to seek backing for a projected trans-Atlantic flight to Italy.

Failing in securing the necessary support, he will attempt a non-stop flight to Mexico, similar to the one in which Emilio Carranza, Mexican ace, lost his life, several days ago.

Daugherty left the airport unaccompanied, although he was to be joined later at McConnellsburg, by Pilot Carl Strickler, in his speedier plane. A little more than a half hour after Daugherty took off, Pilot Strickler was tuning up his plane, making ready to start.

Makes Forced Landing When Engine Halts Fine Handling Saves Plane and Passenger
(*Latrobe Bulletin,* July 28, 1928)

When his plane started earthward like a plummet, causing a woman passenger to faint, C.B. Carroll, of the Hill Airport, remained cool and came down safely in a forced landing, near the Guidas greenhouse at Manito, about 4:15 yesterday afternoon. A wing was smashed and a tire blown out.

Mr. Carroll had taken off from the airport, with a woman from Greensburg as a passenger in the cockpit, a short time before.

As the plane soared over Manito, about a mile from the flying field, the engine suddenly stopped and the plane started earthward.

Overcome with fright, the woman lost consciousness, as the pilot worked coolly to coax the motor back into operation.

He gained control when but a short distance from the ground, and then brought the plane down in a field, a short distance from the greenhouse. The woman was revived a short time later.

Local Flyer Is Killed in Plane Crash
(Hagerstown *Herald-Mail*, November 28/29, 1928)

Carl G. Strickler, 26, test pilot for the Kreider-Reisner Aircraft Company, this city, was fatally injured Wednesday afternoon when the new Challenger plane he was piloting crashed at Laurel Ridge, PA, near Laughlintown, during a blinding storm of snow and sleet . . . .

George W. West, a road worker, witnessed the accident, and was the first to reach the spot. The injured

men were taken to Ligonier, Strickler dying soon after his arrival. The accident, which marked the first fatal crash since the organization of the Kreider-Reisner Company, was caused by conditions over which man has no control. Running into the snow storm, Strickler, a thoroughly competent flyer, and familiar with the locality, found his knowledge of the ground useless in the face of the blinding sleet. Because of the weight of the snow and ice, it was impossible to gain altitude, and he was forced to fly low.

With more than 2,000 flying hours to his credit, Strickler was regarded as one of the most experienced and careful flyers in this section of the country. He was highly esteemed both as a flyer and an instructor, and had many friends in Hagerstown.

Mrs. John Shannon Davenport, local newspaper woman, is probably alive today because she was unable to accept Strickler's invitation to accompany the party on the trip to Chicago. She was on the field, shortly before the planes hopped off and just before Strickler and his mechanic stepped into the plane he again invited her to "hop in."

"I'd love to take a long trip like that it would be thrilling," she replied, "but I've made no arrangements to get away."

"Well, you're missing a wonderful trip," answered Strickler, and a few minutes later the big ship was roaring down the field.

Another reporter, in conversation with Strickler several hours before the fatal accident, was told by the pilot that "stunting" was dangerous for students. "I have a lot of trouble with them," he said. "After they have completed their course, they become careless and begin stunting."

Strickler then told of the new plane he was flying to Chicago.

"We're going to make only one stop and that will be in Cleveland," he said.

"Well, so long and good luck," were the parting words of the reporter.

"Thanks," replied the pilot.

Former Hill Airport Pilot Dies in Crash Member of "Tombstone" Club

(*Greensburg Morning Review*, Friday, November 30, 1928)

Funeral services for Lewis N. "Mickey" DeBurger, former pilot at the Hill Airport, east of Greensburg, are to be held at his home at Indianapolis at 9 o'clock this morning. DeBurger crashed in a tri-motored monoplane in the fog at Spokane Washington last Friday with another pilot. He was employed as mechanician on the plane and had given up parachute work five months ago at Detroit, where he was employed . . . .

The "Tombstone Club," of which DeBurger was a member, will be in charge of the funeral headed by Joe Crane, president, former parachute jumper at the Hill Airport. Originally there were 13 members of the club, with DeBurger the first to die. Steve Burdreaux, Joe Crane, Walter Lens, Russ Brinkley, former manager of the Hill Airport and now associate editor of Air Transportation, a weekly trade journal of commercial aviation published in New York, were the Pennsylvania Members.

Among the organizations DeBurger belonged to are the National Aeronautic Association, the American Society for the Promotion of Aviation, Fraternal Aeronautique Internationale, and the Commercial Aviation League.

Brinkley, Crane and others will fly to Indianapolis by way of the ne

Stout Airline to the attend the funeral. Immediately afterward, Brinkley will go to Scottdale to attend the funeral of Carl Strickler on Sunday.

Funeral of Aviator is Largest Ever Conducted Here

(*Scottdale Independent Observer*, Tuesday, December 4, 1928)

The funeral of Carl Gault Strickler, whose death occurred while flying over the Allegheny mountains, enroute to Bettis Field, on the first hop to the Chicago Aircraft Show, Wednesday afternoon, was the largest ever held in this vicinity.

Fully 2,000 persons were at the church and cemetery combined, when the body of Pilot Strickler, aviation instructor of the Kreider-Reisner Aircraft Corporation, was laid in its final resting place Sunday afternoon.

With hundreds of automobiles at the two places, the casket borne my former co-pilots [*Charlie Carroll, Raymond Elder, Dick Copeland, Clyde Goerring, Clyde Hauger and Jack Frost,* **Ed.**] dressed in snow white jumpers [*Strickler's signature attire,* **Ed.**] and aviation headgear and accoutrements; an airplane circling overhead dropping flowers in the pathway, a most impressive and never-to-be-forgotten scene was enacted. When the casket was opened for the benefit of friends at the Old Tyrone Presbyterian church, it was estimated that fully 1800 persons looked for the last time upon the face of the young pioneer of aviation so well-known here . . . . The high regard with which the young man was held by his late associates at Hagerstown, Maryland, the hundreds from Latrobe and vicinity of the Hill Airport, where he was formerly a pilot, was attested by the grief in evidence on every hand.

L.C. "Red" Gahagan, of Hagerstown, Maryland, piloted the flower plane, one of Charles Carroll's.

Giant Tri-Motor Ford Plane to Haul Local Passengers
(Scottdale Independent Observer, June 28, 1929)

Hetzel-Young Company . . . is one of the Ford dealers in this district sponsoring a 25-mile airplane trip for only five dollars per person, in the new giant Ford Tri-motor Allmetal monoplane . . . .

The huge, fourteen passenger plane is one of a fleet that is carrying passengers all over the United States. This modern airliner, soon to be placed in a trans-continental daily schedule, carrying passengers the same as the railroads, will very likely be piloted over Scottdale, Monday and Tuesday.

Mail Dispatch from Airport At Greensburg
(Greensburg Daily Tribune, September 17, 1929).

With final preparations completed for the official opening of the Greensburg-Pittsburgh Airport, one of the outstanding events of the two day opening is the memorial cachet of air mail which will be picked up here Friday and Saturday afternoons by one of the Clifford Ball airplanes. Government permission, it was learned today, has already been grant-ed, due to the efforts of Congressman Adam M. Wyant, whose dedicatory address on Friday will place Greensburg on the highroads of the air.

Ever since the opening of airports has become an almost daily occurrence, stamp collectors all over the United States have bent their efforts to obtain initial stamp cancellations in the respective cities which are fortunate enough to boast of airports. This has resulted in thousands of letters being sent to cities prior to airport openings with the request that these letters be mailed in the first cachet of air mail to leave that city.

In the present instance, according to H. Raymond Mason, Secretary., more than two thousand letters are now reposing in the offices of the Chamber of Commerce here waiting to be picked up on Friday and Saturday by the mail plane.

For some time Congressman Wyant has been in touch with the Post Office Department at Washington making plans for the Greensburg cachet of air mail. This week W. Irving Clover, second assistant postmaster general, granted permission. As a result the mail plane will pick up the cachet both on Friday and Saturday afternoons, fly it to Pittsburgh where the stamps will be canceled, after which the letters will be sent to their respective destinations. The Chamber of Commerce has already prepared an inscription which will be stamped on every air mail letter leaving here at this time.

For the benefit of those desiring to send air mail during the official grand opening of the new airport, a booth will be erected at the airport by the Clifford Ball Co., of Pittsburgh. Air mail enthusiasts may then purchase stamps and envelopes at the field where they will be mailed. Up until Friday envelopes and stamps may be obtained at the Chamber of Commerce and mailed there.

Plans Completed For Airport Dedication.
(Greensburg Daily Tribune, September 19, 1929).

Greensburg has gone aeronautical! There is no half way point of acceptance about the fact, either. For the past week the scene atop the Dry Ridge port has been a veritable beehive of industry. Contractors have been putting finishing touches to the buildings, engineers have removed every possible flying obstruction from the field, graders have put the actual landing area in apple pie order and tomorrow when this city opens wide its doors to travelers of the air, it has the privilege of boasting of the largest airport in Pennsylvania.

Maurice R. Scharff, president of the Main Aeronautics Co., has spared no single effort in making the official grand opening one that will rank with the finest in the State, and when the drone of motors overhead, from plane arriving from the four points of the compass, announce the much-heralded event, there will be no doubt in the minds of air-enthused citizens that at last Greensburg has become a station on the highroads of the world.

The 712-acre tract of land, which is now the Pittsburgh-Greensburg Airport, represents more than a haven for fliers in the Alleghenies; it is highly indicative of the tremendous strides cities and communities are taking throughout the length and breadth of the land in order that they may have a place in the far-flung, world wide transportation system that is rapidly reaching out to the four corners of the earth. It is not surprising that this city joins hands with others in the most remarkable movement of the age.

An aerial parade over the city in which government and commercial planes will participate will open the

festivities and at 2:30 p.m. Congressman Adam M. Wyant will officially open the new port with a dedicatory address. Following his address the planes of the Army, Navy, and Marine Corps will take to the air for twenty minutes of formation flying.

As soon as Uncle Sam's planes are set down, a special aerobatic flight by Freddie Lund will keep the air enthusiasts busy determining whether he is flying on his back or whether he is just completing one of his outside loops, which is considered one of the most difficult feats to perform in the air. Lund will fly a taper wing Waco, powered by a 300 H. P. Wright Whirlwind motor. Lou Strickler, from Latrobe, and the world's acknowledged youngest licensed pilot, will then be introduced and will in all probability fly one of the ships. Miss Helen Cox, the airport's licensed aviatrix and hostess of the Dry Ridge Tea Room, will be introduced at the same time and will give an exhibition flight in the Avro-Avian plane. Miss Cox comes to Greensburg from Hagerstown, where she was affiliated with the Kreider-Reisner division of the Fairchild Aviation Corp.

One of the most thrilling and educational events of the day will take place when the government planes take off for their warfare maneuvers, lasting for half an hour. If the exhibition which the Army, Navy and Marine pilots at the Cleveland Air Races is any indication, spectators at the grand opening will be treated to more than one thrill as the planes zoom overhead, go into a series of loops and power dives.

More than 20,000 people are expected to witness the program today and accommodations have been made to take care of 25,000 automobiles. Captain D. E. Miller of Troop B State Highway Patrol and

Captain T. J. McLaughlin of Troop A State Police have detailed as many of their men as possible to the airport today. Yesterday afternoon most of the automobiles used the road leading from the Greensburg-Mt. Pleasant road and traffic was very heavy. There are at least two entrances from the Lincoln Highway and many motorists will find it more convenient to take their routes today.

After the aerial parade at 1 o'clock, exhibition flights will be made by the three Navy planes and a number of commercial planes will be made. Then Freddie Lund, world famous stunter, will take to the air and perform his hair-raising aerobatic maneuvers. He will fly a Whirlwind Waco and will do his noted outside loop stunt. Camille Vinet and Robert Clohecy will also entertain with some daring performances.

All afternoon the radio broadcasting amplification systems will be in operation so that announcements can be heard in all parts of the field. During dull moments the crowd will be entertained by music over the amplification system. Livingston Clewell, noted aviation writer, is presiding at the "mike" effectively. He describes everything to the crowd.

In the final event, Joe Crane, winner of the national parachute contest at the National Air Races, will again make a parachute jump. Yesterday he left the plane at 1,000 feet and made a beautiful landing on the field.

A banquet for aviation officials and guests of the Main Aeronautics company will be held at the Penn Albert hotel tonight and will bring to a close the two-day dedication program of the local airport. Congressman S. S. Kendall, of the Somerset-Fayette district, is a guest of Congressman Adam M. Wyant today and he has consented to speak at the banquet tonight.

Many Types of Planes Expected During Day

(*Greensburg Morning Review*, September 20, 1929).

Nature is showering her blessing on Greensburg today for the dedication ceremonies of the Pittsburgh-Greensburg airport of the Main Aeronautics company on Dry Ridge. The program began shortly after 2 o'clock with an aerial parade over the city.

The day is ideal for flying. The sun is shining in all his majesty, the sky is clear, and the wind is moderate. At an elevation of 1,000 feet the countryside is slightly hazy but this condition is expected to disappear in the early afternoon.

At dawn activity began at the airport to have everything in tiptop shape for the formal opening. At 11 o'clock final arrangements had been completed to start the program on scheduled time. More than 300 peo-

ple were present, and cars were coming into the field in droves at 11 o'clock. Approximately 20,000 people are expected to be present at the field this afternoon. Arrangements have been made to provide parking space for more than 25,000 automobiles.

The first plane to arrive at the airport was a Challenger from Dayton, Pa., piloted by M. L. Cunningham and George Reesen. Shortly after *Miss Tydol* piloted by Charles Carroll, of Hill airport, arrived. After 11 o'clock a number of planes were sighted over Greensburg making for the port. Three navy planes, two army planes and a number of visiting planes are expected to arrive early this afternoon.

The first plane to take to the air this morning was a Ryan monoplane piloted by R. J. Clohecy, test pilot of the Fairchild Aircraft Company of Hagerstown, Maryland. Maurice R. Scharff, president of the Aeronautics company, and Helen Cox, Greensburg aviatrix, were the passengers. Shortly after Clohecy took to the air again, with Lieutenant A. J. Oldham and Sergeant Roy Hoover, of the Highway Patrol, and James T. Herald, of the Tribune Review Publishing company, as passengers. On the third trip into the air C. A. Brown, president of the Cornstalk Products Company of New York City, his son, W. K. Brown, and daughter Patty Jane were the passengers. This younger Brown made a film of Greensburg and vicinity while on the trip.

Maurice R. Scharff, president of the Main Aeronautics company, has charge of the field. He is being assisted by Russell J. Brinkley. Richard O. Fay and Corporal F. I. Hildebrand have charge of operations on the flying field. Livingston G. Clewell will have charge of the press and photographers.

Looking Towards Tomorrow . . . . .

On Friday and Saturday, September 20th and 21st, Greensburg will dedicate The Pittsburgh-Greensburg Airport. With tomorrow's travel and commerce following the air routes the forward looking community prepares...with an airport.

We join in congratulating Greensburg.

It was announced this morning that the blimp from the Goodyear Company in Akron would not arrive in Greensburg until 10:30 o'clock tomorrow morning. The wind conditions at Akron prevented the takeoff today as scheduled. The ground crew will arrive in Greensburg shortly after 8 o'clock in the morning.

An aerobatic flight by Freddie Lund is planned as a special feature of the afternoon. He will do an outside loop, one of the most difficult air stunts to perform successfully. Other stunt fliers present will be Hodge Smith, Camille Vinet, Robert Dake, Robert Clohecy.

City Thrives On Aviation As Topic
(*Greensburg Daily Tribune*, Monday, September 23, 1929)

Greensburg people and those of neighboring communities awakened today to find themselves literally "air-minded" and everywhere on went the topic solely was aviation.

The coming of the Main Aeronautics company to this city with its huge port on Dry Ridge, the dedication exercises of Friday and Saturday and the throng which visited the port Sunday when the field

1930. Bob Clohecy (left), the "Flying Coalminer" and chief pilot at Pittsburgh-Greensburg Airport. *Courtesy of Clyde Hauger, Jr.).*

1932. Pittsburgh-Greensburg airport manager Norman "Happy" O'Bryan poses for the camera with a Main Aviation Ryan monoplane. Dick Copeland rummages in the cabin. *(Courtesy of Frank Fox).*

September 21, 1929, Pittsburgh-Greensburg Airport Alfred K. Young poses in the cockpit of his OX5 Challenger after having delivered a shipment of Atwater Kent radios. This was the first air freight delivery for the new airport. *(Courtesy of Frank Fox).*

Lloyd Santmyer (left) and Norman "Happy" O'Bryan with a Ryan monoplane, Pittsburgh-Greensburg Airport. Ryan attracted Sunday crowds by playing the popular song "Deep Purple" over a loudspeaker attached to his plane. *Courtesy of Clyde Hauger, Jr.).*

George Dickson (left), and a youthful Frank Fox with an Aeronca OX5, Pittsburgh-Greensburg Airport. *(Courtesy of Frank Fox).*

officially opened for business has brought out whatever lax interest might have been manifest to this newest of industries.

The trimotored Ford plane of the Pennsylvania Airlines, Inc. was the first ship to land at the port this morning. It was en route from Pittsburgh to Connellsville and landed at 11:20 o'clock and resumed its journey at 11:40.

The airport today settled down to the ordinary routine of affairs although daily many will probably visit the field on the chance that a visiting ship might come in or one of the Main planes depart.

The dedication ceremonies closed in a blaze of glory at a banquet at the Penn Albert Hotel Saturday night. After two days filled with stunt flying and demonstrations by service fliers and commercial pilots, Sunday's flying was, of course, rather tame.

At 11:20 Saturday morning, the Atwater Kent plane of the Johnstown Automobile Company, piloted by Alfred K. Young, arrived at the Pittsburgh-Greensburg Airport with the first consignment of express to arrive at the airport for a local firm. The local shipment consisted of radios consigned to O.M. Deibler and Hochberg's, local dealers for Atwater Kent radios.

Pittsburgh-Greensburg Airport Notes

(Greensburg Daily Tribune, Greensburg Morning Review).

[Editor's note: The following "notes" have been selected to show the enthusiasm of Greensburgers concerning their new airport, and are limited to those which have some connection to the J.D. Hill Airport in Latrobe. The Pittsburgh-Greensburg Airport never fulfilled the hopes and expectations of the planners. "Airport Notes," later " Greensburg Airport Log," gradually faded from the local paper].

(September 25, 1929). Lou Strickler, Latrobe schoolboy pilot who makes his flying headquarters at the new airport, is entered in the Johnstown-Butler air race on Saturday. Strickler expects to fly a Command-Aire, the same plane he used during the airport dedication last week

(September 25, 1929). Livingstone "Pop" Clewell, of Kingston, who has been associated with the publicity department of the Main Aeronautics Company during the past two weeks, is to assist in the organization of the Westmoreland County Flying Club, which is to maintain headquarters at the new airport.

(September 25, 1929). Richard Coulter, III, son of Colonel Henry W. Coulter, is the first purchaser of a plane through the Main Aeronautics Company. Young Mr. Coulter bought a Waco and is at present in Troy, Ohio, to bring his plane home. The first plane owned by Mr. Coulter was a Travel Air.

(September 25, 1929). Archabbot Aurelius Stehle, O.S.B., and Father Victor, of Saint Vincent College, visited the airport yesterday and were quite enthusiastic over it. They conferred with Mr. Scharff and, later Archabbot Aurelius, Father Victor, J.J. Mahady, who handled the real estate transactions for the Main Aeronautics company, and Mr. Scharf, went to Saint Vincent to go over the grounds of that institution. It is likely that he and Mr. Scharf will work out some plan whereby the Main Aeronautics company and Saint Vincent College can cooperate in giving Saint Vincent students practical aviation training.

(September 26, 1929). Bob Clohecy *[Editor's note: the "Flying Coalminer," formerly of Uniontown*

and an instructor at the Carroll School of Aviation.], newly appointed chief pilot of the Pittsburgh-Greensburg Airport, arrived at the local field yesterday, one day ahead of schedule. He buckled down to work soon after his arrival. He made an air trip to Pittsburgh and upon his return made a general inspection of the Main Aeronautics company planes. In the afternoon, he flew with Ted Taney, of the Pittsburgh Airways Company, to Bettis Field in an Avian plane, and then flew the plane back to the local port.

(September 26, 1929). Clohecy intimated that Richard Copeland, son of Judge and Mrs. Charles D. Copeland, will be retained as a pilot by the Main Aeronautics Company. Much of Copeland's instruction in aviation was received from Clohecy and the chief pilot has great respect for Copeland'a ability to handle a plane. *[Editor's note: Copeland received instruction from Clohecy at Longview Flying Field/J.D. Hill Airport. Copeland, in turn, was the first instructor of Earl Metzler].*

(September 27, 1929). Pilot Bert Purnell, formerly connected with the J.D. Hill Airport, was a visitor to the field this morning. He recently opened an air mail route between Omaha and Wichita.

Ford Plane to be Here Sunday

(Greensburg Daily Tribune, Saturday Afternoon, September 23, 1929; September 25, 1929)

Residents of Greensburg and vicinity will have another opportunity to view the big tri-motored Ford plane of the Pennsylvania Airlines Inc., Sunday afternoon at the Pittsburgh-Greensburg airport.

Through the efforts of the Hoffer Motor Car company, arrangements were made to have the plane return

Al Litzenberger. *(Courtesy of Ken Scholter).*

here tomorrow afternoon. The plane was on hand for the opening of the local airport last Friday and Saturday, and also on Sunday. Hundreds of Greensburgers availed themselves of the opportunity to ride in the plane on those days. Many others were unable to take advantage of the opportunity which resulted in arrangements being made by the local company for the return of the Ford plane.

Al Litzenberger, an experienced Ford mail plane pilot, will be at the controls of the plane and it is possible that W.C. Smith, president of the Pennsylvania Airlines, Inc., may come to the local airport with the plane.

The plane will arrive at the local airport about noontime and will carry passengers throughout the entire afternoon

[Dr. W.C. Smith's 14-passenger Ford Tri-motor. Smith used the name "Pennsylvania Airlines" for promotional purposes only, and painted it on the side of the aircraft. Ken Scholter, who flew the plane with Litzenberger and sold tickets to passengers, relates that Clifford Ball bought the plane from Smith simply for the name. Ball would soon form a company called Pennsylvania Airlines]. *(Courtesy of Ken Scholter)*

Aviation in Latrobe
By Charles Carroll,
Proprietor, Hill Airport

(The Latrobe Amplifier,
Latrobe Chamber of Commerce
Newsletter,
May 15, 1930)

The J.D. Hill Airport is located just south of Latrobe on the Lincoln Highway, and has been operated for the past seven years under the same management. During that time, thousands of people have become air-minded by taking a ride in the air, and during that period there has not been the slightest injury to passengers or pilots.

The J.D. Hill Airport is the first landing field west of the Allegheny Mountains, the first airport east being at Gettysburg. These two airports are separated by seven mountains of the Allegheny chain, so this Latrobe Airport is really an important aid to aviation. This airport has been on the Department of Commerce Airway maps for the past five years, and has been used very advantageously by the Army and War Departments on several occasions. The Latrobe Airport is a good emergency field for gas, repairs and so forth.

The Latrobe Hill Airport in the future should play an important part in the development of aviation. It is in closer proximity to the main line of the Pennsylvania Railroad than any airport of any importance in the immediate district west of the Alleghenies, and it may sometime play an important part in combined rail and air transportation. The proposed change in the Lincoln Highway does not affect the airport at all, both the present and the new route touching the north and south ends of the field.

The Latrobe Hill Airport has been made a stop on the airway route of the Pittsburgh Airways, Incorporated, operating between P:ittsburgh, Philadelphia and New York daily. These planes will stop at the Hill Airport, eastward about 2:40 p.m.; westward, 1:25 p.m. Connections are made at Bettis Field, Pittsburgh, for Cleveland, Detroit and Chicago. Through reservations can be made at the airport. Fares are as follows: Pittsburgh to New York, One Way, $35.00. Round Trip $65.00. Pittsburgh to Philadelphia, One Way, $29.50. Round Trip $57.50 New York to Philadelphia, $7.50 Each passenger may carry thirty pounds of baggage free. Excess baggage up to ten pounds carried at fifty cents per pound. Anyone wishing to travel from Latrobe by air, just call the Hill Airport by phone, and they will make the necessary arrangements for you.

Latrobe is fortunate to have an air service of this type.

Elder Makes Quick
Flight to Cleveland

(Scottdale Independent Observer,
July 18, 1930).

Raymond Niles Elder, who is engaged at the Hill Airport with C.B. Carroll as instructor of students and carrying passengers made a successful plane trip to Cleveland Airport Wednesday, flying there in an Alexander Eagle Rock biplane in two hours and ten minutes. Mr. Elder was accompanied in his flight by two passengers, Clyde Hauger of Donegal and William Smith of Greensburg.

The trip to Cleveland was made to enable Mr. Hauger to make a quick delivery of an automobile. Two cars had to be in Donegal at a certain time and the father of Mr. Hauger left the night before to drive one of them. It took him eight hours to drive to Cleveland from Mount Pleasant. The plane had no compass, and Pilot Elder depended on his sense of direction in guiding him to the Ohio Municipal Airport.

Mr. Elder was attracted while at the airport to a group of bronze memorials in honor of flying martyrs and noticed a beautiful one bearing the portrait of James DeWitt Hill, a Scottdale man, who perished on the plane Old Glory in attempting to cross the Atlantic a few years ago. The memorial is located in the lobby of the passenger terminal at the Cleveland Municipal Airport.

The return trip was made successfully, Mr. Elder being accompanied back by Mr. Smith. Considering the type of plane used the time made is considered good.

Hill Airport Will
Signal the Weather

(Scottdale Independent Observer,
August 1, 1930).

C.B. Carroll, owner and operator of Hill Airport, announces that Hill Airport has been officially named one of the four weather stations in the mountainous section of Pennsylvania for the New York-Pittsburgh route of the Pittsburgh Airways line. The weather indicator for pilots has been put into operation. Everett, Stoyestown and McConnellsburg are the other weather stations that have been designated. All four of them are considered necessary to safe flying on the line because of quick weather changes in the mountains. The Hill Airport signal will inform pilots of weather conditions ahead, whether they are just coming out of the mountains to Pittsburgh or flying eastward.

The signal at Hill Airport consists of two pine boards, 20'x12"x1", painted white. When the boards are placed side by side at a distance of three feet apart, the signal to the pilot

is "Proceed, weather OK." If the boards are crossed in the form of an "X" the signal will be "Weather ahead dangerous, land." Daily weather reports will be sent to the Pittsburgh office of the line by Mr. Carroll and telephone communications with Pittsburgh will keep him posted on rapid changes in the weather, east and west. [*Editor's note: Pittsburgh Airways, Inc., was organized in 1929 by James G. Condon, a former navy flier, and Theodore Taney, a retired barnstormer. The company gained financial backing from Oliver M. Kaufmann, the department store owner. The line flew from Bettis Field twice-weekly, and was the first airline to span the Allegheny Mountains. Details of the company may be found in Trimble, 162 ff. and Smith and Harrington, 73ff*].

Second Parachute Comes in Handy

Latrobe Bulletin
(August 20, 1930).

The crowd gathered at the Hill Airport yesterday afternoon to witness the customary Sunday parachute jump by Otto Hoover got a thrill which was not in the program, due to the failure of a parachute to open. The fact that Hoover, in conformity with the law, was provided with two parachutes, saved his life. He had been taken to 2,000 feet by Charles B. Carroll, and the take-off from the plane had been quite uneventful, but almost immediately things began to happen for the jumper. He pulled out the ring of his chute, but it failed to unfurl. For 1,000 feet, Hoover, keeping his head though dropping like a plummet, manipulated with the chute, endeavoring to unfurl it, but it wouldn't open up.

Members of the crowd gasped with horror when they realized that his parachute failed to work. While

Veteran of twenty-one years of parachute jumps, Ott Hoover poses with two friends in 1949. Dorothy Kubish watched Hoover jump at Clyde Hauger and Lloyd Santmyer's Greensburg City Airport at Carbon. Paul Cunningham competed in q contest for free plane rides. Boys with the dirtiest faces won.
(Courtesy of Clyde Hauger, Jr.)

the jumper hurtled downward at an ever-increasing speed, the limp chute trailed behind.

After he had fallen 1,000 feet or more, he pulled the cord on the emergency chute. When he landed safely on the field, Hoover was amused at the anxiety that had been felt for his safety.

"I was safe enough," he explained. "I just delayed opening the second chute until I was sure that the first one wasn't going to work."

Had Lost Their Way in the Haze
(Latrobe Bulletin, August 23, 1930).

The sign on the roof of the freight station was the means by which two flyers, who were lost, located the Hill Airport and made a landing there yesterday afternoon.

One of the pilots was a young woman, Frances Harell, aged about twenty-two, and the other was Cy Younglove. Both are in the employ of the Curtiss Wright Flying Service, and both were operating Travel Air planes, equipped with Wright motors.

Miss Harell and Younglove had hopped off from the Cleveland Airport and were en route to Johnstown, following the William Penn Highway. Upon reaching the mountains, they were forced back because of poor visibility and low-lying clouds.

In the vicinity of New Alexandria, they lost their bearings, and flew around aimlessly for a time, in an attempt to find out where they were.

Flying low, they were able to read a sign, by which they learned that they were near a town called Latrobe. Once above Latrobe, they circled the town several times, and by reading

the sign on the freight station roof, learned the direction to the Hill Airport, and a short time later, landed there, coming to earth about 3:30 or 4:00 p.m.

Attaches at the local airfield said that the woman was an expert pilot as well as the man. Miss Harell landed first.

Both of the fliers expressed pleasure at finding an airport so close to the mountains, declaring that its situation made it especially serviceable to flyers.

After spending about a half hour at the field, the two pilots hopped off again. They intended to go to Bettis field, where they had friends.

Visiting Pilot Cracks Up His Machine
(Latrobe Bulletin, August 26, 1930)

A war-trained aviator cracked up a newly purchased plane, while attempting his first flight in four years at the Hill Airport yesterday.

Both he and C.B. Carroll, of the Hill Airport, who was a passenger with him at the time, escaped injury, when the plane failed to rise sufficiently on the take-off to escape crashing into a tree in the John Kerr orchard at the western corner of the field. The purchaser of the plane is from Connellsville.

Accompanied by several friends who had been invited to witness the flight, the Connellsville man arrived at the field about 7:15 o'clock to take his first ride in the Canuck which he had purchased at the Hill Airport for $900.

Even though it had been four years since he had last had charge of an airship, the new plane owner was confident that he had not forgotten how to handle one.

Declining the offer of a field attendant to take the plane up, with

him as a passenger, in order that he might familiarize himself with the ship before taking charge, he assumed the control at once. Mr. Carroll got in as a passenger.

When the motor was first started it was going at a speed of 1400 revolutions, which would have been sufficient to take it off the ground safely. The Connellsville man, however, reduced the speed to 100 revolutions. As the plane traveled across the field it failed to rise and was skimming but a short distance above the earth when it reached the orchard. It flew into a tree branch and was knocked to earth. The landing gear, one wheel and one wing were smashed.

Carroll's New Alex Airport Dedication October 18 and 19
(Scottdale Independent Observer, October 14, 1930).

Charles B. Carroll, of this place, announces that his New Alexandria airport, located on the William Penn Highway, a mile east of New Alexandria, will be dedicated with appropriate ceremonies next Saturday and Sunday, October 18 and 19. The program will consist of air races, aerial acrobatics, balloon ascension, parachute jumping contest, dead stick landing contest, balloon bursting contest and other aerial activities.

The dedication will take place at 2 o'clock on Saturday afternoon. Prominent speakers of Westmoreland County have been secured. Congressman Adam M. Wyant will get two Keystone bombing planes for exhibition. There will also be a high dive from a 115-foot ladder into a tank of water four and one-half feet deep.

Planes will be present from Pittsburgh, McKeesport, Bridgeville, Aspinwall, Ebensburg, Johnstown,

Altoona, Somerset, Vandergrift, Greensburg, Uniontown, and Donegal. In all, there will be about fifty planes in attendance.

A banquet will be held at New Alexandria on Saturday evening for the flyers. Among the well-known airmen to be present are Bob Dake, transcontinental pilot; Captain Jack Morris; Ted Taney, Sam Bigony, Lieutenant Finay, and others.

The American Legion Post of New Alexandria will have charge of the parking of cars.

....The new airport at New Alexandria is well adapted for a flying field, having a large acreage. There are eight approaches to the field and the shortest runway is 2,000 feet long.

Aviators Had Difficulty Finding Landing Field

(*Latrobe Bulletin*,
October 16, 1930).

Facing a serious situation caused by haze and the approach of dusk, two strange aviators heaved a sigh of relief when they sighted the Hill Airport last evening.

They were unfamiliar with this territory and with daylight fast fading after they had crossed the mountains on their way from New York to Columbus, the airmen feared that night would overtake them before they had located a landing place.

Because of the haze, they were flying so low, searching for a landing place, that residents of Youngstown could hear the shouts of the aviators as they flew over the town.

After their landing at the airport, it was learned that the airmen were A.C. Carl, of Shamokin, PA, and A.K. Owen, of New York, representatives of the New York Airways Company. Both admitted the situation had had them worried before they landed.

Owen, a big man, weighing about 220 pounds, seemed in quite a jolly mood after the anxiety had been removed from his mind.

"I knew there was an airport some place right on the other side of the mountains," he said with a grin, "and, mind you, that was a HAPPY thought!"

Carl and Owen spent last night at a local hotel, planning to take off again some time today.

Hill Airport Site is Sold

(*Latrobe Bulletin*,
April 28, 1931)

[*Editor's note: Apparently, the Bulletin was premature with its announcement. The deal never came off, though its imminence prompted Charlie Carroll to approach the Borough of Latrobe to assume responsibility for the airport, which would occur in 1935, when the Kerr family sold the land to the Borough*].

The tract of land upon which the Hill Airport, at the intersection of the Lincoln Highway and the Latrobe-Manito Road is located has been sold to the Howard Gasoline and Oil Company of Jeannette.

John Kerr, the former owner, has disposed of the entire tract, between sixty-five and seventy acres, to the Jeannette company, which is planning on improvements to the property.

Surveyors are at work on the field now.

C.B. Carroll, proprietor of Hill Airport, who leases the ground, said that officials of the company had told him that they intended to remove the "hump" on the field, which at present makes a larger runway impracticable.

With the "hump" removed, a runway of between 2,400 and 2,500 feet with the prevailing wind would be possible. This is almost 1,000 feet longer than the present runway.

The change in the course of the Lincoln Highway, which is to be made at the field, will necessitate a considerable switching around.

The position of the airplane hangar will have to be changed, while the service station now located there is to be abandoned for that use. It is planned to leave the building stand, with the prospects that it will be used as an office for the airport as the business expands. Michael Peretto, in charge of the airport at the present time, recently let the contract for the erection of a new service station.

He is now seriously considering, but has not definitely decided upon erecting two service stations, one on either side of the new Lincoln Highway at the field.

Using this plan, motorists, no matter in which direction they are traveling, would not be required to cross the highway to get to the service station.

Efforts are to be made, it is understood, to have the airport, in part at least, a Latrobe undertaking. Conferences are to be sought between Cyrus McHenry, secretary of the local Chamber of Commerce, C.B. Carroll, proprietor of the Hill Airport, and officials of the Howard Gasoline and Oil Company, to see if some plan can be worked out.

Noted Stunt Flier Arrives

(*Latrobe Bulletin*,
August 2, 1931)

Eddie Miller came to town yesterday, promising real thrills for everyone who goes to see him perform feats of daring in the air, at the Hill Airport next Sunday afternoon. His stock in trade is something different from the usual run.

Here are a few things he plans to do: hang by his knees from an inner tube suspended below a plane; pick up a handkerchief from the ground as the plane swoops low; hang by one hand from a plane; hang by one foot. He has a number of other stunts in his repertoire.

Charles Robinson, a companion, who was traveling with him, was killed while doing stunts at Peoria, Illinois, four weeks ago.

Parachute Jumper in the Hospital

(Latrobe Bulletin, (August 13, 1931)

Otto Hoover, aged thirty-seven, parachute jumper at Hill Airport, suffered fractures of both bones in his right leg above the ankle at New Alexandria last evening, in the first accident to befall him in more than 1,000 jumps. It was the second accident of occur to a parachute jumper in this vicinity, Joe Crane having had both legs broken when his chute failed to open until he was almost down, at the Hill Airport, five years ago.

Hoover, known as "Last Chance Otto Hoover," ascended in a plane piloted by Dave Patterson, to a distance of 2,200 feet.

His chute opened perfectly and, although a wind was causing his chute to drift, by skillful maneuvering, he seemed to be descending without any trouble.

When he came down in a field near the airport, the chute was still drifting and carried him sideways for a short distance. The tugging of the chute caused him to trip over a rut in the field in such a way that when he fell, his entire weight came down on his right foot, snapping both bones, one of which was protruding from the flesh.

Otto began his career as a parachute jumper in 1922. He is a resident of Uniontown.

Girl Parachute Jumper Coming

(Latrobe Bulletin. August 21, 1931)

Peggy Bramhall, aged nineteen years, the only girl parachute rigger licensed by the government will make a parachute jump at the Hill Airport next Wednesday evening, August 26th, according to an announcement made by Joe Crane.

Joe, a former Hill Airport parachute jumper, and now engaged in a similar capacity at Roosevelt field, N.Y., said that Peggy will accompany him and Mrs. Crane to the National Air Races, and that the party will stop over in Latrobe while en route there.

Miss Bramhall holds the record for women soloing in an airplane. She went aloft alone after three-hours-and-fifteen-minutes instruction. She now holds a private pilot's license. Hoover Sets Parachute Jump Record (Greensburg Morning Review. Monday, July 16, 1934). Two world records in the field of aeronautics were broken in Greensburg Sunday afternoon and early evening, before a crowd of 5,000 persons. Otto Hoover, parachute jumper, made nineteen consecutive jumps between daylight between daylight and 6:30 p.m. breaking the former world record by two jumps. At the same time a Greensburg pilot, Hap O'Bryan, broke the world record for "hauling" a parachute jumper nineteen consecutive times in one day.

The sworn statements of the two, properly attested by a number of witnesses, will be forwarded to the National Aeronautical Association. Since it requires from thirty to thirty-five minutes to properly pack a chute, it is estimated that the actual take-off flight to an altitude of from 1,200 to 1,500 feet and the actual jump itself,

consumed but from five to 10 additional minutes, for Hoover averaged one drop every forty minutes.

He made the first jump in the early morning at 4:30 and his jump from the plane, about 6:30 in the evening.

After Hoover's last jump, which he confined to nineteen because an old leg injury began to trouble him, O'Bryan took Lawrence Bennett, of Pittsburgh, aloft for his first jump. Bennett made a fine jump at 2,000 feet. Don Marshall also jumped during the day. Hoover suffered a fractured leg last year and is wearing a silver plate. It was this injury and the fear of suffering another fracture that made him content to call it a day.

A girl parachute jumper failed to make any jumps during the day.

Flyer Races with Storm, Beats It

(Latrobe Bulletin, July 2, 1932)

Racing with a storm which swept over this section last night, an aviator reached the Hill Airport as sufficient time ahead of the threatened downpour, to make a successful landing.

Before descending here, dark storm clouds had thwarted his efforts to land at two other airports those at McKeesport [Bettis Field] and New Alexandria.

With a fast diminishing supply of gasoline, the aviator headed to the Hill Airport, finally being a victor in his thrilling race with the elements.

He said his name was Williams, and that although he lived in the Pittsburgh district, he was engaged as a pilot at the New Alexandria field. He had hopped off from New Alexandria for McKeesport, after a day's work of hauling passengers was ending.

He found the storm over the

McKeesport field, making it so dark that he could not see clearly enough to make a safe landing.

He returned to New Alexandria and found that the storm had arrived there ahead of him. He then came to Hill Airport. He left his plane there and went to Pittsburgh by train.

Good Will Flyer to Visit Hill Airport
(*Latrobe Bulletin,*
August 6, 1932)

Local business men are making preparations to extend a warm greeting to Alger Graham, war veteran and explorer, when his biplane lands at the Hill Airport . . . .

[Graham and Bob Nesbit] are making an air tour of the principal cities and towns of this section, for the manufacturers of a widely distributed brand of coffee. They will come here from Pittsburgh.

Graham has made a commendable record as an airman and adventurer, and is well-known throughout the country. He is a veteran of the Royal Flying Corps, and saw action on the Western Front during the World War. He is a member of the famous explorers club, having qualified for membership by his distinguished work with the Wilkins Arctic expedition in 1927. He was one of the pilots who took the 6,200 mile National Air Tour, recently completed. In addition to his exploration of the Arctic ice fields with Captain Wilkins, he has made three round trips from Fairbanks, Alaska, to Point Barrow.

The key to Latrobe, made of stainless steel, a hometown product, will be presented to the airman.

New Plane at Hill Airport
(*Latrobe Bulletin,* June 5, 1933)

Piloted by C.B. Carroll, a new Waco plane, just out of the factory, was landed at the Hill Airport, about 2:30 o'clock, yesterday afternoon. It is to be used at the field, and was brought here from Troy, Ohio. There are now four planes, in all, at the local field.

Wind Bowls Over a Parachute Jumper
(*Latrobe Bulletin,*
May 20, 1935).

Patrick "Smiles" O'Timmins, one-armed, one-eyed, and one-legged parachute jumper, is a patient in Latrobe Hospital, suffering from injuries sustained in a jump at the Hill Airport about 7:30 o'clock, last evening.

O'Timmins had almost completed what appeared destined to be a perfect jump when the accident occurred. His chute opened perfectly when he leaped from a plane above the field and he floated gently to earth, near the hangar at the old highway end of the field.
Just as O'Timmins' foot landed on the ground, a gust of wind struck the chute, which pulled him off balance and dragged him for ten feet or more on the ground.

The jumper landed with such force that his back was severely jarred.

O'Timmins was unconscious when field attendants and spectators ran to where he was lying.

C.B. Carroll and others worked with him for ten minutes before the jumper was revived.

He complained of pains in his leg and back. As O'Timmins was being lifted into an automobile to be taken to the hospital he lapsed into unconsciousness again.

The jump during which O'Timmins was injured was his second of the day. In the afternoon he had completed a jump without mishap.

O'Timmins today complained of a numbness in his remaining leg. There are times when he is unable to move it at all. He is not believed to have been seriously injured, however, and is expected to retain the full use of his leg.

O'Timmins was formerly an automobile racer and lost his leg, arm and eye when his automobile was wrecked in a race in the state of Indiana a number of years ago.

Human Bat at Hill Airport
(*Latrobe Bulletin,* October[?], 1935).

Chillie Thomas, the "Human Bat of Pittsburgh" will be a featured attraction at the Hill Airport tomorrow afternoon between the hours of five and six o'clock. Mr. Thomas does a glide from a height of 8,000 feet by means of wing-like contraptions fastened under his arms and between his legs. This daring feat has been performed several times in the west, but this is the first time for it in Pennsylvania.

WPA Proposes to Improve Airport
(*Latrobe Bulletin,*
November 20, 1935).

C.B. Carroll, of the Hill Airport, yesterday received word from Harrisburg that all the WPA airport projects proposed had been approved by the President. The message came from Frank K. McKlveen, airport construction inspector, who received his information from Major J.P. Morris, of Pittsburgh. The approval means that $205,000 will be available for the Hill Airport as soon as the property is in Latrobe's name. The project would give employment to 250 men for many weeks.

It is understood that James Kerr, who owns the land on which the airport is situated, is willing to rent it to the borough and the entire cost to the borough would be very small.

Should the project go through, it would mean that the Latrobe Airport would have facilities for accommodating any air vehicle that might wish to land there. Latrobe is now on the Pennsylvania-Central Air Lines and the Transcontinental and Western Air Lines routes, but few planes can stop here because of lack of accommodations.

The improvements would include new runways, the longest to be 3,300 feet, and a new hangar, 80x100 feet. New lighting would be installed, also, and the airport would be put on a par with other municipal airports throughout the country.

The project was definitely proposed by Major Morris, in charge of WPA aviation developments in the State and McKlveen, of the State Bureau of Aeronautics, at a conference with members of a special committee from the Latrobe Borough Council, held on November 1st. It is understood that the committee is in favor of the project providing sponsors can be secured.

The sponsors would be called upon to supply the material, equipment and superintendence, and the WPA would provide the labor. It is estimated that their share would not exceed $2,000.

At the time of the meeting, Mr. Kerr was not willing to state whether or not he and his brother and sister would be willing to lease the property, but since then it is understood their consent can be gained.

According to Mr. McKlveen, the deadline for taking up the proposition is within the next two weeks.

. . . A New Airport
(*Latrobe Bulletin*, November 30, 1935).

A $205,000 government project for the Hill Airport came a step nearer realization last night when preliminary arrangements for the borough to take over the fifty-five acre flying field were completed at a special meeting of the Latrobe Council.

James and John Kerr (who were present at the meeting last night) and their sister Mary who own the land on which the airport is situated have agreed to deed over the property to Latrobe Borough for a nominal consideration of one dollar, so that the improvements can be accomplished.

Government funds are available for only projects on ground that is municipally or publicly owned.

Council last night decided on taking over the airport. The Kerrs have already signed the deed turning over the property and agreement with the borough.

The papers are now in the hands of Burgess John L. Ackerman, who with the president of council and secretary of council must sign them before they are forwarded to Washington.

Burgess Ackerman is studying the matter before affixing his signature.

The government would provide $132,500 to pay the wages of 280 men for a ten month period, and $58,500 for supplies for hangar, concrete block, etc.

The sponsor, in this case the borough, would be required to provide $5,000 for lighting and engineering, and $9,000 for supervision, foreman, etc. This could be reduced in case the borough could secure some of the materials, etc., which would be credited to their account.

Under the terms of the agreement, the borough would have the privilege of purchasing the airport at the end of fifteen years for $22,500.

Ed Musick Killed. Charley Carroll Was Once Co-Pilot.
(*Scottdale Independent Observer*, January 21, 1938).

Charles B. Carroll, manager of the Latrobe Airport, formerly of Scottdale, was once a copilot with Captain Edwin C. Musick, whose Pan-American Airways Flying boat, the Samoan Clipper, burned and sank with his crew of six near Pago Pago, Tutila Island, American Samoa, on January 11. Mr. Carroll has in his possession a card of the American Airways, Inc., which showed Musick as pilot and Carroll copilot on the plane NC454-E on January 24, 1931, flying between Miami, Key West, and Havana.

A Huge Plane Makes and Easy Landing at the Local Airport
(*Latrobe Bulletin*, April 4, 1938)

A Lockheed all-aluminum two-motored plane valued at $65,000, which landed here on Saturday, took off from the Latrobe Airport yesterday morning with Mrs. Charles Carroll, wife of the local airport manager, and Cecil Smith, of Blairsville, a student pilot, as passengers.

The plane was en route to New York where it is to be loaded aboard a boat to be taken to Czechoslovakia, having been purchased by the government of that country. It is an exact replica of the plane in which Amelia Earhart was lost during an ocean flight.

While the Lockheed was attempting to fly over the mountains

east of here late Saturday, ice started to form on the wings and the pilot turned back as a precautionary measure.

He had intended to come down on the Pittsburgh-Greensburg Airport, but considered the field too small for a good landing, and came down here at the local field instead.

The plane landed at the Latrobe Airport between 5:30 and 6:00 p.m. The pilot, who was the only passenger, spent Saturday night at a local hotel. He offered to take Mrs. Carroll and Mr. Smith to New York for the trip. The plane began its eastward journey from California.

Mr. Smith arrived back here from New York on an early morning train. He said that it had taken the plane only an hour and thirty-five minutes to reach the southern end of Long Island. Mrs. Carroll remained in New York for a visit with relatives.

Scottdale to Cooperate in Air Mail Week

(Scottdale Independent Observer, April 15, 1938)

Plans for Scottdale's participation in National Air Mail week during May 15 to 21 are already under way. Scottdale is one of the boroughs to be offered the privilege of having a special stamp authorized by the Post Office Department for that occasion. The stamp will contain a local picture of a historical nature.

The National Air Mail Week Committee arranged a poster contest for the boys and girls in the high schools and institutions have similar courses of study, according to an announcement by Joseph F. Gallagher, Postmaster of Philadelphia and chairman of the central committee directing Air Mail Week preparation in this state.

The contest will close the last day of this month and a few days there-

May 1938. Charlie Carroll stands on the wing of Merle Moltrup's aircraft as A.R. Parrish of the Postal Department hands up mail bags. Merle flew a load of mail from Bettis Field to Allegheny County Airport, while Charlie flew one from Latrobe. Both pilots were participating in National Air Mail Week. *(Courtesy Lloyd Santmyer).*

after the winner in each of the forty eight states will be announced.

Carroll School of Aviation

(Latrobe Bulletin Editorial,
[?], 1940).

The Carroll School of Aviation at Latrobe Airport offers complete ground and flying instruction for men and women. It also offers charter flying services, sales and service for Piper Cub planes. Saint Vincent College is co-operating with them by taking care of ground work, traffic rules and regulations, meteorology and navigation. The school is under the direction of C.B. Carroll, who has had twenty-one years experience and was formerly a pilot with Pan-American Airways. He is assisted by David S. Patterson, who also has had years of experience.

The Carroll School of Aviation has been established for some time and has built a reputation for thoroughness in its work and now the day of opportunity for its expansion and rapid growth is at hand with the sudden awakening over the world to the fact that flying is to be the mode of travel not only for the many but also for military forces.

There is no field of endeavor that offers such wonderful opportunity as aviation. It is just now coming to the front and aviators are able to secure positions in most any part of the world. To those who desire to be aviators of fortune, and for those who desire to fly in commercial flying there are the fast developing lines over the oceans and the many new lines that are being established. Then there is the great growth in private flying. On all fronts, aviation is coming to the for and offers opportunities unparalleled. Young men who desire to enter a successful and growing business that offers the very highest remuneration will find the way through the Carroll School of Aviation.

Mr. C.B. Carroll and his assistants have made a study of the aircraft of the various countries of the world and are authorities on all new developments. They feature ground work and are prepared to give all the theoretical and scientific instruction. The students are thoroughly grounded in all facts about modern flying and are taught the principles upon which the industry is founded, and every new development is added to the course as soon as it has been perfected and found OK.

Flights are made daily from their flying field as they feature air taxi service. They have cabin planes for charter anytime, anywhere. They use their luxurious, large, comfortable planes for charter flights.

Men of business will find their service saving much time; tourists will find it a pleasant trip and filled with sights of the beautiful local scenery. To all those who desire speed and believe that time is money it is appealing. There is far more comfort in riding the airplane than any other method of transportation.

Council Willing to Transfer the Airport to County Authority

(Latrobe Bulletin,
June 19,1951).

By unanimously approving a conditional resolution last evening, Latrobe Borough Council hopes it has set the stage for the acquisition of a landing field for commercial aircraft within the near future.

It places the borough and council on record as favoring the transfer of the Latrobe Airport to a special Westmoreland County Authority.

The conditions? That the authority "be formed for the primary purpose of developing, extending and operating an airport of a size and having the facilities required for regularly scheduled flights of commercial airlines."

As an indication of the borough's intent, a copy of the resolution is to be furnished the Pennsylvania Aeronautics Commission.

Council president, James M. Underwood, advised that it will probably be considered at a meeting of the PAC in Harrisburg this Thursday.

Redevelopment of the Latrobe Airport into a commercial landing field was discussed at length during a meeting of local officials and the three county commissioners on Monday, June 11. [*Editor's note: Council purchased the Kerr property on November 30, 1950 for $22,500 according to an agreement with the Kerrs established in November 1935*].

On November 30, 1950, the commissioners verbally agreed to lend the authority the sum of $120,000, with the object of securing a like amount from the state, the total of which would be matched by the federal government, making $480,000 available for [construction].

Present at the session were two members of the PAC; State Senator John H. Dent, of Jeannette, and Alan M. Scaife, of Rolling Rock, both of whom are champions of the proposal.

Councilmen OK Transfer of Airport

(Latrobe Bulletin,
March 13, 1956).

Latrobe Borough Council last evening approved a resolution to transfer the borough- owned Latrobe Airport to the Tri-City Municipal Authority of Westmoreland County.

One stipulation contained [in the measure] is that "if at any time prior to the expiration of forty years from the date of said deed, that the said authority should abandon the premises. . . for use as an airport for commercial airlines, that the said premises . . . should revert to the Borough of Latrobe."

[The airport] will be developed into a landing field for commercial aircraft at an estimated cost of $680,000.

The Civil Aeronautics Authority has agreed to provide half this amount and recently made an initial grant of $150,974. The county commissioners have included an appropriation of more than $92,000 in the 1956 budget part of the one-fourth cost of $170,000 so that work can be started in the very near future. The Pennsylvania Aeronautics Authority will provide the other one-fourth.

Authority Sets October 27 Week

(Latrobe Bulletin, October 7, 1958).

Plans for the formal opening of the Latrobe Airport were discussed yesterday at the quarterly meeting of the Tri-City Municipal Authority in Latrobe Borough Council chambers at City Hall.

The authority set the week of October 27 for the opening [*Editor's note: The opening took place on October 30. The contract for construction of the runways was given to Bruno Ferrari*].

Chairman Underwood then read a list of eight applicants for the position of airport manager. They are as follows: Lieutenant Commander Omer C. Bell of Florida and Lieutenant John D. Angus of Mount Pleasant, who would occupy the posi-

tion jointly; Earl Baldwin of Greensburg; Becket Aviation Corporation of Allegheny County Airport; Miller Airlines, Inc.; Mason, Schaller and Rhodes of East McKeesport; J.A. Gill, president of Aviation Sales, Inc., of Pittsburgh; Lauren B. Martin of Greensburg, and C.B. Carroll, present manager at Latrobe [*Editor's note: Charlie Carroll was not offered the position*].

Program Arranged At 11 A.M.

(Latrobe Bulletin, October 21, 1958).

After years of planning and more than a year of construction work, the Latrobe Airport will be opened to public us as a commercial facility at dedication ceremonies scheduled for 11 a.m. on Thursday, October 30.

Principals will be Major General

A 1938 postcard of the North Hangar at Latrobe Airport. The "goal posts" for the air-mail pick-up are in place for practice runs. The world's first official air mail pick-up by All American Aviation will take place the following year. *(Courtesy of the Latrobe Historical Society).*

11438

Latrobe Airport
Latrobe, Pa.

Ronna Bisi, student pilot from Latrobe Senior High School, 1975.
(Courtesy of the Bisi Family).

Anthony J. Drexel Biddle and Mrs. Cordelia Scaife May. General Biddle, adjutant general of the Pennsylvania Aeronautics Commission, will present a brief address as the only speaker, and also represent Governor George M. Leader.

Mrs. May, a resident of Ligonier, is a daughter of the late Alan M. Scaife, who was a member of both the Tri-City Municipal Authority and the PAC. She has agreed to cut the ribbon during ceremonies formally opening the airport.

Among the dignitaries invited to attend are Congressman John H. Dent, Frank Cochrane and W. Everett Noel, members of the Westmoreland County Board of Commissioners when the Tri-City Municipal Authority was chartered. John R. MacFarlane, executive director of the PAC; Richard Puckey, Pennsylvania District airport engineer for the federal government,

other members of the PAC and Civil Aeronautics Board; members of the county authority and Latrobe Borough Council and other dignitaries.

Charles Carroll to be Honored with Dinner Saturday
(Scottdale Independent Observer.
January 29, 1959).

Charles Carroll, a former automobile dealer here, who for many years managed the Latrobe Airport, will be honored by airmen from the Greensburg area at the Jacktown Hotel, near Irwin, Saturday evening. Leading aviators from through the state will take part.

Scheduled to join in giving tribute to Mr. Carroll are Samuel Bigony, president of the OX5 Club of Pennsylvania, an organization made up of men who

won their wings before 1939; Colonel Edgar Allen Goff, Jr., of the "Early Birds," who will present a citation to Carroll listing the highlight of his flying career; John W. "Reds" MacFarlane, executive director of the Aeronautics Commission of Pennsylvania; and Ralph Sloan of Latrobe, president of the Westmoreland Aviation Association.

Many pilots who graduated from Mr. Carroll's School of Aviation will attend the affair.

Latrobe Program Pilot for Aviation in Schools
(Latrobe Bulletin,
March 20, 1975)

High school aviation courses are springing up in the state faster than the speed of an SST.

That doesn't surprise James Taylor, a teacher in Greater Latrobe High School who pioneered Westmoreland County's first high school aviation course six years ago.

Other east suburban districts offering similar programs are Derry Area in Westmoreland County and schools in the McKeesport area.

A total of ninety public high schools and sixty private institutions provides similar aviation courses in Pennsylvania, giving the state the third highest total of high school aviation programs in the country.

Taylor started his course in 1968, the year, according to the State Education Department, Pennsylvania began seeing an upswing in high school aviation programs. What started out as an informal, extracurricular activity for Taylor blossomed into an accredited course which now has forty-two pupils in its fourth year of operation.

"I have friends at various space centers in the country, and we keep up to date on the latest developments in space technology. Our ground

training course for future pilots provides enough information to pass the FAA written test for a pilot's license," said Taylor.

Not many students, however, can afford the average eight-hundred dollar cost of air-time lessons needed to get that license.

One of Taylor's more fortunate pupils is Ronna Bisi of Latrobe. She not only found the necessary funds to take flying lessons, but also learned to fly a plane before she learned to drive a car.

"It was funny because the first time I got in a car I began using the accelerator and brake pedals like rudder controls, until my father yelled," Ronna said.

She's now soloing. Already, she has made it to Detroit and back. Not long ago, she was caught in a storm over West Virginia.

"The tower at Morgantown directed me to a landing," she said. "I was plenty scared."

Ronna, like many of Taylor's students, plans to get into a career in aeronautics.

Some of Taylor's other past students are also training for their commercial pilot licenses or entering careers in rocketry.

Taylor's students take to the air from the Westmoreland County Airport, working with Edward Lavis, chief pilot for Vee Neal, Inc.

Latrobe to Host Aviation Dinner

(*Latrobe Bulletin*,
May 6, 1976).

The OX5 Aviation Pioneers will hold its annual Hall of Fame enshrinement banquet and celebration at Latrobe Airport June 5.

This will be the first time since the Hall of Fame's inception in 1971 that its banquet has not been held at Hammondsport, New York.

Eighteen new inductees will have their names an photographs added to the Hall of Fame plaque. One area man, Lloyd C. Santmyer of New Stanton, formerly of Greensburg and Ligonier, is among the new inductees.

Membership in the Hall of Fame is not limited to pilots. Members are elected on the basis of their contributions to aviation in general. Also among the eighteen who will be inducted at the Latrobe ceremony are Charles A. Lindbergh, Wilbur and Orville Wright, and the late Thomas H. "Doc" Kinkade of Washington, Pennsylvania, who made his name in aviation through experimentation and improvement in fuel and oil for use in aircraft.

OX5 Aviation Pioneers, formerly OX5 Club of America, started its Hall of Fame in 1971. Since then, the Hall of Fame plaque has been held at the Glenn H. Curtiss Museum in Hammondsport, New York.

In March, the plaque was moved to Latrobe Airport, the cradle of the OX5 organization. The club was first organized at Latrobe in 1955, and Santmyer was one of the charter members.

The OX5 organization also is looking on Latrobe as a prospective site for a permanent aviation museum and hall of fame. They have received encouragement from national officers of the organization and from individual members of the Westmoreland County Airport Authority.

One of the OX5 engines now on display at Latrobe Airport, was donated to the club by the late Ray Elder of Scottdale. The engine, a V8 that developed ninety horsepower, was first put on display at Greater Pittsburgh International Airport in 1958. It was moved to Latrobe Airport in 1973 by Evans.

U.S. Team Sets New Flight Record: Latrobe's Arnold Palmer Heads Four-Man Crew

(*Latrobe Bulletin*,
May 20, 1976)

Arnold Palmer stood on a red carpet in Denver sipping champagne and reflecting on his record-setting fifty-seven-hour flight around the world in a business jet.

"All I could think about was getting back here," Palmer said Wednesday night, after landing his sleek red, white and blue jet twenty-eight hours and forty-four minutes ahead of a decade-old record held by a crew which included entertainer Arthur Godfrey.

Palmer, two copilots and a timer-observer averaged 400 miles per hour on their 22,984- mile trip, which included nine stops in seven countries.

"We lost some time because of head winds, but otherwise things went just about as expected," said Palmer. "Probably the only time we had any trouble was going into Paris when we were low on fuel."

Palmer was at the controls as the plane flew low over Arapahoe County Airport in a salute and then touched down in front of a crowd of more than 300. He was clean-shaven and appeared rested as he stepped from the jet into the arms of his wife.

The sun was behind the nearby Rocky Mountains when Palmer donned a brown, suede coat and walked sixty feet across a red carpet for a celebration toast of champagne. He also posed for pictures with crew members James E. Bird, L.L. Purkey, and Robert J. Serling.

Palmer's jet, christened the *200 Yankee*, bore decals from most of the stops that included Paris; Glamorgon, South Wales; Jakarta; Manila; Wake Island, Honolulu, and Ceylon.

Palmer Is Given Hero's Welcome

(Latrobe Bulletin,
May 21, 1976).

Over 1,000 persons were on had at Latrobe Airport yesterday to greet Arnold Palmer, the new holder of the world's record for an around-the-world flight in an executive jet. Shortly after he landed at 2:25 p.m., Ted Simon, chairman of the Westmoreland County Commissioners, presented Palmer with a proclamation stating that hereafter May 20 is Arnold Palmer Recognition Day in Westmoreland County.

In 1924, General Wade flew around the world in 170 days; (this week) Latrobe's Palmer circled the globe in just fifty-seven hours, twenty-five minutes and forty-two seconds, breaking the old record of eighty-six hours, nine minutes and one second established by Arthur Godfrey.

Authority Changes Airport's Name

(Latrobe Bulletin,
December 17, 1977)

At the monthly meeting of the Westmoreland County Airport Authority, it was decided to change the name of the Latrobe Airport to the Westmoreland County Airport.

The purpose of the name change is to more fully reflect the importance of the airport in the daily life of Westmoreland County.

The airport is ideally located in the center of the county about equidistant from Monessen in the south to New Kensington in the north. Operations in and out of the county facility by business aircraft have been increasing steadily as have operations by private pilots. Helicopter traffic has increased markedly this year with impetus coming from coal companies requiring transportation to their various properties. Four years ago there were sixty-five helicopters in western Pennsylvania. Today there are 245.

Commissioners Okay Expansion

(Latrobe Bulletin,
June 9, 1978).

An airport restaurant concession lease amendment between the Airport Authority and Blue Angel, Inc., was approved yesterday by the county commissioners.

The amendment allows expansion of Blue Angel Restaurant, owned by James Monzo and located at the county airport in Latrobe.

Airport Authority officials yesterday told Commissioners Ted Simon, John Regoli and William Davis that expansion plans will allow for a larger bar and banquet area.

The restaurant area will be extended over the entrance hall, while maintaining an entrance hall ceiling height of nine feet.

Authority representatives said Monzo will underwrite the cost of the expansion, which has not yet been set.

While the restaurant owner almost certainly will benefit from the expansion, the county authority also will profit from the plan.

Officials said the that Blue Angel, Inc., pays the county a percentage of its gross. In the first four months this year, they reported, returns to the authority from the restaurant are nearly double the budgeted amount.

Airport Vital to Entire County

(Latrobe Bulletin Editorial,
August 1, 1979).

Westmoreland County Airport is an asset to the county, and anything which is done to improve it is worth the time, effort, and money.

There is a notion that persists among a goodly portion of the populace that the airport serves only a special group and that the benefits are not comprehensively spread to the entire complexion of the county.

This is not so. Primarily, the airport serves as a vital segment of the county's transportation system, which impacts upon the economy of the county. Many of the planes which are based at the airport are utilized by the various businesses and industries. What Westmoreland County Airport is today is the result of many years of work and determination of a number of individuals and local, county, state and federal governments. It is difficult to believe that this modern air facility exists, when it was not so long ago, actually, that it was a "cow pasture" type of operation.

In all candor and honesty, it was the foresight and initiative of men like the late Charlie Carroll (the pioneer in the establishment of the airport); Bruno Ferrari, Latrobe contractor and builder; James M. Underwood, and industrialist and past president of Latrobe Borough Council, and the late General Richard King Mellon, philanthropist and business giant, along with the airport authority members and others, that made Westmoreland County Airport a reality of positive impact upon the county.

And one of the nicer prospects is that the sky is the limit (no pun intended) when it comes to the airport's potential for future growth and service.

Site Is Selected For New Airport Tower

(Latrobe Bulletin,
August 8, 1980).

The Westmoreland County Airport Authority agreed on a location for a new control tower during a meeting Friday. The tower will be built west-northwest of the airports administrative building.

An authority committee two years ago estimated that a new tower would cost $250,000, but there was no estimate on what the cost would be at present prices. Robert Cheffins, airport manager, informed the authority that it will take about sixty days before a bid on the projected tower is considered. The authority plans to use bond issues to finance the construction.

Cheffins also explained that the new site will be both economical and safe.

"We're building in an area that is in good proximity to all our runways," said Cheffins.

Barton ATC Inc., which is under contract to the authority for operating the control tower, has continually advised the authority to renovate the facility.

In November 1979, authority members were told by Toni Luisi, former airport tower chief, that the tower equipment currently in use will be obsolete within two years.

Cheffins calculated that it would take $5,000 to get the tower's radio equipment and transmitters into better shape.

John Glover, and airport tower controller, said that the new tower is long overdue.

He said that the tower's present location does not give the controllers' adequate range over the airport's east ramp.

"Planes will be taxiing around and we can't see where they're going.

"There is also a radio blind spot problem with the old tower complex," he added.

Airport Control Tower is Officially Dedicated

(Latrobe Bulletin,
April 5, 1982).

Local as well as FAA officials and politicians were on hand yesterday during ribbon-cutting ceremonies dedicating the new control tower at Westmoreland County Airport, Latrobe.

Robert Lightcap, representing Lightcap, McDonald, Moore and Mason, solicitors of the Westmoreland County Airport Authority, introduced a number of those attending, including Donald C. Madl, vice-chairman of the Airport Authority; Robert Miller, Westmoreland County Commissioner; Congressman Donald Bailey; State Senator James Kelley; Robert Cheffins, airport manager; Michael J. Fenello, deputy assistant administrator of the FAA, and Joseph Del Balzo, FAA, eastern region.

Madl explained that the original tower, built in 1968, was known as a "portable tower" and its construction was financed through grants from the private sector. It was the first of its kind built, he said, and no state or federal funds were used to build it. Nor has the state or federal government contributed to its operation since. The operation of the airport is funded solely through the authority and the county government.

Fenello, also pleased with the new facility, praised the authority for accomplishing the project without federal funds: "You have shown you can rise to your own needs and do it your own way," he said. "Your tradition . . . is not to wait for others, but to do it yourself."

Airport Charts Development

(Greensburg Tribune-Review,
"Enterprise" Tabloid,
Sunday, February 29, 1983).

Westmoreland County Airport showed many significant developments in 1982, but also experienced one major disappointment.

On the positive note, the year was highlighted by the April 4 dedication of the airport's new $384,000 air traffic control tower.

Airport and county officials were proud to not the sixty-five-foot-high tower was built solely with local funds and no federal or state money.

Other major developments at the airport were an $806,713 runway grooving and taxiway and apron overlay project; the purchase of a $125,000 CFR (Crash, Fire, Rescue) vehicle, and a $98,811 taxiway and ramp lighting improvement project.

All three projects were completed with ninety percent FAA money, five percent state, and five percent local funds.

Scheduled projects for 1983 include the addition of $72,000 worth of snow removal equipment and the addition of a $166,300 storage building to house the CFR vehicle, which is expected to arrive this month, and snow removal equipment.

Loss of the FAA's proposed $1 million flight service center to the Altoona-Blair County Airport was a major disappointment to the authority.

FAA plans to consolidate several flight service stations now operating in southwestern Pennsylvania into one unit. It is expected to create some 200 jobs by 1985.

The Latrobe-based airport, according to FAA officials, finished a close second to the Altoona Airport in the final decision reached in

September. Several other airports including Phillipsburg, Allegheny County and Johnstown were also in the running.

Thousands of fans of the annual county air show were also disappointed when the authority decided to cancel the 1982 show because of airport construction. However, the authority has scheduled this year's show for September 24 and 25.

Perhaps an offshoot of the overall turndown in business, in 1982 the Latrobe facility experienced a eight percent decline in air traffic handled as compared to 1981. The airport handled 69,119 flights las year or a 5,556 from 1981.

However, W. Arthur St. Pierre, air tower chief, said that the majority of the decline was experienced early in the year.

Manager Bob Cheffins noted that traffic in December increased from 3,653 to 4,391 in 1982. St. Pierre said the increase in traffic continued through January.

Development at the airport is expected to continue in 1983, Cheffins said. The authority currently has three funding applications submitted to the FAA for 1983, 1984 and 1985. They include $180,000 for a snow blower; $207,000 for high-intensity runway lights and a $6.75 million request for a 1,500-foot extension to the runway and a 4.5 inch overlay to the existing runway.

Control Tower Dedication To Honor U.S. Representative Dent
(Greensburg Tribune-Review, April 9, 1983).

Former Westmoreland County U.S. Representative John H. Dent will be honored at the Westmoreland County Air Show, September 25,

TOP: Taking part in Westmoreland County Airport's tower dedication ceremonies are (from left) Joseph DelBalzo, FAA Eastern Region; Michael J. Fenello, deputy assistant administrator, FAA; Robert Miller, Westmoreland County commissioner, and Donald C. Madl, vice chairman, Westmoreland County Airport Authority. **ABOVE:** The John Dent Tower. *(Courtesy of Westmoreland County Airport Authority).*

when the airport's recently-constructed traffic control tower will be dedicated in his honor.

Dent, Chairman of the Airport Authority, was surprised at Friday's meeting when Vice Chairman Don Madl asked to take over the chairmanship and then proposed the tower should be named the "John H. Dent Tower."

Runway Plan Would Spare Environment

(*Greensburg Tribune-Review,* May 24, 1983).

There will be no significant environmental impact caused by the proposed 1,500-foot runway extension at the Westmoreland County Airport, Airport Engineer Edward Nasuti told a public hearing Monday.

The hearing on the impact of the proposed runway extension was held at the airport's Blue Angel Restaurant. The extension would be to the southwest, and the existing runway would be extended to 7,000 feet.

Nasuti, of Lee-Simpson Associates of DuBois, explained that the impact on air and water quality, wildlife, plants and farmland was studied. Airport Manager Robert Cheffins emphasized that the extension would not allow the airport to handle larger aircraft, but would improve safety and allow more room for landings. He added that some large jets landing at the airport are currently restricted in operation because of the short stopping distance.

He said the extension would enable those larger jets to land and take off with larger weight capacities. He added that there are no plans to extend the runway past 7,000 feet.

Robert Mills, a resident of the Lawson Heights area near the airport, questioned Nasuti on the noise section of the environmental report. He was concerned that increased noise

December 22, 1984. LEFT TO RIGHT: Airport manager Robert Cheffins, Bruno Ferrari, and acting Authority Chairman Donald C. Madl, review signed contracts for the Westmoreland County Airport's 1,500-foot runway extension. The U.S. Department of Transportation provided $2.3 million for the project.
(*Courtesy of Westmoreland County Airport Authority*).

levels projected in the report will decrease property values.

Nasuti said projections indicate noise levels in the area will increase "with or without" the extension because of increased use.

Authority Solicitor Gene McDonald said, "Property is selling and has sold well since the runway has been in existence." [*Editor's note: Noise pollution in the area has created perennial debate since its early days. In September 1984, the Westmoreland County Airport Authority did receive a USDOT grant totaling $2.38 million for the runway extension. The transaction was reported in the Greensburg Tribune-Review, September 26, 1984*].

County Purchase of Airport Urged

(*Greensburg Tribune-Review,* March 21, 1984).

Westmoreland County Commissioner Robert Miller Tuesday said he will recommend the purchase of the Rostraver Township Airport by the county as part of an overall effort to expand the county's airport system and stimulate industrial development in the Mon Valley.

Miller said a recently completed study by the Southwest Regional Planning Commission shows the Rostraver facility holds the potential for grown and has more planes based there and has more daily flight operations than the Westmoreland County Airport in Latrobe.

But Miller said purchase by the county would be contingent upon

TOP TO BOTTOM: May 12, 1989. "Babe" Krinock commemorates the world's first official air-mail pick-up with a fly-by at the Westmoreland Count Airport in the Stinson Reliant *Old Blue*. Lloyd Santmyer (left) and Clyde Hauger, Jr. pose with *Old Blue*. LEFT TO RIGHT: Don Riggs, "Babe" Krinock, Ed Sabota and Bruno Ferrari review the day's events. LEFT TO RIGHT: Don Rossi, "Babe" Krinock and Don Madl pose with *Old Blue*.

(Courtesy of Westmoreland County Airport Authority).

whether the state will provide the necessary funding to bail out the debt-ridden airport.

The study, sponsored by the Federal Aviation Administration, reviewed airports in six southwestern Pennsylvania counties and listed those with a potential for expansion.

Miller, who is chairman of the SPRPC, said that the development of the Rostraver Airport would be an "integral part: of industrial development in the Mon Valley area.

Andrew H. Solan, Secretary-Manager of Rostraver, said that the township has been paying off an $835,000 bond issue, but is now seeking financial relief from the state.

Solan said the township commissioners are asking the state for $1.8 for the purchase of the airport by the county, and another $1.6 million for water and sewage line extensions. Another $1 million would be needed for upgrading the deteriorating runway.

Miller said that Robert Cheffins, director of the Westmoreland County Airport, will be named the county's Director of Aviation next month, but said the move is not related to the possible takeover of the Rostraver Airport. But Miller said it would

"make sense if the county is considering purchase of the airport. We're not doing anything with industrial development in that part of the county and it does give added attraction to industrial development in that site," Miller said [*Editor's note: The County Commissioners approved the purchase of The Rostraver Airport in August, 1985. The transaction was reported in the Greensburg* Tribune-Review, *August 16, 1985*].

Historic Airmail Flight Re-Enacted
(*Latrobe Bulletin*, May 13, 1989).

A single-engine Stinson aircraft known as "Old Blue," was used Friday morning at Westmoreland County Airport for the re-enactment of a significant event in aviation and local history.

With veteran pilot Eli "Babe" Krinock at the controls, the vintage aircraft made a fly-by to simulate the first scheduled air mail pick-up at the airport May 12, 1939.

The observance, which came off without a hitch despite threatening weather, was sponsored by the Westmoreland County Airport Authority.

With Krinock, aviation enthusiasts Ed Sabota and Bruno Ferrari, owner of Latrobe Construction and Latrobe Aviation, completed the historic re-enactment before a crowd of some 150 spectators.

Taking part in a reception and formal program held immediately following the fly-by were guests from the A.M. 49'ers Club of USAir, local and county officials, OX5 Aviation Pioneers and Westmoreland Historical Society.

The event was also significant to USAir officials, who were on hand in conjunction with the airline's fiftieth anniversary.

Lloyd Santmyer of Ligonier, a pilot with All American Aviation, Inc. was among those who watched as Krinock operated the Stinson. Santmyer worked closely with Clyde Hauger, Sr., a fellow AAA pilot who was killed in a crash in 1957, and Clyde Hauger, Jr. of Donegal, a mechanic with AAA.

"Seeing the old Stinson in flight brings back a lot of aviation memories to me. Somehow it seems like only yesterday when we were making the mail runs to little towns all over the place," Santmyer recalled.

Richard Vidmer, chairman of the County Board of Commissioners, described Friday morning's activities as being "historically significant" not only to the people of Latrobe, but for all the country.

Latrobe Mayor Angelo Caruso said the first scheduled air mail pick-up at Latrobe helped put the community on the map.

Master of ceremonies was Don Riggs, longtime Pittsburgh television personality and aviation enthusiast.

The [49'ers Club] is comprised of employees of All American Aviation, Inc., who were pioneers of the air mail pick-up system and later of All American Airways when the air mail pick-ups stopped and the airline initiated its passenger service [Editor's note: The 49'ers are named after their pick-up route number. The last pick-up occurred in 1949 at Jamestown, New York. Three former pilots from Longview Flying Field and the J.D. Hill Airport were pioneers in the pick-up. They were Raymond Elder, Lloyd Santmyer, and Dave Patterson].

Airport Manager Discusses Growth at County's Sites
Excerpts from an interview with Gene Lakin, Airport Manager.
(*Greensburg Tribune-Review*, May 2, 1994).

At Rostraver, air traffic has increased every year. As we improved that facility, both functionally and in the safety areas, more people are using the field. They've increased from 25,000 operations in 1984 to 45,000 last year. That's a good increase, but it's mostly single- engine airplanes for pleasure flying and pilot training.

[At Latrobe] the numbers have been fairly stable, around 60,000 and 70,000 operations a year over the last five years. But that doesn't mean those numbers haven't improved. We're seeing a better mix of aircraft that use the field. We're at the point where about fifty percent of the operations are being done by twin-engines and jet engines. That tells us there is a good mix of business users and recreational users. The larger airplanes mean more people are coming into the community spending money not only on the airport, but going out and using area businesses, entertainment facilities, recreational facilities, renting cars, hotels and putting dollars into our economy.

[Since the expansion of the runway in the mid-1980s] we've expanded the aprons and really worked hard developing areas for corporate hangar use. Once the airport runway was expanded to 7,000 feet, we felt it was important to anticipate future growth.

[Since acquiring Rostraver in 1986] we've acquired in the neighborhood of $6 million in federal and state funds to rehabilitate what we have. We started with overlaying every square foot of asphalt, then we began with a small public building and the maintenance building. We also opened up twenty hangar sites and since then there's been about twelve hangars built. We just completed a five-unity T-Hangar.

[At Latrobe] The USAir Express started in 1986.Before that we had some small private services from here to Pittsburgh. But those numbers have gone from about 7,500 in 1985 to just under 50,000 in 1993. They've been increasing ten percent every year they've been here. Those numbers are good, but I think it's really only the tip of the iceberg as far as potential goes.

Expansion, Air Show Highlight Year
(*Greensburg Tribune-Review*, February 15, 1998)

The Westmoreland County Airport faces one of the most dynamic years in its sixty-three-year history [*Editor's note: The* Tribune-Review *dates the history from 1935 when the airport became the Latrobe Airport. The airport's actual history dates to 1924, with the founding of Longview Flying Field by Charles B. Carroll*] this year marked by the completion of the $5.3 million terminal expansion and the appearance of the renowned Blue Angels flying team. The three-story addition and renovation project's opening is expected to coincide with the U.S. Navy flight demonstration squadron's appearance at the county air show July 25-6.

In the planning stages for five years, the terminal building project includes the renovation of the existing terminal along with a new 25,000-square-foot addition more than doubling the size of the former facility.

Blue Angels pilots line up and take off, Westmoreland County Airshow, 1998.
(Courtesy of Westmoreland County Airport Authority).

are three primary reasons the expansion was necessary. First, he said the airport needed more space; second, the twenty-five-year-old existing building was in dire need of a face-lift, and third, the expansion will better enable the airport to pursue more commercial flight opportunities.

It's Official: It's Arnie's Airport

(Greensburg Tribune-Review, May 8, 1999).

Move over Jimmy Stewart [*Editor's note: The Jimmy Stewart Airport is located in Indiana, Pennsylvania*]. There's now a new famously named airport in southwestern Pennsylvania.

Westmoreland County commissioners Friday announced their decision to rename the county airport in Latrobe the "Arnold Palmer Regional Airport."

"This is to honor the guy who put Westmoreland County on the map," Commissioner Terry Marolt said, adding the new moniker is also intended to capitalize on the gold pro's internationally famous name "as an economic development tool."

Marolt cited a survey that declared Palmer "one of the two most recognizable names on the planet."

Since boxer Muhammad Ali didn't grow up in Youngstown, Pennsylvania, or serve nearly twenty-five years on the county airport authority, Palmer got the offer.

Palmer said he "appreciated" but declined to lend his name to other facilities. Nonetheless, he officially accepted this one at a press conference yesterday at the county courthouse in Greensburg.

Palmer said he still remembers watching the first official airmail pick-up in the world at the Latrobe Airport, May 12, 1939.

"There aren't many people in this room who can say they actually saw that," said Palmer.

Marolt credited the idea to apply the golf legend's name to the airport to County Common Pleas Judge, John Driscoll.

"This had been on my mind for a long time," Driscoll said. "Arnold Palmer's mark on professional sports is indelible. His name brings honor to the game of golf, to professional sports, and to this community."

The airport authority last year completed a $5.3 million terminal building renovation and expansion project that more than tripled the airport's operational capacity. With Westmoreland County Industrial Development Corporation's plans for a new industrial park adjacent to the airport, the authority is also eying an expansion of the 7,000-foot-long runway and aggressively marketing the facility to several major national airlines.

Palmer has served on the authority since 1995, and previously served for nearly twenty years prior to resigning in 1985 when he acquired

TOP: September 10, 1999, dedication of the Arnold Palmer Regional Airport. LEFT TO RIGHT: Gene McDonald, Phil Morrow, Oland Canterna, Janice Smarto, Mark Gera, Arnold Palmer, John Finfrock, Governor Tom Ridge, Dorothy Zello. *(Courtesy of Westmoreland County Airport Authority).*

ownership of Arnold Palmer Air Service, which was later purchased by Vee Neal Aviation.

"Flying and airports have always been a major part of my life," said the golfer, who is also a pilot and owns a Cessna Citation X private jet. "With the county commissioners and the airport authority working hand in hand, we have one of the soundest airports in the United States."

The statement was somewhat more flattering than one Palmer made last June, when he took the authority to task over the airport's "shoddy" appearance during the renovation project, citing, among other things, the condition of the airport's perimeter fence at the time.

Airport Authority Chairman Philip Morrow apparently remembered the publicized statement yesterday. He thanked Palmer on behalf of the authority and quipped, "Believe it or not, Arnie, we're going to put up a fence, too."

Arnold Palmer poses with "Babe" Krinock, his flight instructor. *(Courtesy of Westmoreland County Airport Authority).*

Gabe Monzo in 1999, when he was Pennsylvania Department of Transportation Bureau of Aviation "Manager of the Year." *(Courtesy of Dorothy Zello).*

Bond Issue Approved; Airport Expansion Set
(Greensburg Tribune-Review)

An expanded and more passenger-friendly terminal at the Westmoreland County Airport in Unity Township could open for business by March 1998.

County commissioners yesterday approved a $1.75 million bond issue, setting in place the final piece of funding for the $4.7million project that will more than double the size of the existing terminal.

Financing for the project includes a $1.2 million grant from the Federal Aviation Administration and another $1.8 million in state funds through PennDOT.

Once completed, the renovated terminal building will be enlarged from 21,000 square feet to nearly 50,000 square feet. Comfort features such as increasing passenger seating in the terminal from about thirty-six to 200 chairs and a larger screening area for pre-flight business will also be part of the project.

"This is the most significant vital progression in Westmoreland County

history. Airport development is coming at the right time because airlines are looking for non-large service centers and we fit the bill," said John Finfrock, chairman of the Westmoreland County Airport Authority.

Airport Official Named Manager of the Year
(Greensburg Tribune-Review, October 4, 1999).

It's not beginner's luck.

Gabe Monzo hasn't been an airport manager for two full years yet. But nearly fifteen years as an assistant manager and twenty-five years as a volunteer firefighter helped him land the title of Airport Manager of the Year.

Demetrius D. Glass, director of [the Pennsylvania Department of Transportation Bureau of Aviation] the bureau, said the award was established "to promote aviation safety and at the same time, to recognize those individuals and organizations that do an exceptional job advancing aviation safety and awareness."

"This award is not only a well-deserved honor for Gabe, but it also

emphasizes our overall commitment to safety," said Gene Lakin, executive director of the Westmoreland County Airport Authority.

"Everything we do...revolves around safety..." Lakin added. "So it's very important to us that [Gabe] is here. And now everyone will know we have a top-of-the-line airport manager."

Monzo, 43, started his career at the county airport as a maintenance worker in 1983.

Two years later, he was named assistant manager under Lakin, who was manager at that time. When Lakin became executive director in 1998, Monzo assumed the manager's post.

Monzo also oversees operations at Rostraver Airport. Lakin said Monzo was hired with the primary duty of instituting an emergency response program here at the airport.

"He has certainly done that, and it was his fire-fighting experience that was beneficial in him taking over the project," Lakin said.

New FBO Facility Open At APRA
(Latrobe Bulletin, April 8, 2000).

Edward and Mary Ann Kilkeary, who own and operate L.J. Aviation, celebrated the grand opening of its new Fixed Base of Operation (FBO) facility at Arnold Palmer Regional Airport on Saturday.

In coordination with the celebration, Bombardier Aerospace sponsored a static aircraft display featuring it s entire Learjet family including the intercontinental Challenger 604, the 31A, the all new 45 and the stand-up cabin 60.

The new facility allows L.J Aviation to cater to corporate jet and turbo prop aircraft landing at the local airport.

L.J. Aviation has been at the airport since 1974. *(Courtesy of L.J. Aviation).*

The project, according to several county and local officials, shows L.J. Aviation's commitment and investment not only to the airport and the community of Latrobe, but also to Westmoreland County and western Pennsylvania.

Members of the Westmoreland County Airport Authority, including Gabe Monzo, Dorothy Zello and Charlie Green, were on hand to congratulate L. J. Aviation. They recognized L.J. Aviation for its years of service to the airport.

FAA Funds Give Latrobe Airport Direction

(Greensburg Tribune-Review April 29, 2001*).*

The Arnold Palmer Regional Airport's receipt of at least $1 million in annual federal funds for the next five years will help smooth plans to extend its primary runway.

U.S. Rep. John Murtha visited the Westmoreland County airport in Unity Township Thursday to announce awarding of the first installment of the annual Federal Aviation Administration entitlement funds.

"In the past, we weren't sure what we would get each year, so airports couldn't plan," the Johnstown Democrat said. "But we (Congress) have worked it out so that rural airports will now know what they are getting."

Noting Arnold Palmer Regional "has made tremendous improvement in recent years" Murtha added the airport authority "can now count on a minimum of $1 million a year and won't have to make contingency plans based on whether applications are approved."

A breakdown of plans for this year's entitlement includes $250,000 to pay for an environmental assessment required for its plan to extend the 7,000-foot-long main runway by 1,500 feet.

The Arnold Palmer Regional Airport terminal building, 2000. *(Courtesy of Westmoreland County Airport Authority).*

[The] proposed extension which would shift the airport's landing zone away from Route 30 and Lawson Heights, a residential community north of Runway 5/23 would "provide a needed safety cushion and help reduce noise levels for the people who live nearby."

"We should have assessment done by the end of this year," authority Executive Director Gene Lakin said. "Hopefully we will enter a design phase in 2002 and begin construction in 2003."

The Sky's the Limit: Rostraver Airport Playing Role in Economic Growth
(Valley Independent, n.d.)

Last month, officials from Rostraver Township interested in the possibility of developing an industrial park at Route 201 and Interstate 70, toured Southpointe to view the success of that site.

While they were impressed with the 586.6-acre site which employees 2,600 in western Washington County, Jack Piatt, owner of Millcraft Industries and a prime developer at Southpointe, was impressed and a little envious of an asset that Rostraver was starting out with the Rostraver Airport.

To Gene Lakin, executive director of the Westmoreland County Airport Authority, such recognition is very encouraging.

"It's good to hear someone else say that," said Lakin. "I've been saying that for fifteen years."

Actually, the state is also recognizing the airport's potential to stimulate economic growth. The Pennsylvania Department of Transportation Bureau of Aviation will release later this year the results of a statewide study of the economic impact of all airports across the state.

Lakin said a preliminary release of figures from that report indicate the economic impact of the Rostraver Airport is $7,841,400 annually.

The airport provides an intrinsic value to economic development efforts. The most visible presence among the companies with hangers at the airport is 84 Lumber owner Joe Hardy.

[Such] firms as Blackwell aviation, Clark Industries, Thermo King, West Penn Communications, Life Flight and Aero Innovations Inc. also maintain hangers at the Rostraver Airport.... There are 120 tenants at Rostraver, including fifteen new hangers in the past ten years, especially significant growth for an airport the size of Rostraver.

Located along Route 51, the 120-acre airport was built in the mid-1960's. The Westmoreland County Airport Authority took over the airport in January 1986.

[Joe] Kirk, [the executive director of the Mon Valley Progress Council] said, "The airport is one selling point when recruiting new businesses to the region. There is a sense that it is a growing airport, that it is on the move."

Aerial view of the Arnold Palmer Regional Airport, 2000. *(Courtesy of Westmoreland County Airport Authority).*

Bibliography

Adams, Willis B. "Dr. Lytle S. Adams and His Airmail Pick-up System. *The Airpost Journal.* (June 1983), 316-320; (July 1983), 384-389; (August, 1983), 460-464; (September 1983), 486-489; (October 1983), 4-10. A comprehensive history of Lytle S. Adams and his pickup system from the earliest days to his collaboration with Richard DuPont. Illustrated with photos and postal covers.

Air Mail Pick-Up "Latrobe Can Claim First Scheduled Pickup," "Inventive Irwin Dentist Extracted Method of Airmail Delivery." *Greensburg Tribune Review* (*Focus Magazine*), May 7, 1989.

Air Mail Pick-Up. "New Air Mail Pickup Begins." *Greensburg Daily Tribune.* May 12, 1939, and "Mail Planes in Operation," May 13, 1939, and "'Flying Post Offices Blaze Airmail Route." *Greensburg Morning Review.* May 13, 1939.

All American Aviation Newsletter. *The Pick-Up.* 1941-1949. Clyde Hauger Collection.

All American Aviation. *Air Pick-Up Handbook.* Wilmington, Delaware: All American Aviation. 1947. Describes new equipment and aircraft to 1947. Photos and line drawings.

All American Aviation Brochure, 1940. [Rare publicity brochure which contains photos of original crews and equipment].

Arnold Palmer Regional Airport. Minutes of Authority Meetings. 1958-Present.

Arnold Palmer Regional Airport. *Latrobe Bulletin* and *Greensburg Tribune-Review* Scrapbooks. Compiled by Robert Cheffins. 1981-1985.

Bettis Field. Elmer Best, "Pittsburgh's Bettis Airport;" Brian Butko, "Some A-B-Cs of Local Aviation;" Scholter, Ken (Trimble interview). *Pittsburgh History.* Vol. 76, no. 4 (Winter 1993/94). 156-1 70.

Flying Schools and Aeronautical Instruction. "A Brief History of Aviation Training at Saint Vincent." Thomas Acklin, OSB. [Saint Vincent College Monastery Archives]. *Saint Vincent Magazine.* 1978..
Flying Schools and Aeronautical Instruction. "Time Flies." *Saint Vincent College Brochure.* 1929. Saint Vincent College Monastery Archives.

Flying Schools and Aeronautical Instruction. *Oral History of Robert Downs.* Recorded September 12, 1999. Archives of the Saint Vincent College Center For Northern Appalachian Studies.

Flying Schools and Aeronautical Instruction. *Correspondence of Father Alcuin W. Tasch and Russell Brinkley.* 1977 to 1978. Saint Vincent College Monastery Archives.

Greensburg, PA. Pittsburgh-Greensburg Airport. *Oral history of Robert Fisher.* Recorded December 12, 1999. Archives of the Saint Vincent College Center For Northern Appalachian Studies.

Hamlen, Joseph R. *Flight Fever.* Doubleday, 1971. pp. 233-45; 254-71; 298. Provides extensive detail to the Old Glory Flight. [Provides details of J.D. Hill's last flight].

Hepler, Robert H. *Airmen of New Alexandria.* Privately printed. March 1994. Westmoreland County Historical Society Library.

Hill, James DeWitt (S). "Bertaud Now Plans Ocean Flight to Rome." *New York Times.* July 7, 1927.

Hill, James DeWitt (S). "Levine Abandons Bellanca Flight." *New York Times.* May 22, 1927.

Hill, James DeWitt (S) "Bertaud Picks Hill for Flight to Rome." *New York Times.* July 14, 1927.

Hill, James DeWitt (S). Articles in the Scottdale, PA Independent Observer. July 12, 1927; July 19, 1927; September 13, 1927; October 14, 1970; October 21, 1970.

Hill, James DeWitt (S). "Hill's Air Service Covers 25 Years." *New York Evening Post.* September 6, 1927.

Hill, James DeWitt "Old Glory Wreckage Found in Atlantic 100 Miles North of Position of SOS Call: No Trace Found of the Three Fliers." *New York Times.* September 13, 1927.

Hill, James DeWitt (S). "Plane Going Fine Says Bertaud Radio." *New York American.* September 7, 1927.

Hill, James DeWitt (S). In West Overton Museum, Scottdale, PA. 1. *Letter from J.D. Hill to His Father.* March 28, 1909; 2. *Letter from J.D. Hill to Giuseppi Bellanca,* June 14, 1927; 3. *Letter from J.D. Hill to Maloney,* June 24, 1927; 4. Pages from Hill family Bible; 5) Portraits of J.D. Hill, Photos of Family Home, Photo of Hill's Experimental Plane Model.

Karant, Max. The Treetop Line. *Flying.* (May 1946), 50-55. [On air mail pick-up].

Oral Histories and transcriptions. Center for Northern Appalachian Studies Archives. Kenneth Scholter, Kip Barraclough, Lloyd Santmyer, Clyde Hauger, Robert Fisher,

Roland Heid, Ed Blend, Josephine Smart, Janet Matchett, James Carroll, Gene McDonald, Gene Lakin, Gabe Monzo, Robert Downs, Mansel Negley, William Strickler, Don Riggs, Marcia Nair.

OX5 Club. *OX5 News.* 1972-2000. Ken Scholter Collection.

OX5 Organization. *OX5 Aviation Pioneers.* Privately Printed by the organization. n.d. [The volume is available from the organization headquarters].

Petee, Frank. *The Triple A Story (1938-1946).* Pittsburgh, PA: Allegheny Airlines, Inc. 1964.

Saint Vincent Archabbey Archives. Boxes 1 and 3. *Aviation at Saint Vincent.* Contains complete history and correspondence of the U.S. Army Air Corps programs at Saint Vincent College and the Latrobe Airport.

Shamburger, Page. "All American Aviation." *American Aviation Historical Society Journal.* (Fall 1964). 198-206.

Smith, Frank Kingston. *Aviation and Pennsylvania.* Franklin Institute, 1981.

Stahl, Earl F. "Treetop Airmail I" and "Treetop Airmail II." *American Aviation Historical Society Journal.* Volume 39, Number 1 (Spring 1994), 3-13, and Volume 39, Number 2 (Summer 1994), 110-123.

Stringer, Harry R., ed. A *Headline History of the Air Pick-Up (1939-1942).* Wilmington/Pittsburgh.

Stringer, Harry R. ed. *Air Pick-Up: A National Policy and Its Fulfillment.* Wilmington, Delaware/Pittsburgh, Pennsylvania: All American Aviation. 1946. Describes developments to 1946, including glider and human pickups.

Trimble, William F. High Frontier: *A History of Aeronautics in Pennsylvania.* University of Pittsburgh Press, 1982.

Trimble, William F. and W. David Lewis. *The Airway to Everywhere: 1937-1953.* University of Pittsburgh Press. 1988.

Index

Notes

Notes

Notes

Notes